# Critical New Perspectives on ADHD

The ADHD phenomenon has reached global proportions, significantly affecting the lives of children, parents and teachers worldwide. Explanations for the growth in diagnoses of the condition are as debatable and contentious as the various treatments available.

*Critical New Perspectives on ADHD* unpicks the myths surrounding the development of this phenomenon, and leaves no stone unturned in its search for answers. The renowned range of contributors, experts in a variety of academic disciplines, explore reasons for the emergence and maintenance of ADHD. They debate such suggested explanations as the dominance of US psychiatric models and the need for new markets for major pharmaceutical companies as well as the functions that ADHD diagnoses fulfil in families, classrooms and communities. This book takes a critical, highly international and frequently controversial perspective on the topic, and raises a number of concerns often not covered by material currently available to parents and practitioners.

In a world where moves to educational inclusion are paradoxically paralleled by the ever-increasing use of medication to control children's behaviour, this book scrutinises current accepted practice and offers alternative perspectives and strategies for teachers and other education professionals. Respect for the unique struggles of children, families and professionals underlies the discussions. Anyone with a serious interest in ADHD and other behavioural difficulties cannot afford to ignore this important new book.

**Gwynedd Lloyd** is Head of Subject at the Department of Educational Studies, University of Edinburgh, UK.

**Joan Stead** is Senior Research Fellow at the University of Edinburgh, UK.

**David Cohen** is Professor of Social Work at Florida International University, USA.

# Critical New Perspectives on ADHD

Edited by
Gwynedd Lloyd,
Joan Stead and David Cohen

Routledge
Taylor & Francis Group

LONDON AND NEW YORK

First published 2006 by Routledge
2 Park Square, Milton Park, Abingdon, Oxon OX14 4RN

Simultaneously published in the USA and Canada
by Routledge
29 West 35th Street, New York, NY 10001

*Routledge is an imprint of the Taylor & Francis Group, an informa business*

Typeset in Baskerville by
Keystroke, Jacaranda Lodge, Wolverhampton
Printed and bound in Great Britain by
The Cromwell Press, Trowbridge, Wiltshire

*British Library Cataloguing in Publication Data*
A catalogue record for this book is available from the British Library

*Library of Congress Cataloging in Publication Data*
Critical new perspectives on ADHD / edited by Gwynedd Lloyd,
Joan Stead & David Cohen.
p. cm.
Includes bibliographical references and index.
1. Attention-deficit hyperactivity disorder. 2. Attention-deficit disordered
children–Education. I. Lloyd, Gwynedd, 1947– II. Stead, Joan.
III. Cohen, David, 1954–
RJ506.H9C75 2006
618.92′8589–dc22
2005026757

ISBN10: 0–415–36036–6 (hbk)
ISBN10: 0–415–36037–4 (pbk)
ISBN10: 0–203–00801–4 (ebk)

ISBN13: 978–0–415–36036–4 (hbk)
ISBN13: 978–0–415–36037–1 (pbk)
ISBN13: 978–0–203–00801–0 (ebk)

# Contents

# Acknowledgements

We are grateful to all the contributors to this book and to Debbie Stasch for her work on the manuscript. Thanks also to Barry, Julia, Bob, Carole, Saskia and Bernard.

# Contributors

**Thomas Armstrong** Ph.D. is now based in Australia and is an author of eleven books, including *The Myth of the A.D.D. Child: 50 Ways to Improve Your Child's Behavior and Attention Span without Drugs, Labels, or Coercion* (New York: Dutton) and *ADD/ADHD Alternatives in the Classroom* (Alexandria, Virginia: Association of Supervision and Curriculum Development). He worked for several years as a special education teacher in the United States and Canada, and for the past eighteen years has lectured extensively in the United States and around the world.

**Maurizio Bonati** graduated from the University of Milan with a degree in Medicine. Since 1973 he has been working at the Mario Negri Research Institute of Milan (an international private foundation for research and education in the biomedical sciences). In 1993 he became Head of the Laboratory for Mother and Child Health, as well as the Director of the Regional Drug Information Centre. Dr Bonati is the author and co-author of hundreds of scientific articles, book chapters and abstracts, and editor of *Ricerca & Pratica*. His main research interests are: monitoring and epidemiological evaluation of drug utilization and effects of drugs and vaccines in motherhood and childhood; research methodology in general hospital and paediatric community practice; transfer of information to the community; epidemiology of paediatric and perinatal care. Dr Bonati has also been active in promoting health projects and research counselling for groups working in developing countries; he carries out part of this work also as advisor for the World Health Organization.

**David Cohen** Ph.D. (co-editor) is currently Professor of Social Work at Florida International University, USA. He has published widely on medicalization, iatrogenic disorders in mental health, and the effects and uses of psychiatric medications in contemporary societies. His books in French and English include *Challenging the Therapeutic State* (1990), *Medicalisation and Social Control* (1994), *The Critical Handbook of Psychiatric Drugs* (1995), and *Your Drug May be Your Problem* (2001).

**John Davis** Ph.D. is a Lecturer in Educational Studies at Moray House School of Education, University of Edinburgh, Scotland. He has carried out ethnographic research projects as a researcher at the University of Edinburgh between 1991 and 2001 in the areas of childhood studies, curriculum innovation, disability, education, health and sport. Having been a Senior Lecturer in Childhood and Disability Studies at the University of Northumbria and Senior Consultant at the Children and Social Inclusion Consultancy, Edinburgh, he rejoined the University of Edinburgh in June 2003 and is now Co-ordinator of the BA in Childhood Studies at Moray House School of Education. He has a wealth of experience of carrying out participatory projects with children and young people for a variety of service providers, voluntary organizations and disabled people's organizations.

**Eva Hjörne** completed her Ph.D. in Education at Göteborg University, Sweden, in 2004 and is now a senior lecturer there. Her main interests are in the analysis of institutional discourse and mediated action with special focus on categorizing and identity formation of pupils in school. Her current research project includes analysis of meetings between experts in school (so-called pupil welfare team meetings) to negotiate and identify who is in need of special support.

**Ken Jacobson** earned his Doctorate in Anthropology from the University of Massachusetts-Amherst. He also earned masters degrees in neuroscience and in anthropology from Brandeis University in Waltham, Massachusetts. His cross-cultural research on Attention Deficit Hyperactivity Disorder was featured in the January 1, 2000, issue of the *New York Times*. Jacobson has presented the results of his project for peer review at numerous professional meetings, and published several papers on the topic. He is in the process of preparing a book-length manuscript. His current research interests focus on power relationships between adults and children, social relationships between children and the ways in which those relationships impact on educational institutions. Jacobson is currently a Research Fellow at Boston University.

**Gwynedd Lloyd** Ph.D. (co-editor) is Head of Subject in the Department of Educational Studies, University of Edinburgh, Scotland. She has published widely on issues of educational exclusion and inclusion, with a particular interest in understandings of educational deviance, ADHD, inter-agency working and support structures in schools. She has recently edited a book entitled *'Problem' Girls: Understanding and Supporting Troubled and Troublesome Girls and Young Women* (published by Routledge 2005) which unpicks and challenges the labelling of some girls and young women who may face or cause difficulties, as 'problems'.

**Nithi Muthukrishna** is Professor in the School of Education and Development, University of Kwa-Zulu Natal, Pietermaritzburg, South Africa. Her research and teaching interests are in the areas of policy and practice related to social inclusion and exclusion; education for social justice and equity; early childhood studies; child health and health promotion in schools. She is a member of the International Advisory Committee of the *Journal of Early Childhood Research*, the editorial board of the *International Journal of Special Education*, and the editorial committee of the *Journal of Education*. She was member of the South African National Commission on Special Needs in Education and Training, 1996–1997, a process that culminated in Education White Paper 6: Special Education – Building an Inclusive Education and Training System, July 2001.

**Üstün Öngel** Ph.D. from Adana, Turkey, became interested in 'cross-cultural' psychology, and this led him to do a critical research project on cross-cultural studies ('The Search for a Valid Paradigm in Cross-Cultural Psychology') for the completion of his doctoral degree at the University of Sussex at Brighton, England. He returned to Turkey in 1995 as lecturer in the school of education at the University of Çukurova. From his background in social and cultural psychology he has become a practising psychologist, providing help mostly to parents with 'ADHD'-diagnosed children. He is critical of much current psychiatric practice in Turkey, and is working on a social psychological-developmental model for understanding and remedying the so-called 'psychiatric illnesses', giving priority to 'ADHD'-related problems.

**Gavin Reid** Ph.D. is a Senior Lecturer in the Department of Educational Studies, Moray House School of Education, University of Edinburgh, Scotland. He is an experienced teacher, educational psychologist, university lecturer, researcher and author. He has made over 500 conference and seminar presentations world-wide. He has held and currently holds appointments as external examiner to universities in the UK and Australia. He has been a consultant to parent groups and charitable bodies in the UK, Europe and New Zealand and is consultant to the Red Rose School for children with specific learning difficulties in St Annes on Sea, Lancashire. Gavin Reid has authored, co-authored and edited fifteen books for teachers and parents. He is the author of *Dyslexia: A Practitioners Handbook* (3rd edition, Wiley 2003), *Dyslexia: A Complete Guide for Parents* (Wiley 2004), *Dyslexia and Inclusion* (David Fulton/NASEN 2005) and *Learning Styles and Inclusion* (Sage Publications 2005). He has also co-authored the Listening and Literacy Index (LLI) and the *Special Needs Assessment Profile* (SNAP) (Hodder and Stoughton 2003).

**Joan Stead** Ph.D. (co-editor) is a Senior Research Fellow at the University of Edinburgh, Scotland. Her research interests include school inclusion/exclusion, school discipline, ADHD and restorative approaches in education. She has published widely in education journals on issues such as inter-agency working in schools; experiences of refugee pupils; the national education debate in Scotland; and school experiences of gypsy traveller pupils. She also is co-author of *Hanging on in there* (published by the National Children's Bureau 2001).

**Gordon Tait** Ph.D. is a Senior Lecturer in the School of Cultural and Language Studies at the Queensland University of Technology, Brisbane Australia. His research interests include education and identity formation, youth and social governance, and the sociology of sport. His most recent work addresses the philosophy of inclusive education.

**David Walker** Ph.D. is Clinical Director of Ani'sahoni (anē' săhōn) Consulting Services, PLLC and provides behavioural health services for the 14 Confederated Tribes of the Yakama Nation and EPIC (Enterprise for Progress In the Community) Youth Services in central Washington. Beginning with the Yakama Indian Health Service, he has been the first and only doctoral-level clinical psychologist in the Yakama Nation community since 2000, aiding in the design and co-ordination of the Pathways to Hope and Healing Conference, Warriors for Life, and the Níix Ttáwaxt (nēx t-tauwawxt) Intervention Program for Native Youth. He received his doctorate degree in clinical psychology at the University of Detroit in 1992 and spent time on the faculties of Oakland University, Eastern Michigan University and Wayne State University Medical School. He currently teaches with the adjunct faculty of Heritage University in Toppenish, Washington, USA.

# Introduction

## Widening our view of ADHD

*Joan Stead, Gwynedd Lloyd and David Cohen*

This book takes a critical perspective on the growing phenomenon of Attention Deficit Hyperactivity Disorder (ADHD). A great many books on ADHD exist but few take a critical view of the concept and associated practices, especially when related to the educational experiences of children in schools. Also, few books on ADHD provide examples, commentary and critiques from outside the USA, Australia and UK. Current literature for parents and children tends to present a diagnosis of ADHD as straightforward, e.g. 'ADHD is a disease caused by biological factors, probably inherited; and stimulant drugs, when used with medical supervision, are usually considered quite safe' (NIMH 2003: 23). Or, 'ADHD is a real biological-based phenomenon, and not just a disorder conjured up by "neurotic" parents' (WWF-UK 2004: 15).

Such biological determinism is not consistent with much of what we know about child development. Where biological predispositions exist for temperament and perhaps for other mental health difficulties these are often expressed in an individual as a result of social and family experiences. So if a biological element turns up as necessary for our understanding of ADHD this biology itself reflects the interaction between the brain and its complex and dynamic individual context of family, social and educational experience. ADHD is therefore a contested concept in that it describes a range of aspects of behaviour clustered together by human judgement into a diagnosis of 'psychiatric disorder', and it is subjectively measured by professionals, with considerable reliance on behaviour checklists. We should therefore question the use of methylphenidate even if it does seem to 'work' for some children. The SIGN Guideline observes that 'The use of psychostimulants remains controversial and there are concerns about prescribing such medication to children' (SIGN 2001: 1). However, in the view of many authors contributing to this edited volume, it appears that medical professionals around the world are nonetheless rushing to prescribe.

This book brings together different views and experiences from countries such as USA, Australia, UK, Sweden, South Africa, Italy and Turkey to further our understandings of, and hopefully fuel the debates over, a diagnosis that is affecting more and more children in schools.

## Brief background

ADHD is a global phenomenon, spreading rapidly as a result of the increasing dominance internationally of US psychiatric models, the need for new markets for major pharmaceutical companies, the increasing use of the Internet by parents and professionals and changing approaches to schooling. In the Western world an increasing recognition of the political and social construction of disability and moves to educational inclusion are paradoxically paralleled by ever-increasing use of psychotropic medication for children (Lloyd and Norris 1999).

The impact of the Internet and of increased international communication between professionals and academics has led to an increasing promotion of labels derived from the psychiatric lexicon. A recent study at the University of Maryland indicated that, in the USA, stimulants prescribed for attention deficit disorder and antidepressants were the most commonly prescribed drugs for children, but also found extremely rapid growth in the use of antipsychotics, so-called mood stabilisers prescribed for mania or aggression, and other classes of potent psychoactive medications (Zito and Rushton 2003). The study confirms that paediatricians and child psychiatrists (and physicians generally), as well as various mental health professionals, are increasingly turning to pharmacology as the treatment of choice for depression, attention disorder, severe anxiety, obsessive disorder, manic depression and other conditions – even when these conditions are diagnosed in pre-schoolers. Recently Prozac was authorised by the US Food and Drug Administration for children as young as 7. Most medications prescribed for child-hood mental disorders, including many of the newer medications, are prescribed 'off-label' because only a few of them have been systematically studied for safety and efficacy in children (Breggin and Cohen 2001).

In the short term it is clear from a multiplicity of research studies that methylphenidate 'works' for many children (indeed it might help many of us concentrate better, as the many thousands of students who obtain it illegally in the USA would argue). However, the US Federal Drug Administration and the International Narcotics Control Board have both frequently stated their concerns about over-prescription and about illegal sale and use of the drug by young people. Other concerns expressed have included the lack of careful monitoring of med-ication and prescription to children who don't meet the criteria or are younger than the recommended minimum age. There is a lack of long-term studies of the impact on children but evidence from the USA does indicate an association with the continued use of psychoactive medication in adulthood.

Labels like ADHD denote which professional knowledge constructs them, and to some extent which professionals attempt to take control. ADHD 'creates a professional discourse', which is excluding. This makes it difficult to challenge by the layperson or by other professionals who do not have access to this specialised discourse (Norris and Lloyd 2000: 508) and it subsequently elevates the status of some 'experts'. However, at the same time, increased access by parents to infor-mation about 'conditions' like ADHD and a growth in organised pressure, in the context of a developing culture of individual responsibility for health as well as a co-existing culture of disability, has created a more challenging client group, with an increased emphasis on a right to diagnosis. It is, however, interesting to note that this 'right to diagnosis' would appear prevalent in some countries and not others.

The critiques offered in the following chapters illustrate some of the concerns mentioned above by discussing such issues as the subjective nature of diagnosis; the medicalisation of behaviour; the pedagogical issues; and labelling. These views are from various perspectives, professional positions and countries. We (as editors) do not necessarily agree with all the authors in this volume, but feel it is important to include this range of diverse views to promote further critical thinking regarding ADHD. It is also important to note that there are views regarding the aetiology and 'treatment' of ADHD which do not appear in this volume.

Although we have stressed the diverse nature of the contributions there are some shared views. One view which emerges in several chapters is the need to change the emphasis, or at least redress the balance between addressing the needs of the individual child in school, and critically examining the systems which are supporting and perpetuating increasing diagnosis of ADHD and the resulting medicalisation of the behaviour of children. For as recognised by Cohen (Chapter 9) even the best intentions of individual actors/professionals can become warped or co-opted by the requirements of systems whose purposes are rarely analysed explicitly.

There is also some agreement (in this volume) of the power of the medical model and how this impinges upon curriculum and pedagogy and disempowers teachers, parents and pupils from responding to a diagnosis of ADHD in a non-medicalised paradigm. The ability of those most affected by the diagnosis to play an active role in decisions and interventions is also discussed both in terms of understandings of power differentials (in particular between adults and children), and from a 'rights' perspective. Both these concepts further highlight the often competing agendas of those involved, including the inclusion agenda. The irony of the increasing medicalization of behaviour in school resulting (inadvertently) in the 'inclusion' of pupils who may otherwise have been excluded from school, is also raised by contributors to this volume.

## Chapter summaries

We begin the book with a chapter by David Cohen who vividly illustrates the phenomenon of ADHD in the USA with the statement: 'Using the keyword "ADHD" for a search in a famous US online bookstore in mid-2005 yielded over 4,800 hits.' But those of us in the UK cannot be complacent, as Cohen highlights the particularly chilling fact that there has been a 7,600 per cent increase in prescriptions in England for methylphenidate during the last ten years (1994–2004). The USA has, however, the somewhat onerous reputation of being the birthplace, or epicentre, of the ADHD diagnosis and so it is appropriate and pertinent that this edited volume begins with Cohen leading us carefully through ten prominent counter-arguments from the USA. The critiques summarised are from sociologists, psychiatrists, paediatric neurologists, paediatricians and psychologists, and provide the reader with a comprehensive overview of not only those who call into question the concept of ADHD, but also those who appear to accept a narrowed version of the concept, while questioning how children with this diagnosis should be managed.

The historical and cultural phenomenon of 'medicalising' behaviours is outlined in the first argument discussed by Cohen. This is a theme which will be further explored by other writers in this book (in particular Walker and Davis), and one which highlights not only the scapegoating of deviance, but the medicalisation of increasingly 'normal' conditions of life resulting from, for example, having educational difficulties, and from being 'an exploratory hands-on child learner' (Walker this volume). When discussing the work of Diller, Cohen describes how the enhancement of 'normal' behaviour has become politically correct, and paradoxically how this is accompanied by 'normalising underperformance' as a disability. This paradox is also discussed by Tait (Chapter 5) who takes the philosophical argument of free will versus determinism to highlight the concerns this raises for schools and for education.

Cohen also discusses the 'rapid fire culture' of America as described by DeGrandpre, and in the following chapter by Thomas Armstrong this analysis is further explored to provide us with a macro view of what Armstrong sees as the cultural underpinnings of the rise in diagnosis of ADHD. Through the analogy of canaries in the coalmine Armstrong sees the phenomenon of increasing diagnosis of ADHD as a cultural issue which should alert us to the need to reform cultural institutions, rather than increasing the medicalisation of our children.

Armstrong describes all of us who have regular access to technology (such as television and computers) as becoming cultures with a 'short attention span'. He locates his analysis in the increasing 'jolts per second' stimuli we receive from our televisions (especially through advertisements) and computer games. He describes how, as the levels of the stimuli increase to perpetuate the 'buzz level', many of our children are finding it difficult to adapt and keep up, and we should be thinking of this in terms of an 'early warning' of cultural instability for all of us. Armstrong does not suggest that there should be some mass movement to reduce, or even halt, the 'jolts per second', but he does suggest that we reduce our use/time spent viewing our televisions or computer games. Proactively he also suggests that there should be a reintroduction of unstructured play for children. By linking biological, social and environmental factors in early child development, Armstrong suggests that dysfunction in the circuitry between emotional and motor activity can be modified through play which is fully socialised, free, spontaneous and unstructured. The idea that we should biologically equip and socially and emotionally empower our children to resist and survive a continuing onslaught of technological stimuli through encouraging unstructured play is also in response to the dangers of methylphenidate, which suppresses the desire to play. Armstrong's view of the importance of unstructured play for children diagnosed with ADHD is in direct contrast to the focus on structure and surveillance as a 'normalising' practice in school (as discussed by Hjörne in Chapter 11).

In Chapter 3 John Davis continues the theme of empowering children by taking an overview of the contemporary dynamic relations between medical science, public policy, children's rights, emancipatory principles and citizenship. This sociological view provides connections between anxiety at the diagnosis of ADHD, to theoretical perspectives in education, disability and childhood studies. Davis argues that whatever approach to ADHD is adopted it should be under-pinned by a well-theorised position that shows awareness of: the tensions between adult control and child self-realisation in Western societies; the pressures placed on children, parents and teachers by social and education systems; the limitations of medical and social constructions of ADHD; the inability of some professionals who work with children to be reflexive; the need to consider a range of causes of ADHD; to consider the recent development of participatory and children's rights approaches; and the ability of children and young people to identify solutions to their own life problems.

Davis uses social constructivist approaches to emphasise the different structural frameworks in which ADHD can be located. In particular he highlights the need for a more reflexive approach to theory (and practice) that questions the assump-tions and interpretations that have been made about children's lives. The rights agenda (also highlighted in a South African context by Muthukrishna in Chapter 6) has foregrounded the rights of children to be consulted and to participate in decisions that affect them. By recognising the capacity and agency of children the complex connections between their actions and wider societal influences can begin to be examined so that they may be encouraged (in partnership with peer group and adults) to play an active role in defining and responding to their own life problems. However, Davis warns that social perspectives should not ignore the influence of biology on children's behaviour, but that solutions to the ADHD crisis are underpinned by appropriate critical thinking from a range of disciplines and perspectives.

David Walker, in his chapter on ADHD and American Indian children, provides us with a cultural history and overview of how labels have been used to marginalise, control and disempower those considered as 'different' and 'other'. As with some other marginal groups, American Indian children have been labelled 'deviant' in some manner by Euro-American culture for hundreds of years. In the case of American Indian children Walker argues that labels such as ADHD have no intercultural utility or validity and he gives the example of the active, exploratory, hands-on Yakama child learner who could be diagnosed as brain diseased and genetically inferior (two of the medical explanations for ADHD). The continued segregation and lowering of academic expectations for American Indian children are also seen by Walker to occur as a result of the pseudo-objectivity of psycho-logical tests for ADHD. Walker is also mindful of the agency of the American Indian child who may actively develop an oppositional identity in which the behaviour and expectations of the public school (state schools in the UK) are seen as a threat to their own cultural identity.

What does appear to be shared across cultures is the hegemonic discourse stemming from the medical model in which many parents, including American Indians, are persuaded to put their children on stimulant drugs. As Walker recognises, this is not to deny that culturally and personally, there are real lived experiences that need to be addressed, for rather than labels obfuscating the actual situations of those so categorised, it is the symptoms that are treated, rather than the cause. Walker is also suggesting there needs to be a step back from seeing the 'problem' as within the child, to looking at the cultural implications of such a diagnosis which perpetuates negative stereotypes of the American Indian child.

Although addressing issues specific to the American Indian, the issues raised in this chapter have many resonances with those raised by other authors here. A rise in the diagnosis of ADHD can be seen through many different lenses and interpreted in many different ways and David Walker provides one such lens that brings into focus issues of race and identity.

Discussions and debates about ADHD may be largely concentrated in medical and sociological discourses, but as Gordon Tait argues (Chapter 5), the phenomenon of ADHD can also exercise the philosophical mind. Tait begins his chapter describing an incident in the USA where a pupil who committed an act of vandalism avoided expulsion from school because of a retrospective diagnosis that he 'had' ADHD. For Tait this raises the notion of truth (is there such as thing as ADHD?) and the notion of moral responsibility (the belief that we all have the capacity to make free choices and we can be held accountable for those choices).

Tait argues that the possible consequences of adopting a particular understanding of the relationship between free will and moral responsibility has some significant implications for the way we educate our children. After leading the reader through an exposition of realism and anti-realism, Tait uses ADHD to illustrate the philosophical debate between free will and determinism, concluding there are now increasing numbers of hard determinist explanations for what was once regarded as 'voluntary conduct'. The resulting erosion of moral responsibility (highlighted by the increasing medicalisation of behaviour) is further exacerbated as more and more categories of behaviour disorders are 'discovered'. Although each disorder has different levels of associated accountability, the increase in diagnosis of these disorders means that more and more students will no longer be held fully accountable for their actions. Tait concludes that by categorising behaviours into smaller and smaller units this exponential increase has significant implications for our ability to hold people accountable for their actions, and we must therefore look for some alternative non-pathologising strategies of childhood regulation and education.

Nithi Muthukrishna (Chapter 6), writing from a South African perspective, takes us into the world of three South African children diagnosed with ADHD and their mothers. This detailed and illuminative account discusses the different contexts in which the school experiences of pupils diagnosed with ADHD are experienced as exclusionary by these children and their parents. As one of the many changes in South Africa, special education has undergone a national paradigm shift, from that of learner deficit and psycho-medical model, to a systemic one. By locating the problem in the system and not in the pupils the principles and values in the new legislation are embedded in a rights discourse. Although little is known about ADHD on the African continent it is estimated that 10 per cent of all South African children may have characteristics associated with ADHD, and there are concerns that drugs such as Ritalin may be over-prescribed. This is a small qualitative study in which the mothers' and children's own narratives inform an understanding of how the label ADHD impacts on their experiences of diagnosis, drug treatment and schooling. Although legislation may be framed in a rights discourse this would not appear to be the overriding experience of these families. The sense of power-lessness is palpable in the narratives of these mothers who are given limited information on which to base decisions that have, as they come to realise, both intended and unintended consequences for the education and well-being of their children. As the mothers reflect on the decisions that they have had to make, it is often serendipitous decisions that have resulted in positive changes (for example, the moving to another school because a placement has ended, and not because of professional advice or for pedagogical reasons). The hegemonic influences of the medical model in many school practices have resulted in educational experiences for these pupils which have often been distressing for them and their mothers. Within a rights discourse it is now hoped that positive, inclusive school experiences will be planned and intended, rather than serendipitous.

Beginning with an absolute negation of the claim that ADHD is biologically or neurologically determined, in Chapter 7 Üstün Öngel looks instead towards characteristics of family and environment that may be associated with the behavioural characteristics of ADHD. In particular he highlights the importance of parenting styles in both the production of and the solution to problems related to ADHD. By outlining the parenting styles associated with Baumrind, Öngel presents a model which places parents at the centre in changing the challenging behaviour of their children. This particular approach is then placed in the Turkish context where an estimated 10,000 children have been diagnosed with ADHD and where psycho-social interventions are described by Öngel as 'non-existent'. Öngel then describes his 'solitary intervention' in objecting to the recent project by the Turkish Ministry of Education to refer children diagnosed with ADHD to psychiatry clinics (and the subsequent prescription of stimulants). In order to reduce the use of stimulants for those diagnosed with ADHD Öngel is a vociferous advocate of the effectiveness of Baumrind's model.

As mentioned by Cohen in the first chapter in this book, there are countries, such as Italy, that have not yet fully embraced the 'notion' of ADHD. In Chapter 8 Maurizio Bonati describes how, prior to 1990, the Italian approach to behavioural difficulties was characterised by an assessment and treatment of 'hyperactivity' based on psychological methods informed by a socio-environmental understanding rather than an organic model. As a result, sales of methylphenidate

(Ritalin) were low and it was withdrawn from the market by the manufacturer (Ciba). The publication of the Diagnostic and Statistical Manual of the American Psychiatric Association, version 4 (DSM IV) (APA 1994) led to several studies in Italy resulting in an estimation that ADHD affected between 1 and 2 per cent of Italian school-aged children and adolescents. This was followed in 2000 by a group of parents with children diagnosed with ADHD lobbying the Ministry of Health for the re-introduction of methylphenidate. A flurry of activity then ensued with national conferences, national guidelines for ADHD diagnosis, and legislative measures that would transfer methylphenidate from the restrictive list to the less restrictive list of prescribed medications. In 2004 a strategic national-level registry was set up through which data on ADHD diagnosis and management could be collected and monitored, and at the beginning of 2005 the marketing authorisation for methylphenidate was granted. Bonati's description of the situation in Italy indicates that there may be an opportunity here for developing a better under-standing of the effects of diagnosis and prescription of methylphenidate for children than has been the case in other countries, most of which failed to monitor prescription patterns.

In Chapter 9 David Cohen discusses how the decision to medicate children diagnosed with ADHD is taken in some Canadian elementary schools. As part of a small team of researchers, Cohen describes how he and colleagues held focus group discussions with parents, teachers, school-based psychosocial professionals, and physicians specialising in the assessment and care of children. Those taking part in the study were agreed that teachers are the first to detect or be concerned by particular behaviours and there was also agreement that schools applied pressure upon parents to consult a physician (with parents feeling that they were obliged to consult a physician, otherwise their children might be placed in a special class or suspended from school). Given the many professionals who may be involved in an assessment it was also recognised there was no consistency of assessment approach. Interestingly, although teachers initiated this process, those who were not special needs teachers saw their participation in assessment as limited and inadequate. Cohen reports that every participant in these focus groups expressed dissatisfaction with the assessment process, and although the importance of conducting contex-tual and multidimensional assessments was recognised, there was agreement that collaboration was lacking. Dissatisfaction with interventions, follow-up and prescription criteria were also raised, but paradoxically, although participants stated emphatically that interventions with children must not rely only upon medication, they recognised just as emphatically that interventions consisted almost exclusively of medication.

As with Tait's conclusion that as more categories and complexity are introduced into societies, the less responsibility the individual retains, Cohen also argues that as social systems become increasingly complex there is a danger that individual and collective human agency is reduced through the increasing use of medication. But whereas Tait was describing the situation for young people diagnosed with ADHD, Cohen is referring to the loss of human agency of professionals who find themselves isolated and powerless to effect change, and of parents who feel they have no choice but to concur with school demands for assessment and resulting medication.

In Chapter 10 Ken Jacobson asks the reader to rethink 'pathology' in terms of adult–child power struggles. This chapter relates to observational field research conducted in USA and England and to a quantitative analysis of behaviours considered characteristic of ADHD. Initially, Jacobson aimed to establish a baseline separating 'normal' pupils from ADHD 'disordered' pupils, but as the research progressed, he came to recognise that there can be no objective standards by which to judge the appropriateness or inappropriateness of any specific behaviour. In this chapter Jacobson takes us on his personal research journey where he describes how children exercise their agency and resistance to adult/school 'rules'. Jacobson observed an apparent lack of difference in behaviours between those pupils in the American school and those in the school in England. Rather, it was the teachers who were described as 'different' in terms of their strategies for maintaining discipline in the classroom. Jacobson concludes that, irrespective of gender or academic success, all children express some ADHD-like behaviours, therefore any attempt to separate 'normal' expression from 'disordered' expression would require setting a standard of normalcy so low that the majority of school children would end up with a diagnosis of ADHD.

In Chapter 11 Eva Hjörne acknowledges the heated debate in Sweden between those who see the rise in diagnosis of AHDH/DAMP as a significant health problem and those who question the diagnosis as not identifiable or verifiable. 'DAMP' (Dysfunction in Attention, Motor control and Perception) is a unique hybrid concept that only very few countries use (it is used in Sweden and Denmark and, to a very limited extent, Norway and the UK), and, as a diagnosis, it is controversial.

This chapter is based on research that asks whether the practices and pedagogy in special classes for pupils with ADHD/DAMP are specifically applicable to this group of pupils and if so, whether they are effective in teaching/encouraging 'normal behaviour' so that the pupil can return to mainstream education. Hjörne provides a detailed and illuminating account of an 'ordinary' school day for one young boy. The description of the layout of the classroom, its location in the school and the dialogue between teacher and pupil highlight issues such as the very high levels of surveillance and control of these pupils (one pupil per teacher) and tension between such disciplinary practices and the long-term aim of returning children to mainstream classes – especially as these practices do not appear to change over time.

Hjörne recognises the irony in a situation where, although there is an increase in the diagnosis [of ADHD/DAMP], there nevertheless remain very few pedagogical strategies that correspond to the diagnosis, and these are no different from strategies used for disruptive pupils generally. This level of perceived homogeneity is reflected in the emphasis on distinct structures and firm routines and is located in a medical perspective of disability which is not grounded in a pedagogical analysis of the pupils' difficulties, needs and strengths: it appears more important for these pupils to be occupied, rather than receiving teaching and a curriculum specific to their needs. Homogeneity of approach for these pupils also promotes a sense of identity and status as a 'DAMP pupil', indeed one of the goals of the DAMP class is for pupils to acquire a 'decent' attitude to their 'handicap' and this is illustrated by teachers and pupils labelling themselves and their actions as 'DAMP'.

It is interesting (and surprising in the Swedish context?) to note that the barriers in the classroom, and the pedagogical practices which aim to reduce the opportunities for these pupils to make choices, are in contrast to the 'rights' agenda, and views expressed by Davis and Muthukrishna (this volume).

Chapter 12 by Gavin Reid focuses on the presenting behaviours of an ADHD diagnosis, rather than on the label itself. By acknowledging the multifaceted dimensions of ADHD Reid argues that no single intervention method is sufficient to produce either short-term or long-term change, and that both within-person factors and systems approaches also need to be considered. Reid stresses that a learning styles approach should also consider the learning environment, as well as the cognitive and curricular implications of the learning experience. Reid highlights the importance of learners attributing positive learning performances to factors within their control because if these positive experiences are attributed to extrinsic factors outside their control (such as the effects of drugs) this dependency will subsequently determine the learning outcome. However, for pupils diagnosed with ADHD it may be necessary for the teacher to take more of an active role in helping them develop their autonomy as learners.

Reid acknowledges the critics of learning styles who see this approach as deterministic, attributing a learning style to an individual as a fixed trait, whereas learning styles should be seen as providing guidance and not replacing one label with another.

In the final chapter of the book Gwynedd Lloyd recognises the challenges for educators who may accept the critiques of ADHD as a 'disorder' of questionable validity and who wish to avoid labelling students but who still have to find the best way to support the particular children and young people in their class and school. Lloyd encourages a recontextualisation of the issue without special emphasis on labels: 'There are no "ADHD" students; there are individual children with very varied family and educational histories, competences, learning styles and preferences.' The chapter suggests that it is possible to identify a range of effective strategies for supporting children and parents but argues that these should be developed within a more humanistic and less technicist approach to children and young people with difficulties in their lives. Lloyd also shows that although the literature on methods for 'ADHD students' makes very strong claims for specialist intervention, such interventions in fact do not differ from interventions aimed at improving learning or managing behaviour generally. She argues for schools to explore the ways that their curricula, pedagogy and assessment strategies may contribute to difficulties in learning or behaviour that become characterised as 'disorders'.

## Conclusion

There is much evidence in this book of a rapid move in many countries towards discussing the behaviour of children within a medical discourse, resulting in increasing diagnosis of ADHD (and apparently co-morbid conditions such as Oppositional Defiant Disorder and Conduct Disorder), and the prescription of psychotropic medicines. But this pathologising of behaviour does not, and cannot, address the complex range of reasons why children's behaviour may be challenging, or why they may experience difficulties in school and/or at home.

This edited volume aims, by presenting a wide range of views and perspectives, to challenge narrow notions of the idea of ADHD, what 'causes' ADHD, and how it may be 'cured'. Some contributors discuss key ideas and research, others describe experiences 'on the ground' in schools and in families, comment on those concerns that cross cultures and professional discourses such as the subjectivity and ethnocentricity of diagnosis, and consider the macro-level concerns of cultural stability and 'norms' which impact upon our thinking and our actions. The book asks readers to stop and think, to reconsider and reconceptualise the question of ADHD and the question of parents', teachers', and other professionals' responses to children so diagnosed. Surely we owe this to our children?

## References

American Psychiatric Association (APA) (1994) *Diagnostic and Statistical Manual of Mental Disorders* (4th edition). Washington, DC: American Psychiatric Association.

Breggin, P.R. and Cohen, D. (2001) *Your Drug May be Your Problem: How and why to stop taking psychiatric medication*. Cambridge: Perseus Books.

Lloyd, G. and Norris, C. (1999) 'Including ADHD?' *Disability & Society*, 14(4): 505–51.

NIMH (National Institute of Mental Health) (2003) *Attention Deficit Hyperactivity Disorder*. Available <http://www.nimh.nih.gov.publicat/adhd.cfm> (accessed 6 September 2004).

Norris, C. and Lloyd, G. (2000) 'Parents, professionals and ADHD: what the papers say.' *European Journal of Special Needs Education*, 15(2): 123–37.

SIGN (2001) *Attention Deficit and Hyperkinetic Disorders in Children and Young People. A national clinical guideline*. Edinburgh: Scottish Intercollegiate Guidelines Network.

WWF-UK (World Wildlife Fund UK) (2004) *Compromising our Children: Chemical impacts on children's intelligence and behaviour*. A WWF-UK Chemicals and Health Campaign Briefing. Available <http://www.wwf.org.uk>.

Zito, J.M. and Rushton, M.D. (2003) 'Psychotropic practices for youth: a 10-year perspective'. *Archives of Pediatrics & Adolescent Medicine*, 157: 17–25.

# Chapter 1

# Critiques of the 'ADHD' enterprise

*David Cohen*

At first glance, the reality of 'Attention-Deficit/Hyperactivity Disorder' (ADD or ADHD) seems obvious. The world's 'psychiatric bible,' the *Diagnostic and Statistical Manual of Mental Disorders* (fourth edition) (DSM-IV, American Psychiatric Association 1994) describes the mental disorder ADHD in detail. The manual lists four distinct ADHD diagnoses that can be derived using combinations from among eighteen behavioral signs. According to the DSM-IV, ADHD is a discrete member of the class of 'Disruptive Behavior Disorders.' It is characterized by persistent inattention and/or hyperactivity/impulsivity occurring in several settings and more frequently and severely than adults judge to be typical for children at the same chronological stage of development. Symptoms are said to begin before age seven and to cause serious difficulties in home, school, or work life. Based on these and previous DSM criteria, approximately two dozen behavioral checklists are in use by teachers, parents, physicians, and other health, mental health, and social service professionals to assess or 'test for' ADHD – although no actual test of any sort besides a behavioral checklist establishes or confirms the diagnosis. Nonetheless, Russell Barkley (1998: 67), a leader in the field, gives the latest definition of ADHD as a 'developmental failure in the brain circuitry that underlies inhibition and self-control.'

Like many other medical-psychiatric-educational labels, the ADHD label gives meaning to countless activities and leaves large traces. It is applied to millions of children around the world and recorded in millions of computerized and paper records in government and insurance company data banks, in educational institutions of all types and sizes, doctors' offices, clinics and hospitals, residential treatment centers, and in courts.

To millions of modern families, the label provides a legitimate justification to 'outsource' some responsibilities related to raising children, a task whose objectives, rules, and methods have changed dramatically over the last half-century, along with the typical composition of families. Messages about ADHD destined for parents have strong guilt-dissolving, 'natural calamity' components, as in Consumer Reports' health website (MedicalGuide.org): 'Learning that your child has ADHD can be distressing. But ADHD is nobody's fault. Nothing you or your child has done has caused it.'

The ADHD label serves to justify the disbursement of substantial public and private funds (about \$3.5–4.0 billion annually by the end of the 1990s) to fund special services in schools in the United States (Hinshaw *et al.* 1999). The label also provides schools yet another alibi to explain why they regularly fail to make some children fit in the only societal institution designed exclusively for children.

The ADHD label spurs enormous research activities and programs: thousands of drug treatment studies and experimental pharmacology and neuroscience studies of ADHD have been published since the 1960s. Each month, about twenty articles related to ADHD appear in scientific journals internationally. Hundreds of investigators from the health and social sciences currently study the cognitive performances of children diagnosed with ADHD. As of this writing, clinical trials conducted at the National Institute of Mental Health in the US are recruiting participants for investigations in the genetics of ADHD, brain processes in ADHD, herbal treatments for ADHD, and preventive interventions for ADHD. Using the keyword 'ADHD' for a search in a famous US online bookstore in mid-2005 yielded over 4,800 hits.

Last but not least, the ADHD label fuels the manufacture, promotion, regulation, and prescription of a dozen psychotropic pharmaceuticals, such as Ritalin and Concerta (two brand names for methylphenidate), Adderall (a mixture of four amphetamine salts), and Strattera (a 'non-stimulant' norepineprine reuptake inhibitor) in a worldwide market estimated to exceed \$3 billion annually (CNS Drug Discoveries 2004). A parallel industry of herbal, natural, complementary, and other 'alternative' diagnostics and remedies for ADHD also flourishes.

Together, these and other social facts too numerous to list make ADHD as tangible as any condition can be. They are the social bodyguards of ADHD, surrounding and protecting its integrity as an actual discrete entity, as an abnormality or disorder of childhood development and functioning, or as a 'severe neurobehavioral disorder,' as ADHD is regularly described in popular and professional literature. These social facts serve to dissuade would-be critics from analyzing the concept ADHD too critically and from scrutinizing it logically, ethically, sociologically. Commenting solely on the number of monthly scientific publications related to ADHD, Barkley and colleagues (2004: 65) write that 'the genuineness of ADHD as a disorder appears to be alive, well, and on solid scientific ground . . . Any "debate" over the legitimacy of ADHD as a valid disorder exists only in some segments of the popular media, not in the scientific community.' Put another way, the myriad activities undertaken to manage ADHD in familial, educational, clinical, scientific, bureaucratic, and commercial systems constitute insurmountable evidence pointing to a single conclusion: ADHD exists!

Yet the very popularity of ADHD has given rise to accounts expressing great skepticism that so many children in our cognitively and educationally affluent societies should be afflicted with a disorder rarely if ever mentioned merely 25 years ago. Raising and teaching children is something about which everyone has an opinion, usually a firm opinion, and the idea of ADHD leaves few people neutral.

Every effort to cement ADHD into the social consciousness has been resisted or derided to some extent. The notion of ADHD as a disorder or disease of childhood evokes resistance because it defies the common twin beliefs that *all* children are hyperactive, impulsive, and inattentive and that adults' primary task is precisely to raise them to act differently (Oas 2001). Besides an undercurrent of lay resistance, some sociologists, psychologists, pediatricians, psychiatrists, and psychologists have vigorously questioned the existence of a genuine condition 'ADHD' in all its previous and actual definitions since the 1960s. Facing psychologist Russell Barkley's (1995: 17) claim that 'ADHD is real, a real disorder, a real problem, often a real obstacle' stands neurologist Fred Baughman's (1998) counterclaim that 'ADHD is total, 100% fraud.'

The US, epicenter of the ADHD enterprise, is also epicenter of critiques of the ADHD enterprise. In this chapter, I summarize ten arguments emanating from North American authors and researchers who show one fault or another with various assumptions or conclusions concerning ADHD – its nature, its manifestations, its recognition, and its treatment via medications.

Not all countries have embraced the ADHD construct. My selective reading of the scant and necessarily retrospective epidemiological evidence suggests that at present, the construct is well established in the US, Canada, Australia, New Zealand, Switzerland, Norway, Sweden, Denmark, the United Kingdom, Germany, Holland, Israel, Spain, and Taiwan. In parallel, great international disparities exist in the use of stimulants as treatments for ADHD. It is estimated that fully 97 percent of the global sales of drugs for ADHD were derived from the US only, the rest from Europe (CNS Drug Discoveries 2004). Notably, certain countries with high rates of adult psychiatric drug use, such as France and Italy, appear so far to have resisted using stimulants with children in any significant manner, although in both countries key medical and educational institutions and parents' groups are just beginning to promote them – and the ADHD construct – vigorously (Bonati, this volume; Cohen 2000; Saget 2003). Systematic explanations of these puzzling international differences are still lacking. Possibly, the 'reality' of ADHD might assume different forms in nations just beginning to embrace the construct. The present summary of critiques of ADHD constitutes a modest effort toward the goal of shaping such alternative realities.

So far, the diagnosis of ADHD and the prescription of stimulants are inseparable phenomena. Without historical analysis, it is difficult to ascertain which preceded which, but it is reasonable to argue that the diagnosis is frequently a *post hoc* justification for the use of stimulants (Cohen, this volume; Conrad 1976). The figures from England (i.e. not Scotland, Wales, or Northern Ireland) illustrate just how rapidly their use can flourish on virgin soil: from 6,000 prescriptions for stimulants in 1994 to 186,200 in 2000, to 458,200 in 2004 (Prescription Cost Analysis 2005). To my knowledge, this 7600 percent increase in one decade represents the fastest ever anywhere on record. Taking into account their respective populations, England in 2004 still used stimulants about five times less than the US, where about 13 million prescriptions were written in 2003. If recent growth rates persist, however, there is every reason to expect England's rate of use to equal or exceed that of the US when this book appears in print.

The use of drugs increases the popularity of the ADHD label, which in turn reinforces the use of drugs and other interventions. Given the considerable short-term benefits that accrue from these practices to the influential mental health, educational, and drug industry communities, their members are likely to increase proclamations that those who question the validity of ADHD as a genuine disorder requiring lifelong treatment are flat-earthers.

The critiques included in this chapter were chosen mostly on the basis of their familiarity to this author; they do not represent the full spectrum of opposition and critical analysis (see, for example, Kiger 1985; Armstrong 1995; Maté 1999; Stein 1999; Timimi 2003). Broadly speaking, the critiques emanate from the fields of sociology, medicine (pediatrics, neurology, psychiatry), psychology, and clinical epidemiology. I have included authors who completely call into question the valid-ity of the ADHD construct along with authors who appear to accept the construct while questioning how ADHD-diagnosed children are managed. Some critiques emphasize broad societal tendencies, others focus on methodological shortcomings of studies purporting to identify brain differences between ADHD and normal children. Most are scholarly critiques, in the sense that their authors have spent considerable time marshalling evidence and constructing logical arguments and submitting them to peer or public review. Together, these critiques represent what I believe is a compelling case for continuing critical examination of, and skepticism toward, the 'ADHD enterprise.'

## ADHD as result of socio-cultural mutations

### Medicalizing deviant and ordinary behavior

In *Medicalization of Deviance: From Badness to Sickness* (first edition 1980), sociologists Peter Conrad and Joseph Schneider argued that several socially problematic conducts formerly characterized as sins or crimes, such as homosexuality, excessive drinking, and suicide, had been or were in the process of being medicalized. Conrad and Scheider defined medicalization as defining or describing a socially deviant condition using medical terms, attributing a medical cause to it, or managing it with medical means such as hospitalization, drugs, or psychotherapy.

Conrad and Schneider hypothesized a series of sequential steps in the med-icalization of deviance, from initial 'claims-staking' by early proponents to the final 'institutionalization' of the fully medicalized 'condition.' Interestingly, before publishing the complete theory of medicalization, Conrad's first case study of the phenomenon focused on what he termed the modern medical 'discovery' of hyperkinesis. Conrad (1976) argued that this discovery was built principally around the use of behavior-controlling drugs such as the stimulants.

In the intervening period since Conrad's study, and as reflected in American psychiatry's third edition of its *Diagnostic and Statistical Manual of Mental Disorders*

(American Psychiatric Association 1980), hyperkinesis eventually became 'Attention-Deficit/Hyperactivity Disorder,' to be defined using eighteen different behavioral signs. As some critics have pointed out, taken singly, these eighteen components of ADHD represent instances of *ordinary*, normal childhood behavior that would not be expected to cause distress or impairment to any individual manifesting them. With DSM-III, the actual diagnostic signs became a *frequency and combination* of signs.

Moreover, the continued extension of medical boundaries that theoretically characterizes medicalization appears in the emergence, in the mid-1990s, of the category of 'ADHD adults' (Hallowell and Ratey 1994). This grouping, arguably designating certain forms of adult incompetence and vocational failure, remarkably allows 'for the inclusion of an entire population of people and their problems that were excluded by the original conception of hyperactive children' (Conrad and Potter 2000: 559). Over the last few years in the US, the validity of 'adult ADD' has been promoted in skillfully crafted television commercials by Eli Lilly and Company, the manufacturers of Strattera (atomoxetine), a drug specifically marketed for adults with this 'treatable medical disorder'. Within a year of its lauching in November 2003, Strattera had captured a full 15 percent of the ADHD market for drugs (Breitstein 2004).

Some of the first conceptions of medicalization (by psychiatrist Thomas Szasz, sociologist Irving Zola) viewed it as an inexorable consequence of the merging, on the one hand, of ancient tribal urges to scapegoat deviants with, on the other, imperatives of secularism, scientism, and technological progress. In later conceptions, analysts described how medicalization was being applied not only to the classic cases of deviance (alcoholism, suicide, homosexuality, insanity), but increasingly to ordinary, normal conditions of life (such as menopause, educational difficulties, incurring excessive debts by shopping, violence, homelessness, excessive gambling, racial prejudice) (Cohen 2001). Top-down scapegoating as motive for medicalization gave way to bottom-up, diffuse, subtle, citizen-inspired initiatives filling various needs in complex and fluid societies. More recent conceptions of the dynamics of medicalization have included the corporate nature of medicine, the individualization of risk via genetic theorizing, as well as other features of health care systems in advanced post-industrial societies (Clarke *et al.* 2003).

In all its versions, however, medicalization never implied conspiracies by medical professionals seeking to increase their power and influence. On the contrary, the original claims-makers in the medicalization process are usually non-medical professionals or laypersons. Throughout the periods that saw changing labels applied to the condition that concerns us here, such as 'hyperkinesis' and 'hyperactivity' (early 1970s), 'minimal brain damage' (late 1970s), 'attention-deficit disorder' (early 1980s) or 'attention-deficit/hyperactivity disorder' (late 1980s), teachers and educational psychologists appear as the pioneers of medicalization, at least in the US and Canada. In the UK, the reverse appears to have been true, with evidence suggesting that, initially, teachers typically resisted medicalization, rejected the label and refused to encourage the medicating of children (Malacrida 2004). In contrast, in the case of 'ADHD adults,' long after the cementing of ADHD as a condition of childhood, the expanded diagnostic category received support from a broad combination of lay, professional, and media claims.

The last step in the medicalization process, termed 'institutionalization' by Conrad and Schneider (1980), consists in the now fully medicalized category being consecrated by most mainstream official and scientific instances. The existence of one or more bureaucracies devoted to perpetuating and expanding the boundaries of the category, and to actively suppressing alternative claims, illustrates institutionalization, which is where ADHD rests securely today in the handful of developed nations mentioned earlier. There exist degrees of medicalization, limits to medicalization, and some rare instances of demedicalization (Conrad 1992). However, by any indicator, medicalization of children's deviant and ordinary (but problematic-for-adults) behavior continues unabated.

### Rapid-fire culture and rapid-fire consciousness

Psychologist and independent drug scholar Richard DeGrandpre proposed in *Ritalin Nation: Rapid-fire Culture and the Transformation of Human Consciousness* (1999) that the US suffers from being a 'hurried society.' DeGrandpre describes America as 'a nation strung out on excitement,' where 'the pleasures of slowness' have disappeared. As America increasingly sought to conquer excitement and speed, the pace of American life in all its dimensions accelerated and continues to accelerate. Further, this acceleration of culture has itself been accelerating. This is illustrated, among other things, by a bewildering proliferation of technologies designed with a single aim: to make people go through all activities of their life faster. DeGrandpre's characterization recalls descriptions of the acceleration of other tendencies in modern society, such as urbanization, or the accumulation of information and waste – where each change creates circumstances requiring faster change, the process seeming to feed on itself.

Illustrating the slogan 'The personal is political,' DeGrandpre links these supra-societal changes to individuals' internal states. He believes that 'as society goes faster, so do the rhythms of our own consciousness. This is especially true for children, who grow up in concert with the latest speed' (1998: 19). Cognitive and emotional adaptation to quickening pace, however, has produced an unexpected effect, one that evokes paradoxes resulting from societies' previous marches toward perceived utopias. DeGrandpre suggests that the 'transformation of human consciousness actually has the unanticipated effect of neutralizing its intended rewards. We pursue newness and change yet quickly come to experience these changes as no more stimulating than before.' In other words, 'We're not just moving through our lives faster; we're also acquiring a heightened need for speed' (1998: 24). DeGrandpre's thesis focuses not on the advent of technology *per se*; it emphasizes the impact of technology on our attention, awareness, desires, and frustrations.

Many children in the modern world are filled with sensory stimulation almost 24 hours a day. The least expensive source of stimulation, television, accounts for most of it. Television watching, according to DeGrandpre, illustrates how easy it is even for adults to forfeit self-control (spending hours clicking a remote control device, from channel to boring channel) and succumb to a never-ending provider of effortless stimulation.

Young children suffer most from television because the more they watch it the less likely they are to develop other ways to occupy themselves, to develop other habits and other skills, such as dramatic play, reading, and physical activity (Eastman 2004). It is of course crucially important for children to learn these other habits and skills in order to control themselves. DeGrandpre's thesis recently received support from a longitudinal study of 1,300 pre-schoolers, where the number of hours of television watched daily at age 1 and 3 years was linearly associated to the likelihood of exhibiting attentional problems at age 7 years (when 10 percent of the sample exhibited such problems) (Christakis *et al.* 2004).

Here is how DeGrandpre summarizes the development of 'ADHD':

> As rapid-fire culture gives rise to a rapid-fire consciousness – and, for children, an inability to regulate their own behavior – sensory addictions develop, motivating us to engage in more stimulus-seeking behaviors. At the heart of this developmental problem lies the emergence of a phenomenological experience of unsettledness, characterized by feelings of restlessness, anxiety, and impulsivity. Hyperactivity and the inability to attend to mundane activities exemplify the type of escape behavior that the 'sensory addicted' child or adult uses in order to maintain his or her needed stream of stimulation.
>
> (1998: 32)

In sum, DeGrandpre describes what he believes to be a series of unique, late twentieth-century sensory addictions among Americans, some of which constitute what is labeled as ADHD. These addictions are at root cultural problems that have a way of becoming psychological ones and perhaps biological ones as well. A close variation of DeGrandpre's thesis, applied to the consumptive behaviors fostered in modern adults, is developed in a book with the telling title of *American Mania: When More is Not Enough* (Whybrow 2005).

### The cult of performance – in a pill

In *Running on Ritalin: A Physician Reflects on Children, Society, and Performance in a Pill*, pediatrician Lawrence Diller (1998) discussed how the idea of enhancing normal performance became somewhat politically correct over the last two decades. Formerly, enhancing performance was only a preoccupation among elite athletes ('doping'), artists, or warriors. By the mid-1990s, however, enhancing performance had become planted within suburbia and the middle-class, fertilized in part by the Prozac-induced seduction of 'cosmetic psychopharmacology' (Kramer 1993). Cosmetic psychopharmacology, originally defined by psychiatrist Peter Kramer, resembles the magic potion of fairy tales in that it refers to the possibility of changing one's inner emotional and cognitive states at will and harmlessly by means of modern psychotropic drugs.

According to Diller, one of the principal messages conveyed by American culture is that one should be successful and happy. In this culture, 'persistent difficulty, disappointment, and sadness are not acceptable parts of the human condition: rather, they are subversive enemies which we must defeat' (Diller 1998: 316). However, Diller also sees an 'emerging culture of disability' that seeks – despite the dominant 'cultural rejection of underperformance' – to normalize and to accept underperformance.

Despite increases in the use of psychiatric diagnosing and drug treatment of poor children and children from ethnic and racial minorities in the US (Breggin and Breggin 1998; Zito et al. 2003), the use of stimulants in this country appeared to remain throughout the 1990s mostly a phenomenon of white, suburban, middle- and upper-middle-class children. According to Diller (1998: 317): 'It's in this slice of society, of course, that expectations run highest and anxieties about performance shortfalls lately have become acute. It's this group of parents who worry that their children's future may be jeopardized by not getting into the right preschool. Little wonder that they so often see the wisdom in Ritalin.'

Because of other cultural contradictions, however, such as the extraordinary prizing of individual achievement but the expectation of conformity, the desire for performance enhancement cannot be announced openly; it remains repressed, socially frowned upon. In the US, performance enhancement, in contrast to physical enhancement (via implants, surgery, hormones) still appears too much like gaining an unfair advantage over others who choose to 'play by the rules.' Craving legitimacy, the performance enhancers thus have little recourse but to assert ever more forcefully that ADHD is a genuine medical disorder or deficit like diabetes or poor vision, and that the regular use of stimulants is as *bona fide* a treatment for it as insulin maintenance or the wearing of eye glasses is legitimate for these latter disorders and deficits.

Some cultural trends change rapidly, and performance enhancement is becoming more socially acceptable as different rationales and justifications for uses of pharmaceuticals are voiced by consumers (Cohen et al. 2001). In many anecdotal accounts appearing on the Internet, and in my own contacts with families, parents often cite performance enhancement as the primary reason for continuing their children on stimulants: their children's grades have improved. Occasionally, in medical journals, academic performance enhancement is specifically stated, without comment, as the reason for prescription (Cohen and Leo 2002). It would seem that this justification of the use of stimulants – as short-term school performance enhancers for children – deserves open discussion rather than remain camouflaged behind the label of an ostensibly medical condition. If that were the case, parents and social actors would undoubtedly be in a better position to assess the merits and the drawbacks of enhancing educational performance with drugs (just as, for example, they are able to assess the strategy of physical punishment or that of token rewards) on its *own* ethical, educational, and developmental terms, uncontaminated by medicalesque explanations and justifications.

## Disorder? What disorder?

### 'Total, 100% fraud'

ADHD is regularly described, in medical literature, as a 'neurological,' 'neurobe-havioral,' or 'neurodevelopmental' disorder or disease. Yet, pediatric neurologist Fred Baughman, Jr, has repeated, in a series of short articles, letters to the editors of medical publications, and commentaries in newspapers and on his website (www.adhdfraud.com), that the diagnosis of ADHD constitutes 'total, 100% fraud.' Baughman ceaselessly reminds his colleagues in unambiguous language that children diagnosed with ADHD have no detectable abnormality specific to that diagnosis.

According to Baughman, physicians learn in medical school that a fundamental difference distinguishes disease from non-disease. To diagnose disease, the physician must find confirmatory evidence *in each individual patient* of the physical abnormality or abnormalities that characterize the disease and that are described in the scientifically validated literature. Baughman likes to remind his audience that he is well qualified to pass these judgments as he himself has discovered a true disease, a rare birth defect – curly hair-anklyoblepharon (fused eyelids)-nail dysplasia syndrome – whose genetic origin he also later helped to discover and describe in publications. In contrast, no characteristic abnormality has yet been identified or validated for ADHD. As the DSM-IV (American Psychiatric Association 1994: 81) states in its description of ADHD, under the heading 'Associated Laboratory Findings,' 'There are no laboratory tests that have been established as diagnostic in the clinical assessment of Attention-Deficit/Hyperactivity Disorder.' Hence, physicians cannot and do not detect any abnormality in their patients during their patients' life – or after death, at autopsy, as with most physical diseases – that can be reliably associated with the diagnosis of ADHD.

Nevertheless, Baughman charges, physicians routinely violate scientific and ethical tenets of medicine by diagnosing individuals as suffering from a disease called ADHD and by prescribing potentially toxic drugs to these individuals. The scientific misconduct lies in diagnosing disease in the absence of any confirmatory evidence of disease. The ethical misconduct lies in not informing parents or patients of this fact while obtaining their 'informed consent' to receive a 'treatment.'

Baughman ceaselessly emphasizes that children diagnosed ADHD must be considered *physically normal*: 'It is as simple as this: if no physical examination, lab test, X-ray, scan or biopsy shows an abnormality in your child, [your child is] normal.' Baughman cautions, however, that 'Once Ritalin or any other psychiatric drug courses through their system, day-in and day-out, [children] are no longer physically normal.' Baughman can be even more categorical: 'The Nuremberg

Code does not allow the abrogation of informed consent (*de facto* medical malpractice) or the drugging of normal, disease-free, children. We are not mis-diagnosing or over-diagnosing, mis-treating or over-treating ADHD. It has been a total, 100% fraud throughout it's [*sic*] 35 year history.'

Baughman's singular emphasis on the absence of demonstrated physical abnormalities makes him a true adherent, rather than an opponent, of the 'medical model.' His argument resembles a major thesis of Thomas Szasz, the iconoclastic psychiatrist who has also argued for several decades that, absent confirmatory evidence of physical etiopathology, 'problems in living,' no matter how troublesome and painful, must remain just that (Szasz 2001). Baughman's argument could be extended from ADHD to most of the hundreds of diagnoses in the DSM. Indeed, are not all psychiatric conditions (certain dementias and substance-abuse problems excepted) diagnosed in the absence of any laboratory tests, by simply 'eyeballing' and talking with the ostensible patient? Baughman's argument is completely inassailable on the facts but will remain marginalized until laypersons and professionals are ready to re-evaluate physicians' 'unique expertise' in the diagnosis of *all* problems in living.

## 'ADHD' as annoying behavior

Throughout the 1980s and 1990s, psychiatrist Peter Breggin has been the leading critic of biological psychiatry. He is the most prolific and outspoken detractor of the concept of ADHD, its diagnosis, and its drug treatment, and has authored four books specifically dealing with ADHD, children, and psychiatry.

In a popular book on stimulants, Breggin succinctly expresses the idea that the DSM diagnosis of ADHD simply *cannot* have any validity as a label for a genuine biological dysfunction. In his view, 'The very nature of the ADHD diagnosis renders absurd the idea of finding a common biological or genetic basis. The ADHD diagnosis is nothing more than a list of all the behaviors that annoy teachers and require extra attention in the classroom.' He illustrates: 'Key items in the diagnosis such as "often fidgets with hands or feet or squirms in seat," "often leaves seat in classroom," "often blurts out answers," and "often has difficulty waiting turn" have in common that they make life more difficult for teachers and other adults trying to manage groups of children' (2002: 126). Breggin thus radically contextualizes the criteria for the ADHD diagnosis: the behaviors are normal and have no meaning outside of the structured, regimented demands of a typical classroom. The only difference between these behaviors exhibited by normal children and by 'ADHD' children, as the DSM-IV recognizes, is found in the word 'often.' Breggin's argument suggests we ask simply: What sort of biological cause would know the difference between 'normal' and 'often' before a given teacher, in a given classroom, or in a given culture?

The DSM-IV states that 'Signs of the disorder may be minimal or absent when the person is under strict control, is in a novel setting, is engaged in especially interesting activities, is in a one-to-one situation (e.g. in the clinician's office), or while the person experiences frequent rewards for appropriate behaviors' (American Psychiatric Association 1994: 79). Breggin (1999: 230) seizes upon this statement to remark: 'This extraordinary admission indicates that ADHD is a 'disorder' quite unlike other disorders. It *disappears* when the child gets proper attention. Multiple sclerosis, cerebral palsy, genetic mental retardation, and other genuine neurological disorders would not so readily disappear under improved environmental circumstances.'

### Ignoring, yet pathologizing, temperament

William Carey, Clinical Professor of Pediatrics at the University of Pennsylvania, earned his principal reputation for his studies of children's temperament (e.g. Carey 1985, 1992) and co-authored a popular book on the subject for parents and teachers (Carey and Jablow 1997). For Carey, temperament can be divided into at least nine dimensions, including activity, adaptibility, distractibility, initial reaction, intensity, mood, persistence/attention span, regularity, and sensitivity. Carey believes that about half of temperament is of genetic origin and may be resistant to change, and the other half is fully malleable by the environment. Though it is more difficult to measure as a child ages, temperament, Carey holds, becomes more stable and remains a key factor influencing the quality of child–adult relationships.

In his presentation at the 1998 US National Institutes of Health Consensus Conference on ADHD and its treatment, Carey argued that ADHD represents nothing more – or less – than normal variation of temperament, but that professionals ignore the issue of temperament when discussing ADHD:

> My concern with the problem of ADHD was sparked by the abundant evidence that behavioral scientists and practitioners have, in distressing numbers, failed to recognize the existence and importance of temperamental variations. Common patterns in professional thinking have been to ignore, trivialize, or pathologize temperament. DSM-IV does not even mention it.
>
> (Carey 2002: 4)

First, Carey argues that the DSM-IV,

> which makes the diagnosis when a certain number of troublesome behaviors are present (and other criteria met), overlooks that these behaviors are probably usually normal . . . temperamental traits that lead to dysfunction not by their total numbers but when any number of them generates dissonant interactions between the child and his/her incompatible setting.
>
> (Ibid.: 5–6)

Second, Carey emphasizes the absence of clear evidence that symptoms of ADHD are related to brain malfunction. He raises the point, made in previous publications (e.g. Carey 1992), that different but normal temperamental differences can be shown to have a genetic basis as well as biochemical correlates. He finds that 'the assumption of brain malfunction in inattentive, active school children suffers from too narrow an evolutionary and anthropological perspective of what is normal in human brain function' (ibid.: 11).

Third, Carey criticizes the neglect of the role of the environment and interactions with it as factors in causing the 'symptoms' to appear: 'The whole body of the temperament research of the last 30 years [concurs that] . . . the outcome of children with "difficult" temperament depends on whether the parents and other essential elements of the environment provide a harmonious fit or one that gen-erates excessive conflict and stress . . .' (ibid.: 7).

Finally, Carey observes that the widely used ADHD diagnostic questionnaires are highly subjective and impressionistic. 'Their items are phrased such as "talks too much", "often fidgets", and "messy work". The rater is not advised how much is too much, how much motion and how often under what circumstances constitutes fidgetiness, and so on' (2002: 8). Carey believes that these questionnaires 'should be regarded as no more than the perceptions and discomforts of parents and teachers' (ibid.: 9). This view has recently received empirical support in a study by Barnes *et al.* (2003). In a large urban university, 115 students filled out a questionnaire using language similar to that found in widely used ADHD rating scales. Subjects were asked to judge just how frequently a behavior needs to occur before it should be rated as 'often.' Barnes and colleagues' results show that individuals are consistent with themselves in their view of 'often,' but that this view varies considerably from individual to individual. This suggests that when applied to individual children, ADHD behavior rating scales may not have much validity.

A good summary of Carey's position may be found in the following passage:

> What appears to be going on with most children being diagnosed with ADHD today is normal variations, especially of temperament, in neurologically intact individuals, especially low adaptibility and low persistence/attention span . . . The dysfunction appears to be in the interaction between child and environment, both of which may be normal but incompatible with each other. . . . That does not mean, however, that there is an underlying disorder in the child.
>
> (2002: 13)

## Confusing symptoms with cause

Neurologist and psychiatrist Sidney Walker III attempts to distinguish the symp-toms of a disease from the cause of the disease. In a book entitled *The Hyperactivity Hoax* (1998), Walker charges that physicians today diagnose ADHD and prescribe treatments without engaging in differential diagnosis, that is, without seeking to determine whether known medical problems might explain the presenting problems (the 'symptoms'). Merely checking a list of symptoms and naming a child as 'hyperactive' or 'inattentive' *explains* nothing. Walker believes that 'The unanswered question, obviously, is, "What is causing your child to be hyperactive?" Or, "What is causing your child to have attention problems?"' According to Walker:

> It's a critical question. Children with early-stage brain tumors can develop symptoms of hyperactivity or poor attention. So can lead- or pesticide-poisoned children. So can children with early-onset diabetes, heart disease, worms, viral or bacterial infections, malnutrition, head injuries, genetic disorders, allergies, mercury or manganese exposure, petit mal seizures, and hundreds – yes, *hundreds* – of other minor, major, or even life-threatening medical problems. Yet, all of these children are labeled hyperactive or ADD.
>
> (1998: 6)

In a manner reminiscent of Fred Baughman, the other neurologist critic in this group, Walker continues:

> Furthermore, hundreds of thousands of *perfectly normal* children are labeled hyperactive or attention disordered, though there's nothing at all wrong with them. These children are lumped in with the truly ill children . . . and all are medicated willy-nilly with potent and dangerous drugs.
>
> (Ibid.: 6–7)

This occurs, according to Walker, because physicians have recently been taught to believe that the *symptoms* of hyperactivity and inattention are signs of a genuine disease. Believing that they have identified the genuine cause, when they have merely confounded symptoms with the cause, physicians usually go no further in their 15-minute examination than a cursory exploration of eye or vision problems.

Squarely conforming to the tradition of clinical medicine, Walker argues that symptoms never explain themselves (Taylor 2000). Relying merely on symptom presentation to conclude something about the nature of a disorder is a profound fallacy, as countless different diseases share symptoms. The task of the clinician is that of the detective: to ferret out the cause of the symptoms. Yet, lip service to 'differential diagnosis' and to 'ruling out organic causes' aside, the majority of ADHD diagnoses are posed when clinicians merely establish that various informants agree that a certain number of symptoms are present.

### Brain abnormality in ADHD: genuine or artifact?

The website of Children and Adults with Attention-Deficit Disorder (CHADD), an international ADHD lobby group that receives significant funding from the pharmaceutical industry and collaborates with the Center for Disease Control to disseminate information about ADHD, defines ADHD as a 'severe neurobiological disorder.' Such a disorder would be expected to leave observable traces in the central nervous system of affected individuals, and this expectation is just what guides studies of ADHD patients using modern neuroimaging technology such as MRI and PET scanning (which images the functioning of the brain non-invasively). Pictures of such scans, showing a 'normal' brain and an 'ADHD brain' (really, a composite of many pictures of brains) clearly distinguished by different colors, spots, and shadows, have appeared in numerous professional and popular publications.

Although no one can tell apart, on the basis of a brain scan, the brain of a normal person from the brain of an ADHD-diagnosed person, and although neuroimaging has no place in the diagnosis of ADHD – as it would if it identified valid biological markers of ADHD – a review of over 30 neuroimaging studies by Giedd and colleagues (2001) concluded: 'Taken together, the results of the imaging and neuropsychological studies suggest right frontal-striatal circuitry involvement in ADHD with a modulating influence from the cerebellum' (2001: 44). In their review, however, Giedd *et al.* did not provide information on a crucial question: were the ADHD subjects in these neuroimaging studies medicated?

This is a crucial question because an astronomical number of studies show that psychotropic medications impact the brain, alter its function and structure, and are more likely to do so in younger subjects with developing brains than older subjects. Studies of Ritalin in humans show that it induces large volume changes in dopamine in brain regions within one hour of ingestion (Volkow *et al.* 2002). In rodents, early drug administration leads to about 50 percent less dopamine receptors by adulthood, long after termination of the drug (Moll *et al.* 2001). Thus, having ADHD subjects on stimulants for varying durations and then scanning their brain is a truly confounding factor in brain-imaging research. If some subtle abnormality is detected in the ADHD subjects but not in the control subjects, how can we rule out the influence of the drugs?

When neurological scientist Jonathan Leo and I examined all the studies included in Giedd *et al.*'s review (Leo and Cohen 2003) we were astounded to find that most subjects in the ADHD groups were on medication or had been medicated prior to the scans, though this issue was rarely discussed by the investigators. For example, in fourteen studies that used MRI, three studies gave no information on medication status. The remaining eleven studies involved 259 patients and 271 controls, with 247 (95 percent) of patients having prior or current medication use. In only two reports was this issue actually discussed, but neither devoted more than two sentences to it. Our findings were similar for other types and more recent brain-imaging studies (Cohen and Leo 2004).

Then appeared a major study, funded by the NIMH and conducted by Castellanos and colleagues (2002), that finally did what no other study had done before: not only was it huge (291 participants), not only did it last ten years, but one-third of the ADHD children had never received medication. Here, finally, was the opportunity to compare medicated with unmedicated ADHD patients. The findings, widely reported, were to the effect that the brains of ADHD children were about 3–5 percent smaller compared to those of controls. The important question: What about the brains of the *unmedicated* ADHD children? Castellanos reported that they were smaller too. But when Leo and I analyzed the study, we found that the unmedicated patients were on average 2.5 years younger, were shorter, and were lighter than the medicated patients. These age, height, and weight differences could in themselves entirely explain any observed difference: think of an average 8-year-old and an average 11-year-old; the older child is likely to have a slightly larger brain, a 3–5 percent larger brain . . . Until the Castellanos study, brain-imaging studies using ADHD patient groups were flawed in almost every study, as they used mostly medicated patients. With the Castellanos study, the *control* group was inappropriate. In any case, one US newspaper, the *Detroit News*, announced the results of Castellanos' study on December 12, 2002 with the following headline: 'Ritalin is safe, and it works: Study finds it actually helps brain grow.'

## Treatment? What treatment?

### Confusing adverse drug reactions with behavioral improvement

Psychiatrist Peter Breggin's second distinctive contribution to critiques of the ADHD enterprise may be found in his conclusions concerning the effects of stimulant drugs on human and animal behavior. Breggin has provided a forceful explanation for the perceived 'effectiveness' of stimulants to reduce overactivity and inattention, or to increase 'on-task' behavior and 'focusing.' This explanation is consistent with the 'brain-disabling' hypothesis that Breggin has formulated in earlier publications.

Breggin has emphasized that a large body of animal literature points to two basic and closely related behavioral effects of stimulant drugs:

> First, *stimulants suppress normal spontaneous or self-generated activity, including social-ization* [references omitted]. Exploration, novelty seeking, curiosity, purposeful locomotion, and escape behaviors are diminished. Inhibitions in socialization are demonstrated by reductions in approach behavior, interactions, mutual grooming, and vocalizations. . . . Second, *stimulants promote stereotyped, obsessive/compulsive, overly focused behaviors that are often repetitive or meaningless* [references omitted]. The effects may be demonstrated by limited or constricted pacing, reduced or localized self-grooming, staring out of the cage, staring at small objects, repetitive head movements, and other compulsive behaviors, such as picking, scratching, gnawing, or licking limited areas of the body or objects.
>
> (1999: 222, italics in original)

Breggin's next step is to propose that these expressions of what he calls the 'continuum of stimulant-induced toxicity' represent precisely what is misperceived as 'improvements in the behavior of children diagnosed as ADHD. That is, they can be potentially misinterpreted as "beneficial"' (ibid.: 225). In other words, drug-induced suppression of spontaneous behavior and drug-induced enforcement of obsessive physical and cognitive behavior are adverse drug reactions (ADRs), easily recognizable in animal research as deviations from normal, spontaneous motor and social behavior. In settings requiring conformity from children, however, these same effects appear as:

> increased willingness of children to do school work and chores that they would ordinarily find boring, meaningless, or frustrating. By struggling compulsively over their work, they may have seemed to be learning, even when they are not. . . . 'Social Withdrawal ADRs' describes drug reactions that render children more quiet, less seemingly needy, and less troublesome. . . . 'Behaviorally Suppressive ADRs' includes behaviors related to enforced compliance, submissiveness, and apathy. If the children are 'out of control' due to improper discipline, boredom, or other psychological and social problems, their behavior will nonetheless be suppressed so that they appear 'more normal.'
>
> (Ibid.: 227–228)

Just as stimulant-induced behavioral changes occur in healthy animals, stimulant effects on humans are independent of any psychiatric diagnosis or disorder: 'They represent a specific drug effect on all children [references omitted]. Whether or not children seem to be overactive, impulsive, or distractible, psychostimulants will subdue these behaviors' (ibid.: 225).

### Treatment studies: low-quality, short-term effects only

In 1999, the US Agency for Health Care Policy and Research (AHCPR) reached a sobering conclusion regarding trials of treatments for attention-deficit/ hyperactivity disorder (ADHD). Among hundreds of treatment studies, researchers selected 92 so-called 'gold standard' randomized controlled trials (RCTs). These are studies where subjects diagnosed with ADHD were randomly assigned to receive either a treatment (mostly stimulants) or a placebo, and where subjects and investigators were expected to be blind about treatment status. The reviewers for the AHCPR found that 'Most studies did not clearly describe clinically important information such as the primary outcomes of interest . . . The small sample size of most studies limited their power to detect meaningful clinically important differences among the interventions' (1999: 3). In addition, 97 percent of the studies did not describe how subjects were randomized, 95 percent did not describe how investigators were kept blind about the patients' treatment status, and 87 percent gave no details on dropouts and reasons for dropouts in each treatment group. These methodological failings, of course, indicate poor-quality studies, because they prevent us from ruling out alternative explanations for any reported positive effects of treatments.

Schachter and colleagues (2001) also conducted a meta-analysis of 62 carefully selected RCTs of short-acting Ritalin as a treatment for ADHD. Their observations match those of the AHCPR, with the additional detail that *less than half of the trials lasted more than 10 days*, and average duration was three weeks. This extremely short duration would prevent observers from making valid judgments about longer-term effects of stimulants, which are often prescribed for months and years. Only seven studies had more than 80 subjects in total. Interestingly, although Schachter *et al.* (2001) found a statistically significant clinical effect for Ritalin in the short-term treatment of ADHD diagnosed youth, they concluded that this effect was not robust concerning efficacy on 'core ADD features.'

These two meta-analyses identify methodological failings that suggest one conclusion: from a scientific point of view, most positive effects attributed to ADHD treatments are exaggerated. Unless a study meets certain basic criteria, which include the detailed description of methodological procedures, it may be considered a low-quality study. Low-quality studies have been shown regularly to overestimate the effects of treatments (Khan *et al.* 1996). That is why precisely why reviewers pay special attention to the methodological failings identified above. The more a study deviates from the ideal conduct and reporting of an RCT, the less confidence one can have in its findings.

What about longer-term studies of treatments for ADHD? The only significant review of long-term studies was conducted by Schachar and colleagues (2002). Searching exhaustively in the entire known medical literature, these investigators were able to locate only fourteen controlled studies lasting longer than three months. Because so few of the studies were of high quality, and because the outcome measures differed so much from study to study, Schachar and colleagues were unable to conduct a meta-analysis, relying instead of a detailed qualitative analysis. Altogether, the fourteen studies involved 1379 participants, with 549 (42 percent) coming from a single study, the Multi-Modal Treatment Study of ADHD (MTA). Four studies had less than ten subjects per group. Only three studies exceeded one year. It is extraordinary that more than three decades after millions of children had been medicated with stimulants, only three treatment studies following children for more than one year had been published.

Quality-wise, the studies were quite poor: thirteen of fourteen did not describe the method of randomization, nor the primary outcome of interest; nine of thirteen did not describe how the blind was protected, and poorly described dropouts and withdrawals. In the largest study, the MTA, the raters for the primary outcomes, parents and teachers, were not blind to the children's treatment status. This would prevent one from ruling out the potential confounding of raters' expectations on the ratings.

Of the fourteen studies, only six tested stimulants compared to placebo. Methylphenidate or dexedrine was superior to placebo in reducing ADHD symptoms in four studies, but did not exceed placebo in two. Seven studies measured academic performance but only three reported a slight effect favoring drugs. Schachar and colleagues concluded: there is 'little evidence that stimulants improve academic attainment, even after as long as 1 year of treatment' (2002: 346). Nine studies measured social behavior and aggressivity: there, six studies showed an effect – consistent with Breggin's interpretation of the classic effects of the 'continuum of stimulant-induced neurotoxicity' (see earlier). Five studies examined 'internalizing symptoms' such as sadness, crying, self-esteem: only two studies reported improvement in self-esteem. Schachar and colleagues (2002) conclude: 'Rigorous treatment research among representative sample of ADHD individuals is needed.' It is worth mentioning here that neither the AHCPR nor the authors of the analyses just summarized give any indication of believing that the ADHD label is not valid – on the contrary, they make several assertions indicating otherwise.

Many authors have discussed why clinical studies of psychiatric drugs, whether they be antipsychotics (Thornley and Adams 1998), antidepressants (Kirsch *et al.* 2002; Jureidini *et al.* 2004), or as we have shown here, stimulants, consistently demonstrate serious methodological failings. This body of evidence thus cannot confidently be used to guide social policy on such a wide scale as these drugs are used today. The principal reasons for the 'debasement' of the clinical trial over the last 50 years involve conflicts of interests between commercial and scientific imperatives, the inappropriate involvement of product sponsors into the clinical trial enterprise, and publication bias or the use of various methods to censor and suppress findings reflecting negatively on a product (review by Cohen 2005). Overall, this line of argument – which so far has been taken seriously only with respect to the recent research involving antidepressants for children (Medawar and Hardon 2004) – suggests strongly that the practice of medicating children with stimulants is not as evidence-tested as many people believe or want to believe.

## Conclusion

This selective review suggests that contemporary critiques of the ADHD enterprise differ in their meanings and conclusions. Some critics, like Baughman and Breggin, completely reject the concept of ADHD and the idea that children need to be treated for 'it.' Others, like Carey, Diller, and DeGrandpre, appear to believe that a narrowed ADHD concept may have some descriptive utility but that dominant educational and treatment practices have vastly outpaced any legitimate significance of such a concept. Still others, like Schachter and Schachar, reviewers of the drug treatment studies, fully accept the validity of ADHD but lament that the quality of most treatment studies means that clinicians who prescribe drugs are still basically shooting in the dark.

The diagnosis of ADHD and the drug Ritalin marked the beginning of the full-scale psychiatric colonization of childhood. Today, not only ADHD, but the whole range of psychiatric labels – including as of this writing, the fastest-growing one for children, bipolar disorder – are now applied to children, some of whom are barely old enough to talk. Not only stimulants, but the full panoply of psychiatric drugs – antidepressants, anticonvulsants, antipsychotics, and tranquilizers – are now given to children, some of whom have just learned to walk.

It is difficult, if not impossible, to find historical precedents for medically sanctioned mass drugging of youth to alter their behavior or improve their performance. Never before have we labeled as biologically and cognitively defective such a large proportion of children. If previous large-scale but controversial social experiments involving children serve as guides, the most important consequences of the ADHD experiment will probably be unanticipated, and will probably leave our successors shaking their heads at the delusions that animated their mental-health imbued predecessors. One of these notable large-scale social experiments was that of child labor in the West from the eighteenth to the early twentieth century. Child labor in factories revealed that our dreams of an ideal industrial society led to endangering the health and lives of children. At least on the surface, identifying and suppressing deviance, dissent, and distress in children with medical labels and drugs seem part of a utopic quest for the ideal performance society. It is appropriate, therefore, to focus on the limitations of the ADHD enterprise and to ask what will be its cost.

# References

Agency for Health Care Policy and Research (1999) *Treatment of Attention-Deficit/Hyperactivity Disorder* (AHCPR Publication No. 99–E017) Rockville, MD: AHCPR.

American Psychiatric Association (1980) *Diagnostic and Statistical Manual of Mental Disorders*, 3rd edition. Washington, DC: American Psychiatric Association.

American Psychiatric Association (1994) *Diagnostic and Statistical Manual of Mental Disorders*, 4th edition. Washington, DC: American Psychiatric Association.

Armstrong, T. (1995) *The Myth of the A.D.D. Child: 50 Ways to Improve your Child's Behavior and Attention Span without Drugs, Labels, or Coercion.* New York: Dutton Books.

Barkley, R. A. (1995) *Taking Charge of ADHD: The Complete and Authoritative Guide for Parents.* New York: Guilford.

Barkley, R. A. (1998) *Attention-deficit Hyperactivity Disorder: A Handbook for Diagnosis and Treatment*, 2nd edition. New York: Guilford.

Barkley, R. A. and 20 coendorsers (2004) 'Critique or misrepresentation? A reply to Timimi *et al.*' *Clinical Child and Family Psychology Review*, 7(1): 65–69.

Barnes, G. R., Cerrito, P. B. and Levi, I. (2003) 'An examination of the variability of understanding of language used in ADHD behavior rating scales'. *Ethical Human Sciences and Services*, 5(1): 195–208.

Baughman, F. A., Jr. (1998) 'The totality of the ADD/ADHD fraud'. Consulted May 18, 2003 from http://www.adhdfraud.com.

Breggin, P. R. (1999) 'Psychostimulants in the treatment of children diagnosed with ADHD: Part II – Adverse effects on brain and behavior'. *Ethical Human Sciences and Services*, 1: 213–241.

Breggin, P. R. (2002) *The Stimulant Fact Book.* Cambridge, MA: Perseus Books.

Breggin, P. R. and Breggin, G. R. (1998) *The War against Children of Color: Psychiatry Targets Inner-city Youth.* Monroe, ME: Common Courage Press.

Breitstein, J. (2004) 'Think small, grow big'. *Pharmaceutical Executive*, 1 July 2004. Consulted 9 January 2005 at http://www.pharmexec.com.

Carey, W. B. (1985) 'Clinical use of temperament data in pediatrics'. *Journal of Developmental and Behavioral Pediatrics*, 6(3): 137–142.

Carey, W. B. (1992) 'Temperament issues in the school aged child'. *Pediatric Clinics of North America*, 39(3): 569–584.

Carey, W. B. (2002) 'Is ADHD a valid disorder?' In P. S. Jensen and J. R. Cooper (eds.), *Attention Deficit Hyperactivity Disorder: State of the Science. Best Practices.* Kingston, NJ: Civic Research Institute.

Carey, W. B., and Jablow, M. M. (1997) *Understanding Your Child's Temperament.* New York: Macmillan.

Castellanos, F. X., Lee, P. P., Sharp, W., Jeffries, N. O., Greenstein, D. K. and Clasen, L. S. *et al.* (2002) 'Developmental trajectories of brain volume abnormalities in children and adolescents with attention-deficit hyperactivity disorder'. *Journal of the American Medical Association,* 288: 1740–1748.

Christakis, D. A., Zimmerman, F. J., DiGiuseppe, D. L. and McCarty, C. A. (2004) 'Early television exposure and subsequent attentional problems in children'. *Pediatrics,* 113: 708–713.

Clarke, A. E., Shim, J. K., Mamo, L., Fosket, J. R. and Fishman, J. R. (2003) 'Biomedicalization: Technoscientific transformation of health, illness, and US biomedicine'. *American Sociological Review,* 68: 161–194.

CNS Drug Discoveries (2004) Princeton, NJ: Epsicom.

Cohen, D. (2000) 'Social dynamics of stimulant prescriptions to school children in France and the United States'. Pediatrics Grand Rounds, Boston Medical Center, Nov. 16.

Cohen, D. (2001) 'La médicalisation'. In H. Dorvil and R. Mayer (eds.), *Problèmes sociaux: Théories et méthodologies* [Social problems: Theories and methodologies]. Montreal: University of Quebec Press: 217–231.

Cohen, D. (2005) 'Clinical psychopharmacology trials: 'Gold standard' or fool's gold?' In S. Kirk (ed.), *Mental Disorders in the Social Environment: Critical Perspectives.* New York: Columbia University Press: 347–367.

Cohen, D. and Leo, J., with commentaries by T. Stanton, D. Smith, K. McCready, D. B. Stein, P. Oas, M. Laing, B. Kean and S. Parry (2002) 'A boy who stops taking stimulants for "ADHD": Commentaries on a pediatrics case study'. *Ethical Human Sciences and Services,* 4: 189–209.

Cohen, D. and Leo, J. (2004) 'ADHD and neuroimaging: An update'. *Journal of Mind and Behavior,* 25: 161–166.

Cohen, D., Collin, J., McCubbin, M. and Pérodeau, G. (2001) 'Medications as social phenomena'. *Health,* 5: 441–469.

Conrad, P. (1976) 'The discovery of hyperkinesis: Notes on the medicalization of deviant behavior'. *Social Problems,* 23: 12–21.

Conrad, P. (1992) 'Medicalization and social control'. *Annual Review of Sociology,* 18: 209–232.

Conrad, P. and Potter, D. (2000) 'From hyperactive children to ADHD adults: Observations on the expansion of medical categories'. *Social Problems,* 47: 559–582.

Conrad, P. and Schneider, J. W. (1980) *Medicalization of Deviance: From Badness to Sickness.* St. Louis, MO: Mosby (2nd expanded edition published 1992).

DeGrandpre, R. (1999) *Ritalin Nation: Rapid-fire Culture and the Transformation of Human Consciousness.* New York and London: W.W. Norton and Company.

Diller, L. H. (1998) *Running on Ritalin: A Physician Reflects on Children, Society, and Performance in a Pill.* New York: Bantam Books.

Eastman, W. (2004) 'Beginnings and beyond: The relationship between television violence and neurodevelopment of young children'. *College Quarterly,* 7(3). Retrieved May 17, 2005 from www.collegequarterly.ca/2004–vol07-num03-summer/eastman.html

Giedd, J. N., Blumenthal, J., Molloy, E. and Castellanos, F. X. (2001) 'Brain imaging of attention deficit/hyperactivity disorder'. In J. Wassertein, L. E. Wolf, and F. F. Lefever (eds.), *Adult Attention Deficit Disorder: Brain Mechanisms and Life Outcomes*, 931: 33–49. New York: New York Academy of Sciences.

Hallowell, E. M. and Ratey, J. J. (1994) *Driven to Distraction: Recognizing and Coping with Attention Deficit Disorder from Childhood to Adulthood*. New York: Pantheon Press.

Hinshaw, S., Peele, P. and Danielson, L. (1999, May 17) 'Public health issues in ADHD: Individual, system, and cost burden of the disorder workshop'. Retrieved April 24, 2004 from Center for Disease Control website: http://www.cdc.gov/ncbddd/adhd/dadburden.htm.

Jureidini, J. N., Doecke, C. J., Mansfield, P. R., Haby, M. M., Menkes, D. B. and Tonkin, A. L. (2004) 'Efficacy and safety of antidepressants for children and adolescents'. *British Medical Journal*, 328: 879–883.

Khan, K. S., Daya, S. and Jadad, A. R. (1996) 'The importance of quality of primary studies in producing unbiased systematic review'. *Archives of Internal Medicine*, 156: 661–666.

Kiger, G. (1985) 'Economic transformation and processing of hyperactive school children'. *Mid-American Review of Sociology*, 10: 65–85.

Kirsch, I., Moore, T. J., Scoboria, A. and Nicholls, S. N. (2002) 'The Emperor's new drugs: An analysis of antidepressant medication data submitted to the U.S. Food and Drug Administration'. *Prevention and Treatment*, 5(23). Available on World Wide Web: http://journals.apa.org/prevention/volume5/toc-jul15-02.htm.

Kramer, P. (1993) *Listening to Prozac*. New York: Viking.

Leo, J. and Cohen, D. (2003) 'Neuroimaging studies of ADHD: Broken brains or flawed research?' *Journal of Mind and Behavior*, 24: (29–56).

Malacrida, C. (2004) 'Medicalization, ambivalence, and social control: Mothers' descriptions of educators and ADD/ADHD'. *Health*, 8: 61–80.

Maté, G. (1999) *Scattered Minds: A New Look at the Origins and Healing of Attention Deficit Disorder*. Toronto: Alfred A. Knopf Canada.

Medawar, C. and Hardon, A. (2004) *Medicines Out of Control? Antidepressants and the Conspiracy of Goodwill*. London: Aksant Academic Publishers/Transaction.

Moll, G. H., Hause, S., Ruther, E., Rothenberger, A. and Huether, G. (2001) 'Early methylphenidate administration to young rats causes a persistent reduction in the density of striatal dopamine transporters'. *Journal of Child and Adolescent Psychopharmacology*, 11: 15–24.

Oas, P. T. (2001) *Curing ADD/ADHD Children*. Raleigh, NC: Pentland Press.

Prescription Cost Analysis (2005) England 2004. Department of Health, NHSE. Prepared by the Government Statistical Service, Statistics Division, Branch SD1E.

Saget, E. (2003, June 2) 'Docteur, mon enfant est agité' [Doctor, my child is agitated]. *L'Express Magazine*.

Schachar, R., Jadad, A. R., Gauld, M., Boyle, M., Booker, L., Snider, A., Kim, M. and Cunningham, C. (2002) 'Attention-deficit hyperactivity disorder: Critical appraisal of extended treatment studies'. *Canadian Journal of Psychiatry*, 47: 337–348.

Schachter, H. M., Phan, B., King, J., Langford, S. and Moher, D. (2001) 'How efficacious and safe is short-acting methylphenidate for the treatment of attention-deficit disorder in children and adolescents? A meta-analysis'. *Canadian Medical Association Journal*, 165: 1475–1488.

Stein, D. B. (1999) *Ritalin is not the Answer: A Drug-free, Practical Program for Children Diagnosed with ADD or ADHD*. San Francisco, CA: Jossey-Bass Publishers.

Szasz, T. S. (2001) *Pharmacracy: Medicine and Politics in America*. New York: Praeger.

Taylor, R. L. (2000) *Mind or Body: Distinguishing Psychological from Organic Disorders* (2nd edition). New York: Springer.

Thornley, B. and Adams, C. (1998) 'Content and quality of 2000 controlled trials in schizophrenia over 50 years'. *British Medical Journal*, 317: 1181–1184.

Timimi, S. (2003) *Pathological Child Psychiatry and the Medicalization of Childhood*. London: Brunner Routledge.

Volkow, N. D., Wang, G. J., Fowler, J. S., Logan, J. *et al.* (2002) 'Relationship between blockade of dopamine transporters by oral methylphenidate and the increases in extracellular dopamine: Therapeutic implications'. *Synapse*, 43: 181–187.

Walker, S. III. (1998) *The Hyperactivity Hoax: How to Stop Drugging your Child and Find Real Medical Help*. New York: St. Martin's Books.

Whybrow, P. C. (2005) *American Mania: When More is not Enough*. New York and London: Norton.

Zito, J. M., Safer D. J., dosReis, S., Gardner J.F., Madger, L. *et al* (2003) 'Psychotropic practice patterns for youth: A 10-year perspective'. Archives of *Pediatric and Adolescent Medicine*, 157: 17–25.

# Chapter 2

# Canaries in the coal mine

## The symptoms of children labeled 'ADHD' as biocultural feedback

*Thomas Armstrong*

Were the field of attention deficit hyperactivity disorder to have a 'poster boy' to promote its cause (in the way that muscular dystrophy or cerebral palsy organizations have a child with the disorder appearing on television during fund-raising campaigns), it would surely have to be Calvin from the celebrated comic strip Calvin and Hobbes® by Bill Watterson.[1] In one of my favorite Calvin and Hobbes strips, Calvin is sitting at a school desk, utterly bored. Finally, he shouts out to the teacher and all of his classmates: 'BO-RING!' In the last panel, we see Calvin being sent to the principal, saying: 'Yeh yeh . . . kill the messenger.'

This particular comic strip symbolizes for me how children who have been labeled 'ADHD' are the messengers of today's frenetic stressed-out culture. Optimally, they should be characterized by educators and mental health professionals, not as intrinsically dysfunctional or biologically damaged organisms, but rather as a kind of early warning signal for cultural instability. Canaries have been traditionally used in British coal mines as an early warning system for detecting potentially poisonous gases such as carbon monoxide. Miners would see the canaries fall off their perches and know that they still had time to get out of the mines safely. Similarly, I believe that children labeled ADHD are the canaries in today's noxious cultural climate, and are responding in a natural way to the social conditions of the times by developing the symptoms of hyperactivity, distractibility, and impulsivity that are characteristic of ADHD. Instead of 'blaming the victim,' that is, diagnosing ADHD 'within the child,' we ought instead, to be reading their behaviors as symptoms of a wider dysfunction and using that information to make substantial reforms in our cultural institutions. In this chapter, I will make the case for how the so-called ADHD child's behaviors reveal much more about the context in which we live than about the specific mechanisms that reside within an individual brain.

## Short attention span culture

It has always fascinated me that so much research money in education, psychology, and psychiatry has been spent on investigating short attention span in individual children, but no money has been invested by these fields in looking at short attention span in the broader culture. When I put the phrase 'short attention span culture' in PsychInfo, an online search engine of the American Psychological Association (of which I've been a member since 1985), I discovered that since I have been a member of the APA, there has been only *one* article written on this topic (in 1985), and ironically it defended television as a positive contribution to children's cognitive development. A similar search for the term 'ADHD' yielded 4,428 documents over the same period of time. On the other hand, research in investigating short attention span in the broader culture has received *considerable* financial support from the field of advertising. As so often happens in fields that operate according to different paradigms, however, there is quite a different phrase used in commercial media advertising to characterize this investigation: 'jolts per minute.' The Center for Media Literacy of the Ontario Ministry of Education defines this term as follows:

> 'Jolts per minute' programming is often cited as a principle – almost a first law – of commercial television. 'Jolt' refers to the moment of excitement generated by a laugh, a violent act, a car chase, a quick film cut – any fast-paced episode that lures the viewer into the program. Television and screen writers often inject a jolt into their scripts to liven up the action or pick up the pace of a story.

Readers can investigate for themselves how the number of 'jolts per minute' on commercial television has increased over the past several decades. Watch a television show made in the 1950s and count the number of 'jolts per minute' (as noted above, this would include camera changes, noises, laughs, etc.). Then compare this number to that of any current television program or commercial. The increased tempo is immediately obvious. It has come to the point where advertisers now talk about 'jolts per second.' One media commentator, for example, refers to: 'MTV-style hyper-visuals, *where anything less than a dozen jolts per second is considered boring*' [my italics].

The reason for the dramatic increase in 'jolts per second' in television programming over the past many years (and we should add, in other media sources, including video games, computer software, and the Internet) should be obvious to the reader. Television programmers need to grab the attention of their viewers in order to sell their products. Advertising money is the grease that makes the world of commercial television run. To make a living, programmers use this trick of 'jolts per minute/second' to grab their viewers' attention. This is essentially Pavlovian conditioning. It was the Russian physiologist Ivan Pavlov who, in 1927, described what he called 'the orienting response.' This describes our instinctive biological reaction to any sudden or novel stimulus, and includes dilation of the blood vessels to the brain and constriction of blood vessels to major muscles groups. During the orienting response, mental arousal becomes heightened and visual and auditory perceptions are sharpened. The orienting response evolved in part to help protect human beings (and other living creatures) from sudden environmental changes, such as a mountain lion about to strike. Television programmers (and manufacturers of video games and computer software) use this powerful and important evolutionary gift, not to save us from being eaten by lions and tigers, but to sell their products. They are essentially exploiting a several-million-year-old evolutionary adaptation for short-term commercial gain.

What happens, however, is that over time our attention becomes habituated to this stimuli. Like the people who heard the boy cry 'wolf!', we discover that there really *isn't* a mountain lion waiting to eat us and that we've been fooled. The next time we hear that loud sound, or see that blast of light, or experience that sudden camera shift, we know better. And we stop paying attention. In order to get our attention back, media programmers have to *up the ante* and increase the number of jolts per second. Thus, over a period of years, we've seen an exponential growth in the tempo and intensity of stimulation on television and in video games. At the same time, we've seen a steady decrease in the ability of viewers to maintain any kind of sustained attention. In short, we've become a short attention span culture.

An important component of this culture are the children who have been labeled ADHD. In attempting to build a case for a 'medical disorder' existing *inside* of individual children, ADHD advocates have repeatedly pointed to the neurotransmitter dopamine as a key factor in its etiology. Dopamine is a chemical in the brain that plays a central role in the modulation of *stimulus seeking*. When dopaminergic pathways are disrupted, an individual can develop an insatiability for stimuli. This is what researchers have typically seen in many children identified as ADHD: they require higher levels of stimulation than the average person. Ritalin and other psychostimulants help to provide this missing stimulation in chemical form. There is evidence that video games and other media may actually facilitate the release of dopamine in the striatum, a part of the basal ganglia that is regarded as a crucial structure in the etiology of ADHD. Mass media may serve to overly stimulate and exhaust the dopaminergic system in vulnerable individuals. One study saw a correlation between the number of hours of television viewed each day at ages 1 and 3 and later attentional problems at age 7. Other studies have linked media viewing to violent behaviors, and to physiological responses such as 'TV-induced fright,' 'video-game epilepsy,' and 'television addiction' that is comparable to substance abuse. It is plausible to suggest that viewing television and other media in excess can have an effect upon neurological development in children. The average child in the United States watches four hours of television a day, and 20,000 commercials a year. This may be part of the reason why the American Academy of Pediatrics has recommended that children below the age of 24 months not be exposed to *any* television, and that older children watch a maximum of one or two hours a day of nonviolent educational programming (e.g. without commercials).

Despite of all this, ADHD researchers have typically discounted any assertion that mass media may have any significant role to play in the etiology of the disorder. One recent consensus statement on ADHD signed by 74 international scientists working in the field of ADHD assails those who suggest that 'behavior problems associated with ADHD are merely the result of . . . [among other things] . . . excessive viewing of TV or playing of video games.' However, it is significant that the growth of the concept of attention deficit disorder since its 'discovery' in the early 1970s parallels the increased tempo of mass media in our lives. While correlation is not causation, it has become almost a cliché to say that people in today's world have shorter attention spans and live life at a faster pace. That there might be a subtle and intricate interrelationship between biology and culture with regard to mass media and ADHD, therefore, should not be such an astounding assertion to make. Children labeled ADHD may be the canaries in this high tech coal mine, possessing greater neurological sensitivity than average to powerful media stimuli, and thus be the first to drop off their perch when placed into a frenetic mass media culture. We might, therefore, be smart to spend at least part of our time as educators, researchers, and mental health professionals interpreting the behaviors of these children as a kind of biocultural feedback.

## The disappearance of play

Another strong social undercurrent that deserves attention with regard to ADHD symptoms is the gradual decline of free unstructured play in our time. As play expert Brian Sutton-Smith (2001) puts it:

> American children's freedom for freewheeling play once took place in rural fields and city streets, using equipment of their own making. Today, play is increasingly confined to back yards, basements, playrooms and bedrooms, and derives much of its content from video games, television dramas, and Saturday morning cartoons.

Where children once made up games that they played over a distance of several city blocks, or engaged in rough-and-tumble wrestling, or created imaginative scenarios played out with simple props found around the house, kids now spend more time indoors playing with their action toys, or engaging in highly competitive games and sports supervised by adults, or doing their homework, or watching TV, the Internet, or video games. One report issued by the National Association for Sport and Physical Recreation recommends that children engage in one or two hours of physical activity every day, yet increasingly schools are cutting back on physical education programs and recess periods in order to dedicate more time to academic achievement (often spent in front of a computer), and to make matters worse, research suggests that children are not making up the physical activity they are losing in school by increasing their physical activities after school. The reasons for the decline in play are numerous: fears of parents concerning strangers in the neighborhood, legal liability for 'unsafe' playground equipment, increased academic demands, and, of course, the rise of technologies described above. This failure to play in active ways, however, may be taking a significant toll on our children's neurological development.

Research in ADHD has focused on problems with the executive function in children with this label, that is, the ability to reflect, plan, inhibit impulses, and set goals, among other tasks. Areas of the brain typically referred to in the ADHD literature as the locus of the disorder include the frontal lobes, striatum, limbic system, and cerebellum. Essentially, there appears to be a dysfunction in the circuitry between emotional and motor activity in the limbic system and cerebellum, and the higher cognitive areas of the frontal cortex. The striatum, in particular, which appears to mediate motor and emotional responses and influence inhibitory control over those responses, is a key component in what appears to malfunction in children labeled ADHD. While the causes of this breakdown are typically viewed in the ADHD literature as genetic and therefore fixed at birth, a richer interpretation must include environmental influences as a key factor in the smooth functioning of this circuitry. Free unstructured play appears to have an important role in this process. There is evidence that the kinds of social adaptations and learning experiences that young children acquire through play actually modify brain structure and functioning from a very early age. It has even been suggested by some researchers that the evolution of the frontal lobes in primates occurred in part as a result of the experience of play. As children play, they learn to modulate their cerebellar motor movements and their limbic system impulses as they create imaginative play scenarios, practice 'faking out' an opponent in a wrestling game, plan a game strategy, or organize their play experiences as spontaneous and yet fully socialized events. These activities, then, serve to mediate between frontal lobe thinking and inhibitory functions and the highly motoric and emotional processes of sub-cortical structures. As neuroscientist Jaak Panksepp (1998) has pointed out:

> Indeed 'youth' may have evolved to give complex organisms time to play and thereby exercise the natural skills they will need as adults. We already know that as the frontal lobes mature, frequency of play goes down, and animals with damaged frontal lobes tend to be more playful . . . Might access to rough-and-tumble play promote frontal lobe maturation?
>
> (Panksepp 1998)

Panksepp indicates that '[t]he explosion of ADHD diagnoses may largely reflect the fact that more and more of our children no longer have adequate spaces and opportunities to express this natural biological need – to play with each other in vigorous rough-and-tumble ways, each and every day.' In a series of controlled experiments with rats, Panksepp and his colleagues have discovered a number of interesting effects regarding play, including significantly elevated brain-derived neurotrophic factor (BDNF) (a key modulator of neuronal development, plasticity, and survival) in rats who played. He has also done studies suggesting that methylphenidate or Ritalin inhibits play behavior in rats.

These studies raise some troubling issues regarding current approaches to ADHD treatment. If some children exhibit ADHD symptoms because of the loss of rough-and-tumble play in our culture, and then undergo methylphenidate treatment which further suppresses the drive to play, then these children may be receiving a double dose of harm from society. Add to this what we have observed in the first part of this chapter – that play-starved children are sitting in front of highly stimulating fast-tempo television, video games, and computers without being able to respond with large motor movements and playful responses – and it becomes easier to understand how ADHD symptoms could indeed be a form of biocultural feedback. As we saw above, the most neurologically sensitive ones – the ADHD canaries – will be the first to show up on the radar screen, but the wise professional will understand and interpret these symptoms as a comment, as well, about the broader culture and its need for more play in early childhood development for *all* children.

## Pushing back developmental timetables

Another cultural phenomenon that deserves our careful scrutiny in understanding the cultural underpinnings of ADHD symptoms in children is the way in which expectations for reaching developmental milestones have been pushed back to earlier and earlier ages by parents, educators, and researchers over the past three decades. Simply put, younger children these days are increasingly being asked by adults to do things they are not developmentally ready for. In my work as a teacher-trainer in the United States I have heard preschool teachers say something like: 'I really don't like using an overhead projector, worksheets, and lots of sitting time with my little ones, but it gets really rough next year in kindergarten, and I've got to get them ready for it!' My wife, who is a psychotherapist, reports on kindergarten-aged children coming to her practice and saying that they have two hours of home-work to get done that night. These kinds of pressures were unthinkable in the 1950s, when a kindergarten was what is really means in German: a 'children's garden,' where playing, singing, painting, dancing, storytelling, and nap time were the order of the day.

However, in the late 1960s in the United States, American education underwent a profound and lasting change. Stung by the 1966 landmark report *Equality of Educational Opportunity* written by sociologist James Coleman, which indicted America's schools for their lack of equal educational opportunity for people of color, more emphasis began to be placed upon the concept of *accountability* as an important goal for American education. Education historian Diane Ravitch (2002) writes:

> In the wake of this report . . . policymakers, public officials, community activists, and parents started to conclude that many of the problems [in American education] were structural consequences of the bureaucratic . . . system of public education and could only be addressed by market competition or structural changes. This shift in focus from inputs (resources) to outputs (results) was facilitated by the increasing availability of test scores. The establishment of the National Assessment of Educational Progress (NAEP) in 1970

provided cumulative new data and trend lines to document the educational achievement of American students.

(Ravitch 2002)

It is telling that the accountability push in American education in the early 1970s coincided with the original formulation of attention deficit disorder in 1972 by Canadian psychologist Virginia Douglas.

The availability of comparative test data in turn set loose a new set of demands on teachers to boost test scores. These pressures were in turn visited upon students, who were prodded to succeed in a more rigorous academic *curriculum* (a Latin word, meaning 'racetrack'), and who were viewed with concern by parents if they not did score at or above *grade level*, which became a more important measure of a child's overall competence than his IQ score. At the same time, American educators beseiged the Swiss developmental psychologist Jean Piaget and asked him how his cognitive stages of development could be *speeded up*, a problem he regarded as 'the American question.' One unintended outcome of this American drive for speed and achievement was a new phenomenon termed by developmental researcher David Elkind (1987) (who was a disciple of Piaget), 'the hurried child syndrome.' Elkind argued that the push over the past three decades to maximize a child's potential at an early age had created a situation where preschool children were being given a watered-down version of the first through third grade curriculum. This trend, he warned, set the stage for the 'hurried child syndrome,' which included physical symptoms (headaches, nausea, irritability), learning dysfunction, attentional difficulties, and behavioral problems.

These symptoms of the 'hurried child syndrome' are in many cases indistinguishable from the symptoms of ADHD. Many cases of ADHD may, in fact, arise from these underlying cultural pressures on children to achieve before they are developmentally ready. It is actually quite interesting to regard children labeled ADHD from a developmental perspective. It turns out that many children identified as ADHD exhibit traits characteristic of children younger than they are. We should note here that the symptoms of ADHD are developmentally *normal* for infants. Every healthy baby is hyperactive, distractible, and impulsive, often to the chagrin of many a mom! These traits are generally seen as abnormal, or as examples of 'developmental immaturity,' when they appear in older individuals. The question is at what age should they be considered abnormal, and can this age shift from one historical period to another? If culture has indeed pushed back the developmental milestones for a child's growth to an earlier age, then these behaviors will be seen as abnormal at an earlier age as well, and many children who decades ago might have been seen as exhibiting normal behavior, or even somewhat lagging development (but within normal levels), are now regarded as ADHD for these same types of behaviors that are now set against a different cultural backdrop.

Another factor to consider is that the so-called developmental immaturity of some children labeled ADHD may actually be a *good* thing for society. Here we must introduce the concept of *neoteny* (a Greek term meaning 'holding youth'), which refers to the retention of childlike traits into adulthood. Evolutionary thinkers such as Stephen Jay Gould (1985) and Ashley Montagu (1983) have characterized neoteny as an evolutionary *advance* (e.g. *homo sapiens* has a greater tendency to retain youthful characteristics into adulthood than do chimpanzees, bonobos, or gorillas). As it turns out, many highly creative adult thinkers, including Einstein, have been seen to possess childlike (and sometimes 'childish') qualities that were integral to their great discoveries. Einstein said, for example, 'I never grew up.' One has to ask the question here whether the so-called 'developmental immaturity' of some children labeled as ADHD is really a problem or whether it may actually be an evolutionary *advantage*.

While many kids labeled ADHD have childlike or neotenous qualities that continue into adulthood, in other cases these traits disappear with time. As normal myelination processes occur in the brain, many ADHD behaviors slip into the sub-clinical realm, and may disappear entirely. The flailing arms and legs of the hyperactive 8-year-old become the nervously tapping fingers and toes of the 40-year-old, and vanish forever in the 60-year-old. One study suggested that the rate of ADHD in any given age group appears to decline by 50 percent approximately every five years. Thus, assuming an ADHD prevalence rate of 4 percent in childhood, the estimated rate of adult ADHD would be 0.8 percent at age 20 and 0.05 percent at age 40. Many children labeled ADHD may simply be individuals who mature later than the norm, and yet, in a culture that has pushed back developmental timetables to earlier and earlier ages, they are viewed as having a disorder. One of the great champions of childhood development in the 1950s, Louise Bates Ames (1985) of the famed Gesell Institute, wrote about a boy who had been referred to her clinic in the 1980s by an evaluator who had seen him as potentially a future 'learning disabled child with emotional problems' because he had thrown objects and couldn't concentrate. He was 56 weeks old! Elsewhere, Ames (1968) suggested that if children entered school when they were developmentally ready, rather than according to when they were born (the usual methods of determining placement) we might eliminate 50 percent of all learning disabilities in the country. Ames' suggestion came before ADHD had wreaked its vengeance upon the United States, and it seems likely that she would say very much the same thing about ADHD if she were alive today.

## Conclusion: the need for a biocultural approach in ADHD research

The three issues discussed above – the impact of mass media, the disappearance of play, and the pushing back of developmental timetables for children's development – are only a starting point in examining the deeper cultural roots of ADHD symptoms in children. Many other issues could be looked at as well, including the breakdown in the nuclear family over the past several decades, the increase in violence in schools and neighborhoods, and the creeping medicalization of human behavior in contemporary society. What is important, however, is that a beginning be made in establishing a biocultural basis for research in the field of ADHD. As noted above, ADHD researchers are generally blind to these influences. They are not necessarily to be faulted for this, since their training does not usually include a strong component of anthropology, sociology, or systems theory. It is simply not possible to use the current tools of the ADHD researcher to investigate many of the claims made above. You simply can't roll the clock back to 1956, when mass media ran at a slower rate, and measure the number of children who would qualify for an ADHD diagnosis. The fact that one cannot run controlled scientific studies like those done in typical ADHD research, however, does not invalidate these claims. Rather, it requires that a different set of tools be brought to bear upon the issue. One can, for example, investigate contemporary cultures where mass media has been slower to develop. In one such study in the 1980s, for example, sociologists tracked the changes that occurred in a mountain community in Canada after it acquired access to television for the first time. Over a period of two years, the adults and children in the community became less able to persevere at tasks, less able to engage in creative problem-solving, and less tolerant of unstructured time.

Similarly, one can investigate these questions by essentially *creating a mini-culture*, that is, by changing the existing environment in some significant way. One study, for example, provided children labeled ADHD with therapy balls to sit on rather than chairs in school, and discovered an improved ability to concentrate on their school work. Another study investigated children identified as ADHD in outdoor natural or 'green' settings compared to indoor or formal outdoor environments, and discovered that green outdoor activities reduced ADHD-related symptoms. The problem for ADHD researchers is that these studies were done outside of the field of ADHD (in the fields of communications, occupational therapy, and public health), and like a foreign object intruding upon the membrane of a cell, have been not absorbed into the ADHD collective body of work. What is required are researchers in the field of ADHD who possess interdisciplinary minds, who can bring to bear the tools of other fields of study – especially those that investigate biology at the cultural level – upon the problems of children who can't sit still, concentrate, or make good decisions. Or perhaps we need to envision this process in reverse. Perhaps it is the ADHD field itself that has become too narrow in its focus, too focused upon its limited methodologies – scanning the brains of children engaged in artificially contrived learning tasks, evaluating the pros and cons of different medications, and testing the effectiveness of lock-step cognitive-behavioral training programs on children's symptoms – to effectively see the forest for the trees. Perhaps the ADHD field itself needs to be turned inside out, or even upside down, so that fresh research methodologies, novel intervention strategies, and new ways of looking at children can revivify the work of those who seek to help the Calvins of this world experience joy and vitality in school and in life.

## Notes

1  The Calvin and Hobbes comic strip appeared in over 2,300 newspapers worldwide over the period 1985 to 1995. Calvin is a boy of about 7 or 8 whose energy, according to creator Watterson, 'is unhindered by common sense.' Hobbes is his 'imaginary' friend, a stuffed tiger that frequently comes to life.

## Bibliography

American Academy of Pediatrics, 'Television and the family,' online position statement: http://www.aap.org/family/tv1.htm.

Ames, L.B. (1968) 'Learning disabilities often result from sheer immaturity,' *Journal of Learning Disabilities*, March, 1(3): 207–212.

Ames, L.B. (1985) 'Learning disability: very big around here,' *Research Communications on Psychology, Psychiatry, and Behavior*, 10(142): 17–34.

Armstrong, T. (1997) *The Myth of the A.D.D. Child: 50 Ways to Improve Your Child's Behavior and Attention Span without Drugs, Labels, or Coercion*. New York: Plume.

Armstrong, T. (1999) *ADD/ADHD Alternatives in the Classroom*. Alexandria, VA: Association for Supervision and Curriculum Development.

Armstrong, T. (2003) 'Attention deficit hyperactivity disorder: one consequence of the rise in technologies and demise of play?' In Sharna Olfman (ed.), *All Work and No Play: How Educational Reforms Are Harming Our Preschoolers*. Westport, CT: Praeger Publishers.

Barkley, R.A. *et al.* (2002) 'International consensus statement on ADHD,' *Clinical Child and Family Psychology Review*, June, 5(2): 89–111.

Brasted, P.J., Robbins, T.W. and Dunnett, S.B. (1999) 'Distinct roles for striatal subregions in mediating response processing revealed by focal excitotoxic lesions,' *Behavioral Neuroscience*, April, 113(2): 253–264.

Christakis, D.A., Zimmerman, F.J., DiGiuseppe, D.L. and McCarty, C.A. (2004) 'Early television exposure and subsequent attentional problems in children,' *Pediatrics*, April, 113(4): 708–713.

Clark, R.W. (1984) *Einstein: The Life and Times*. New York: Avon.

Coleman, J.S. *et al.* (1966) *Equality of Educational Opportunity*. Washington, DC: US Department of Health, Education, and Welfare: US Government Printing Office.

Dale, D., Corbin, D.B. and Dale, K.S. (2000) 'Restricting opportunities to be active during school time: do children compensate by increasing physical activity levels after school?' *Research Quarterly for Exercise and Sport*, September, 71: 240.

DeGrandpre, R. (2000) *Ritalin Nation: Rapid-fire Culture and the Transformation of Consciousness*. New York: W.W. Norton.

Diamond, M. and Hopson, J. (1998) *Magic Trees of the Mind: How to Nurture Your Child's Intelligence, Creativity, and Health Emotions from Birth through Adolescence*. New York: Dutton.

Douglas, V.I. (1972) 'Stop, look and listen: the problem of sustained attention and impulse control in hyperactive and normal children,' *Canadian Journal of Behavioural Science*, 4: 259–282.

Duckworth, E. (1979) 'Either we're too early and they can't learn it or we're too late and they know it already: the dilemma of applying Piaget,' *Harvard Educational Review*, August, 49(3): 297–312.

Elkind, D. (1981) *The Hurried Child: Growing Up Too Fast Too Soon*. Reading, MA: Addison-Wesley.

Elkind, D. (1987) *Miseducation: Preschoolers at Risk.* New York: Alfred A. Knopf.

Furlow, B. 'Kids need the playground just as much as the classroom: having fun builds bigger, better brains,' *New Scientist,* June 9, 2001.

Fylan, F., Harding, G.F. and Webb, R.M. (1999) 'Mechanisms of video-game epilepsy,' *Epilepsia,* 40: 28–30.

Gleick, J. (2000) *Faster: The Acceleration of Just About Everything.* New York: Vintage.

Gordon, N., Burke, S., Stanley, H.A., Watson, J. and Penksepp, J. (2003) 'Socially-induced brain 'fertilization': play promotes brain derived neurotrophic factor transcription in the amygdala and dorsolateral frontal cortex in juvenile rats,' *Neuroscience Letters,* 341: 17–20.

Gould, S.J. (1985) *Ontogeny and Phylogeny.* Cambridge, MA: Belknap Press.

Hansen, L.A. (1998) 'Where we play and who we are,' *Illinois Parks and Recreation,* March/April, 29(2): 22–25.

Hill, J.C. and Schoener, E.P. (1996) 'Age-dependent decline of attention deficit hyperactivity disorder,' *American Journal of Psychiatry,* 154(9): 1323–1325.

Koepp, M.J. *et al.* (1998) 'Evidence for striatal dopamine release during a video game,' *Nature,* May, 393(6682): 266–268.

Kubey, R. and Csikszentmihalyi, M. (2002) 'Television addiction is no mere metaphor,' *Scientific American,* February, 286(2): 64–80.

Kuo, F.E. and Taylor, A.F. (2004) 'A potential natural treatment for attention-deficit/hyperactivity disorder: evidence from a national study,' *American Journal of Public Health,* September, 94(9): 1580–1586.

Montagu, A. (1983) *Growing Young.* New York: McGraw Hill.

Nylund, D. (2002) *Treating Huckleberry Finn: A New Narrative Approach to Kids Diagnosed ADD/ADHD.* San Francisco, CA: Jossey-Bass.

Panksepp, J. (1998) 'Attention deficit hyperactivity disorders, psychostimulants, and intolerance of childhood playfulness: a tragedy in the making?' *Current Directions in Psychological Science,* 7: 98.

Panksepp, J., Burgdorf, J., Gordon, N. and Turner, C. (2002) 'Treatment of ADHD with methylphenidate may sensitize brain substrates of desire: implications for changes in drug abuse potential from an animal model.' *Consciousness and Emotion,* 3(1): 7–19.

Ravitch, D. (2002) 'A brief history of testing and accountability,' *Hoover Digest,* Fall, No. 4. http://www.hooverdigest.org.

Roth, R.M. and Saykin, A.J. (2004) 'Executive dysfunction in attention-deficit/hyperactivity disorder: cognitive and neuroimaging findings,' *Psychiatric Clinics of North America,* 27(1): 83–96.

Schilling, D.L., Washington, K., Billingsley, F.F. and Deitz, J. (2003) 'Classroom seating for children with attention deficit hyperactivity disorder: therapy balls versus chairs,' *American Journal of Occupational Therapy,* September–October, 57(5): 534–541.

Sutton-Smith, B. (2001) *The Ambiguity of Play.* Harvard: Harvard University Press.

Valkenburg, P.M., Cantor, J. and Peters, A.L. (2000) 'Fright reactions to television: a child survey,' *Communication Research,* February, 27(1): 82–97.

Volkow, A.D. *et al.* (2004) 'Evidence that methylphenidate enhances the saliency of a mathematical task by increasing dopamine in the human brain,' *American Journal of Psychiatry,* July, 161(7): 1173–1180.

Williams, T.B. (1986) *The Impact of Television: A Natural Experiment in Three Communities.* Orlando, FL: Academic Press.

# Chapter 3

# Disability, childhood studies and the construction of medical discourses

## Questioning attention deficit hyperactivity disorder: a theoretical perspective

*John Davis*

This chapter employs sociological perspective from childhood studies and disability studies within the UK to question the identification and diagnosis of children with attention deficit hyperactivity disorder. It investigates the contemporary dynamic relations between medical science, public policy, children's rights, emancipatory principles and citizenship. This investigation highlights a contrast between medical literature/public policy guidelines on ADHD and human rights perspectives. By critically examining the sociological context that underpins the identification of problematic childhood behaviour a number of questions are raised regarding the diagnoses of children and young people labelled as having ADHD. The chapter concludes that, at present, diagnostic approaches to ADHD do not sufficiently engage with the sociological issues that influence children's and young people's lives and therefore do not give enough consideration to how children and young people can take charge of resolving their own life issues.

The definition of attention deficit hyperactivity disorder originates in the USA. It is used as a label to describe children and young people whose behaviour is perceived by adults to be impulsive, overactive and/or inattentive, who behave in ways that do not concur with their developmental age and who lack the experience of social and educational achievement (BPS 1996). The term is constantly being reviewed not least because in the UK there are differences between the way that child psychiatrists and clinicians (e.g. paediatricians) diagnose it.

A range of academics, professionals and policy-makers have been involved in discussions concerning the diagnosis of children and young people thought to have ADHD. Possible causes are thought to be:

- Dietary
- Genetic
- Neurological
- Psycho-social
- Environmental

Concerns about the validity of these causes and of ADHD as a medical category have been highlighted by a range of writers (see Safer *et al.* 1996; Gilmore *et al.* 1998; Orford 1998; Zametkin and Liotta 1998; Lloyd and Norris 1999; Zametkin and Minique 1999; Conrad and Potter 2000; SIGN 2001). This chapter links these concerns to specific theoretical perspectives within academic writing. Specifically it:

- Links anxiety over the diagnosis of ADHD to theoretical perspectives in education, disability and childhood studies;
- Relates arguments over the causes of ADHD to long-term debates within disability studies over the difference between medical and social models of disability;
- Connects anxiety concerning who benefits from the diagnosis of ADHD to writing in educational studies that discusses the conflict between managerialism and inclusion;
- Explains apprehension over the effects of drug-based solutions and unease concerning the subjective nature of ADHD to debates in childhood studies that examine the conflict between regimes of control and values of self-realisation.

By comparing different theoretical perspectives and ideas in childhood, disability and educational studies it is possible to highlight the potential for the development of progressive holistic approaches to ADHD. It is concluded that whatever approach to ADHD is adopted it should be underpinned by a well-theorised position that shows awareness of:

- The tensions between adult control and child self-realisation in Western societies;
- The pressures placed on children, parents and teachers by social and education systems;
- The limitations of medical and social constructions of ADHD;
- The inability of some professionals that work with children to be reflexive;
- The need to consider a range of causes of ADHD;
- The recent development of participatory and children's rights approaches;
- The ability of children and young people to work in partnership with adults to identify solutions to their own life problems.

## Disability studies

Arguments over the lack of a clear medical cause for ADHD can be linked to discussions in disability studies in the UK concerning the distinction between medical and social 'models' of disability. In the case of ADHD it is argued that a medical model approach enables drug companies to make huge profits by encouraging vulnerable parents to believe that their children have an innate biological impairment that can only be addressed by a chemical solution (Lloyd and Norris 1999; Singh 2002). In an attempt to challenge the medical model of ADHD, many writers have suggested that children's behaviour is rooted in social causes. This argument is very familiar to scholars within disability studies. For well over a century disabled people in the UK have fought the 'medical model' perspective that represented them as deficient, tragic, vulnerable and lacking agency. They have argued that these discourses have enabled medical professionals to monopolise resources and power and create a culture of dependency.

The change from medical to social perspectives is underpinned by a redefinition of the word *disability*. Since the 1970s disabled people have sought to redefine this word to highlight the inequalities they experience within society. The Union of the Physically Impaired Against Segregation stated that disability is:

> the disadvantage or restriction of activity caused by a contemporary social organisation which takes little or no account of people who have . . . impairments and thus excludes them from participation in the mainstream of social activities.
>
> (UPIAS 1976)

Over the years this statement has underpinned collective action that has successfully enabled disabled people in the UK to contrast individualised and medicalised impairment-based presumptions about their apparent inabilities with more social perspectives that characterise inability as caused by attitudes and structures within society. This shift has enabled disability to be recharacterised as a form of social oppression that prevents disabled people's inclusion in society (Abberley 1987; Oliver 1990; Barnes 1991; Finkelstein 1993; Campbell and Oliver 1996; Barnes *et al.* 1999; and see, for example, Linton 1998 for a slightly different North American angle on the 'social model').

Since the 1990s a number of writers have attempted to make the social model more sophisticated to take account of post-structural perspectives. This has led to disability no longer only being viewed as something that you 'are' in relation to social location but as something that you 'experience' in different ways, times and places. This shift has enabled writers to represent the fluid nature of oppression and to illustrate disabled people's capacity to resist oppressive discourses, people, groups and organisations. It has also led to the suggestion that there are a number of social models of disability (Corker and Shakespeare 2002). This chapter mainly uses the term 'social model' in the traditional sense to highlight the structural context of disability. In so doing, the chapter is able to examine the social construction ADHD.

## ADHD as a social construct: the parent, socialisation and morality

The social model of disability can be employed to underpin the suggestion that ADHD is purely a social construct. Some writers argue that it is a label of forgiveness for parents or that it is useful because it brings parents financial rewards (Slee 1995; Lloyd and Norris 1999). These arguments shift the emphasis for the increase in diagnosis of ADHD from medical to psycho-social explanations. The suggestion is that parents whose children don't behave well avoid criticism when their child is found to have a medical impairment. But where does this potential criticism stem from? Many authors argue that this potential criticism of parents relates to traditional views of families, theories of socialisation and issues of morality/social control.

Traditionally, functionalist writers argued, in a deterministic manner, that the family functioned to integrate the child into society. It was believed that the child had to be taught the correct way to behave otherwise it would be a threat to society (Parsons and Bales 1955). These perspectives promoted the need for society to appropriate the child, take it over and mould it primarily through processes of socialisation (Corsaro 1997; James *et al.* 1998). Socialisation was defined as:

> The process through which an individual learns to be a member of society is called socialisation . . . [S]ocialisation is the imposition of social patterns on behaviour.
>
> (Berger and Berger 1991: 4)

Berger and Berger (1991) suggested that powerful adults could impose language, rules and behavioural patterns in an absolute way in order to shape their children's identities. 'Behaviourist' psychologists stressed the importance of learning, nurture rules, rewards and punishments (Stanton-Rogers 2001b). They argued that children could be controlled by giving them rewards such as sweets or watching television and that skills had to be gradually learned and refined.

Concepts of socialisation in sociology and psychology have been criticised for ignoring the role of the individual being socialised and for neglecting:

> The worlds that children design by themselves for themselves. It fails to examine children's ideas and activities as their ways of being in the world. Furthermore, these omissions are not shortcomings of the concept itself and cannot be rectified by modifying the concept; they are necessary consequences of the fact that socialisation is only one way of looking at children.
>
> (Waksler 1991: 21–22)

It has been argued that individuals do not have to follow all the rules they have learned. That is, that the process of internalisation is complex and critical rather than absolute (Wrong 1961; Waksler 1991). This does not mean that society and parents can't influence childhood. Rather, it suggests that there is interplay between individual agency and wider issues.

Notwithstanding this critique, some authors argue that top-down socialisation perspectives still inordinately influence beliefs and practices within health, social care and education (Alderson 2000). It is argued that women are coerced into collaborating with professionals to: carry out surveillance of children's development; shield children from the dangers of society; define acceptable behaviour at different age stages; and strengthen children's ability to become productive adults who are able to engage with a wider social world (Mayall 1996). Central to this collaboration is the idea that a women's role is to ensure that her children behave in ways that fit with social norms (see Sing 2002 for further discussion of the history of processes of normalisation).

In the USA it is argued that despite a complicated history (including a century of changing diagnostic labels, symptoms and aetiology) ADHD is still underpinned by an association between problem boy and problem mother:

> Modern American mothers are historically programmed to worry about their sons' behaviours and to blame themselves when those behaviours do not meet normative standards of achievement and success.
>
> (SIGN 2001: 597)

These writers suggest that the pressure on parents (particularly mothers) to ensure their children meet societal norms comes from a specific discourse which is to be found replicated time and again in professional practices, staff/student training resources, the marketing materials of drug companies, local and national policies, women's magazines, television programmes and so forth. This discourse enables some commentators to blame children's lack of educational achievement on a decline in moral standards. It is argued that this decline in moral standards is perpetuated by irresponsible parents (specifically teenage and single mothers), an unchecked media and the disintegration of social ties within communities (Murray 1990). In this extremely 'moral' discourse, problems related to class, family status and generation are employed as explanations for children's educational failure.

This type of thinking is worrisome when considered in relation to the work of writers who suggest that the majority of children with ADHD underachieve at school and that children who experience problematic social, cultural and economic factors are disproportionately diagnosed with ADHD (Fischer et al. 1993; Searight and McLaren 1998; SIGN 2001). At its most extreme, this moral discourse is believed to pressurise parents into using drugs to control their children's behaviour. It would appear that the increase in the diagnosis of ADHD may be an indicator of a wider social problem that relates to a family's location within society.

## ADHD and childhood studies: the child, society and control

A number of writers have examined the influence of material or social structures on childhood (e.g. adults, schools, economic systems, etc.) and presented children as the products of socio-economic, political and macro-cultural processes (this led to them being labelled as constructing a *social structural child*, James *et al.* 1998). For example, Qvortrup (1994, 2000) promoted the case for a materialist understanding of childhood. He stated that: 'No child can evade the impact of economic or spatial forces, nor ideologies about children and the family, let alone political and economic ideologies and realities' (2000: 79). He argued that it was only through a macro analysis that explanatory instances could be identified and that whilst a focus on society, mode of production, culture and historical periods could not explain everything, it enabled sociologists to empirically explain the influence on children of phenomena such as education, wealth, health, housing, institutionalisation and urbanisation.

Qvortrup (2000) asserted that we need explanatory parameters at the societal level in order to understand the major forces that account for the common features of childhood. He argued that we should employ quantitative studies to examine the structures and broader political contexts within which children live. This type of writing has been referred to as a 'reproductive model' because it suggested that childhood reproduces divisions in society (Corsaro 1997). This type of writing also requires us to examine the social systems within which the rise in diagnosis of ADHD has taken place.

Many authors have suggested that our social world has changed and that we as actors are subjected to discourses of control and surveillance. Some writers have suggested that children are now subjected to greater discourses of control that are deeply political and that underpin ideas such as curfews, national testing and guidelines for nursery provision (Stanton-Rogers 2001a). Some have argued that new technology has led to the creation of new forms of autonomy and independence for and by children (Lee 2001). Other writers argue that the child in post-modern society has had to react to changes in family structures, post-Fordist modes of production, concepts of risk, labelling processes of child welfare professionals, *inter alia* (Finn 2001). These writers contrast the post-modern child with its parents' generation who first encountered such things as mass education and mass consumption (Jenks 1996; Heiman 2001; Lee 2001). This contrast has led to the suggestion that new forms of technology have shattered the innocence of childhood because children are now able to easily access information on all manner of issues (Postman 1982). Jenks (1996, drawing from Beck 1992) suggests that in post-modern society the project of childhood involves the pursuit of independence and that children are symbolic of adult powerlessness.

At the heart of this perspective is the suggestion that adults have become more and more concerned with protecting children because of the breakdown of their own adult authority (e.g. Jenks 1996; Males 1999). Some authors have suggested that this has led to professionals (e.g. social workers) and other adults (e.g. parents) creating a 'curious' middle-class solidarity that enables them to define youth 'normality' and 'deviance' and where required, prescribe programmes to counteract youth deviance (Finn 2001). This work seems to suggest that the increase in diagnosis of ADHD does not only relate to expectations placed on mothers (which historically have always been there) but also is explained by specific recent changes in society that are related to globalisation.

In particular the need for education systems to respond to a fast-moving global employment market is believed to have recently further increased the pressure on professionals, parents and children. Many authors argue that schooling enables consensus between state and family and that childhood is controlled by the state through family and school-based socialisation. It is suggested that children benefit more from the education system if they are perceived to be 'good' pupils and that this suits the requirements of the state to have future productive workers and citizens (Shamgar-Handelman 1994).

This virtuous cycle of good childhood – good education – good employment contrasts the vicious cycle of lack of opportunity – bad childhood – poor employment prospects promoted by social capital theorists such as Putnam et al. (1993) and Coleman (1998). Social capital theorists suggest that poverty relates to children's educational, economic, social and environmental inheritance. Szreter (1999) argued:

> Social capital flows from the endowment of mutually respecting and trusting relationships that enable a group to pursue its shared goals more effectively than would otherwise be possible. Social capital therefore depends on the quality of the set of relationships of a social group. It can never be reduced to the mere possession or attribute of an individual. It results from the communicative capacities of a group: something shared in common and in which all participate.
>
> (Szreter 1999: 57)

In the UK, the concept of poverty is also closely related to ideas concerning social inclusion which suggest that specific groups experience marginalisation within society (Levitas 1998). It is suggested that a community's ability to develop social capital is determined by their material location. Parental material insecurity is believed to prevent children from developing relationships of trust, positive networks and ties of co-operation (Putnam et al. 1993). Children/young people are believed to fail at school because they do not have sufficient support networks to enable them to access systems of reward within education and subsequently opportunity for employment as adults (and in turn their children subsequently fail in the education system). This argument, like that of the social model of disability, brings into question the belief that ADHD has a medical cause. The suggestion is that children do not behave appropriately in school because they fail to experience social and emotional support and that this has to be rectified in order to protect adults, the viability of the economy and the long-term stability of society. It would appear that the need for good children, normal young people and future productive citizens underpins the emergence of ADHD as a category.

This type of analysis locates the causes of ADHD in the social sphere. It suggests that if the label ADHD is to have any use at all it should not be considered as a specific medical condition (see Davis and Watson 2000, 2001, 2002 for further debate in disability studies concerning whether labels have any utility). It is argued that medical model solutions to ADHD, such as the prescription of drugs, fail to treat the root social causes of ADHD (Lloyd and Norris 1999). It is possible to hypothesise that social solutions to ADHD might include restructuring of the school system. However, school restructuring is not an easy thing to achieve. For example, worthy attempts to challenge structural inequality by developing more inclusive schooling may have accidentally led to increases in diagnosis of ADHD in the UK.

## Inclusive education and ADHD

The promotion of inclusive schooling is linked to social capital debates on the basis that if more children can access mainstream education they are less likely to experience social exclusion and poor employment prospects as adults. However, ironically this very push towards inclusion may also be responsible for the increased numbers of children being diagnosed with ADHD.

Greater awareness of the social model of disability has led to more disabled children being included and/or integrated in mainstream schools. In order to achieve this change particular emphasis has been placed on considering/removing barriers created by market-place educational policy (Slee 1996; Riddell 1996; Ainscow 1992); reconsidering the power relationships between adults and disabled children (Alderson and Goodey 1999; Davis and Watson 2000); reviews of knowledge and practice in schools (Corker 1999; Adams *et al.* 2000); assessments of risk and safety (Rowley 1992); development of training and resources (Clark *et al.* 1997); and the need to properly assess, plan and resource children's requirements (Armstrong and Galloway 1994).

Central to this change has been an idea that managers who organise schools and staff that work in schools can make the necessary changes to ensure that disabled children and young people experience inclusion. Many disabled children have experienced difficulties with inclusion and not all staff, head teachers or local authorities have been able to meet their requirements (Davis and Watson 2000).

In addition to inclusion policies, the education systems of the UK have been under substantial pressure for over 20 years to take more of a market-based approach to enabling and evaluating performance. For example, there have been a number of policy changes aimed at improving standards, increasing managerialism and centralising control of curriculum and assessment. The nature of schooling has changed in contradictory ways. At the same time as schools have been encouraged to develop policies of inclusive education, restructuring of education policy has also created a separate pressure to increase standards and student performance (Brown 1990; Bondi 1991). At the centre of the managerialist agenda has been devolved management of school budgets, national testing of children at specific ages and the development of league tables of test/exam results to enable parents/politicians to differentiate between schools (Dale 1989; Hargreaves 1989; Lawton 1989). Changes to mainstream schooling have resulted in a change in the population of 'special' schools. More children and young people with physical impairments have become included in mainstream schools; however, more children labelled as 'disruptive' (particularly boys from families who have less access to material resources) have been sent to special schools (Riddell 1996). Many writers believe that the pressure on schools to both raise attainment and develop inclusion has had a negative effect on disabled children's education (Davis and Watson 2001). It has also been argued that inclusion will only fully prosper when:

- Teachers receive greater opportunities for training and peer exchange;
- The structure and balance (i.e. how much is taught on specific content) of the curriculum is reviewed;
- The range of opportunities for vocational subjects is increased;
- Pupils and parents are enabled to genuinely participate in decision-making about school rules, rewards and sanctions; and
- Schools are evaluated on quality of experience as well as quantity of attainment (Munn 2000).

The rise in cases of ADHD may simply symbolise the inability of education systems in the countries that make up the UK to cope with the requirements of inclusive education policy and attempts to raise attainment. Some writers specifically suggest that the self-controlled behaviour required of post-modern compulsory education may explain the increase in diagnosis of ADHD (Hinshaw 1994; Cooper and Ideus 1995, 1996).

Statistical analysis of the rise in ADHD has demonstrated that it is regularly diagnosed in children who have other learning difficulties and impairments (BPS 2000). A diagnosis requires that a child exhibit 'unusual behaviour' in more than one setting and that the child's behaviour has impeded academic progress. It is possible to theorise that increases in the number of children being diagnosed with ADHD may relate to the education system's inability to include disabled children or children who don't fit with specific norms that are required to boost attainment. This lack of fit may well be exacerbated by the belief systems of those involved in a diagnosis. For example, adults (including teachers, parents and a range of health professionals) are required to identify a number of behavioural signs, including hyperactivity (e.g. roaming around, talking, inability to sit through lesson); inattention (levels of distraction and inability to follow direction); and impulsivity (acting without thinking, shortness of temper, yelling and hitting) (APA 1994). This process requires adults to interpret the meaning of the behaviour of children. In recent years the development of the new social studies of childhood has seen the emergence of a considerable body of literature on research with children. This literature has been employed in a variety of stand-alone and accredited training. There is great debate concerning ethics, roles and tools that are best employed by adults to enable them to interpret the meanings of children's behaviour. Central to this debate have been discussions that highlight the need for adults to be reflexive when interpreting children's behaviour (Davis 1998). This rigorous qualitative research technique requires adults to consider how their own professional and personal preconceptions and beliefs affect the process of interpretation. It also requires adults to observe children over a sustained time period in a large variety of social contexts, not just the two required of ADHD (Davis 2000; Davis and Watson 2000; Davis et al. 2000). It is believed that only a sustained approach to observations enables adults to identify the connections between children's individual ways of being and wider cultural and structural influences on their lives (e.g. the role of peer group, neighbourhood, ethnic identity and so forth: Davis 2000; Davis and Watson 2000).

There is absolutely no evidence that the adults who are tasked with diagnosing ADHD are capable of employing reflexive techniques over a sustained period of time to support processes of interpretation and diagnosis. Indeed, there is evidence that some adults who work with disabled children consistently fail to question their long-held assumptions that are based on medical model perspectives of disability (Davis et al. 2000; Davis and Watson 2000).

Sustained ethnographic research with disabled children in schools suggests that as well as experiencing positive relationships with pupils and teachers, they also routinely experience bullying, do not receive appropriate access to the curriculum, have their different learning requirements stigmatised, and are excluded from social and cultural processes (Davis and Watson 2001 – please note this is not an argument against inclusive school but a suggestion that more efforts could be made to improve the nature of inclusive schooling). When disabled children express their resistance to this experience by being inattentive, angry or agitated they run the risk of their impairment being rediagnosed as ADHD (Corker and Davis 2000, 2001).

Therefore the grounds used for the diagnosis of ADHD are totally inadequate because they:

- Take little notice of the social context of the school;
- Overlook the relationship between pupil behaviour and the actions of fellow pupils, teachers and parents;
- Fail to employ rigorous and sustained observation;
- Only require observation to be carried out in a few locations by people who have little knowledge of how to analyse the social context of childhood;
- Are carried out by people who lack experience of qualitative and reflexive research methods;
- Take little account of the power relations between adults and children.

A further crucial point is that the process of diagnosis may take little account of children's own views on the causes of their behaviour. This raises an important issue. Medical models of childhood have been criticised for failing to consider the views of children (Davis and Watson 2000, 2001). Yet structuralist writers on childhood have also experienced the same criticism and early social model theorists in disability studies have been criticised for concentrating on adult perspectives of disability (Shakespeare and Watson 1998). This suggests that both medical and social structural constructs of ADHD have their faults.

## ADHD and children's rights

Structural, developmental and medical theories of childhood have been critiqued because they have reduced children to the state of passive objects; overlooked children's capacity to generate their own capital; ignored the influence of peer groups; failed to investigate children's own indicators of material inequality; and overlooked the two-way nature of adult-child relations (Davis forthcoming; Morrow 1999; Mayall 2000). For example, Prout (2000: 7) argues that children are 'limited by the conditions of their social lives, but they find ways of creatively managing, negotiating and extending the possibilities'.

This poses a problem for writers who are tempted to argue that the rise in ADHD is merely symptomatic of a change in the power relationships between children and adults within Western societies. Recent attempts to characterise 'modern' global youth as sharing a 'troubled' experience have been challenged within youth studies because they overemphasise UK/USA-based structuralist and social constructionist narratives and underplay the tension between control and self-realisation in childhood (Griffin 2001).

In childhood studies Prout (2000) critiques social constructionists because they often represent childhood bodies as purely discursive. (An example of this would be the way that Jenks (1996) concentrates on the meta-narrative of adult power-lessness in relation to child abuse at the expense of considering the lived reality of the child experiencing abuse.)

Prout (2000) suggested that social constructionist perspectives unintentionally reinforce discourses of powerlessness:

> Whilst the anti-foundationalist view of children's bodies speaks to the role of professions such as medicine and their role in the creation of frameworks through which the body is understood, it has little to say about the childhood body in these terms. On the contrary the person with a body is generally construed quite passively: acted upon, regulated, disciplined and determined.
>
> (Prout 2000: 7)

This critique encourages us to move beyond the polar nature of medical v. social debates to examine the complex interplay of different influences on children's lives (e.g. their own agency, social forces, medical/biological issues). In contrast to social constructionist perspectives, there are a number of examples in childhood studies of texts that illustrate the complex connections between the actions of children/young people and wider influences. For example, Pribilsky (2001) con-nected illness among young people in the Equadorian Andes to a complex mixture of issues such as young people's perceptions of self, economic migration by fathers, emotional and physical exhaustion, parenting styles and changes in community relationships. Robinson and Delahooke (2001), drawing from actor network theory, illustrate the complex fusion of issues in everyday school life. For example, impair-ment issues (asthma), technology (an inhaler), symbolic exchange (the performance of using of the inhaler), cultural juxtaposition (the comparison between different coloured inhalers and coloured belts in Karate) and peer relational issues (an inhaler being stolen).

In relation to ADHD, this type of work encourages us to theorise that ADHD may not have a single medical or social cause. It also requires us to recognise that, as social agents, children who are labelled with ADHD have a role to play in processes of 'diagnosis' and resolution. As such, they should be encouraged to define their own life problems that have led to them being labelled ADHD and reflect on the solutions to their experiences.

The notion that children can contribute to decision-making processes that impact on their lives is enshrined in the UN Convention on Rights of the Child. This document underpins children's rights perspectives. There appears to be a number of strands to the children's rights perspective. The first strand promotes the use of legislation (e.g. the Factory Act 1802) to protect vulnerable children from cruelty and/or lack of consideration (Mills 2000). The second strand challenges the historic assumption that children are non-rational, cannot take significant decisions about their lives, and need to be protected by adults who will take responsibility and make choices on their behalf. This strand promotes the provision of legislation to encourage adults to recognise the individual child's capacity to make choices in their own interest in a variety of settings and contexts (e.g. Archard 1993; Marshall 1997; Foley *et al.* 2001; Franklin 2002).

For example, Article 12 states that children not only have a right to articulate their opinions with regard to issues that affect them but that they also have a right to have these opinions heard. Article 13 declares that the child has a right to seek, receive and impart information and ideas of all kinds (Alderson 1995; Morrow and Richards 1996). The Children's Act 1989 and Children (Scotland) Act 1995 emphasise that children's opinions should be sought with regard to matters/decisions concerning their welfare (Beresford 1997). Despite this legislation, writing which connects ideas in disability and childhood studies suggests that medical model perspectives invariably characterise children as not being competent to make decisions.

In the most part, this has occurred because a perception exists that children are unable to put forward their own views and that they lack competency and agency (Robinson 1997; Shakespeare and Watson 1998; Corker and Davis 2000; Davis and Watson 2000; Bricher 2001). In contrast, it has been argued that children are very capable of making their views known when adults make the effort to learn the different ways in which they communicate (Davis *et al.* 2000).

In disability studies, it is argued that medical model perspectives prevent adults from viewing disabled children as agents. It is suggested that very often parents and children are initiated by medical professionals into a medical culture which does not allow space for them to challenge traditional orthodoxy and that fails to recognise conflicts of interests between children, parents and professionals (Mayall 1998; Shakespeare and Watson 1998; Avery 1999). In the main, adults are deemed 'experts' and children are assumed to be unable to put forward their own solutions to their own life problems. This very often leads adults to make decisions about children's lives without consulting them, or to assume that they know what is best for children. Children's problems are identified and resolved by parents and/or professionals and ownership of their own choices is taken away from children (Davis and Watson 2000).

In the health field too much emphasis is placed on adults/parents' views at the expense of understanding the things that disabled children and teenagers want to change about the services that they encounter. There is little or no evidence that children are being consulted about their opinions of the identification, diagnosis treatment and management of ADHD (Cooper and Shea 2000; Lloyd and Norris 1999; Norris and Lloyd 2000). For example, some studies suggest that effective management of ADHD should be based on clinicians establishing good working relationships with schools and families (Williams *et al.* 1999). More could be done to highlight the importance of including children as participants in these processes.

It has been argued that a lack of participation relates to the tendency for assessment procedures (of a variety of services) and academic research (e.g. in health, education and psychology) to concentrate on illustrating the things that children cannot do (e.g. how they fail to achieve developmental 'norms'), rather than understanding their skills and abilities (Priestly 1998; Alderson 2000; Woodhead and Faulkner 2000; Bricher 2001).

In contrast to medical discourses a number of writers have demonstrated that children are capable of making complex medical decisions (Alderson 1993; Bricher 2001). Others have urged us to recognise children's knowledge and ability to negotiate and collaborate on making decisions about health matters (Mayall 1996, 1998). However, the shift to collaborative practice requires a cultural shift in the practices and perceptions of professionals that work with children. It also requires those of us that work with children to be open about the possible causes of ADHD. For example, social perspectives should not ignore the influence of biological issues on children's behaviour. It is important that solutions to the ADHD crisis are underpinned by appropriate thinking from a range of disciplines (e.g. psychology, social policy, sociology, anthropology, childhood studies, social work, education and health) and that they take account of individual, group, organisational, biological and material contexts. The need for openness is central to the participatory approaches that have recently emerged in childhood studies. There is no point talking to children about issues in their lives (e.g. symptoms of ADHD) if you have already made up your mind what the causes and solutions are.

Children may come up with a range of explanations for their own behaviour that might include issues such as diet, self-esteem, relationships with others, environmental issues (e.g. noise pollution), structural issues (e.g. the structure of schooling) and cultural issues (e.g. the practices of teachers and parents). It is important that they are enabled to participate freely in discussions to identify the causes of their behaviour, to decide if their behaviour is appropriate and work in partnership to plan strategies of resolution where they deem this to be necessary. It is worth noting that these strategies should not simply concentrate on changes the child has to enact. They should also consider how the behaviour and practices of adults might be altered. This does not mean that children's rights should be recognised in opposition to and at the expense of adult rights (Cockburn 1998; Davis and Watson 2001; Pupavac 2001). Rather it is a plea for adults and children to exercise rights and choices in partnership (Cockburn 1998; Davis and Watson 2001; Pinkerton 2001). In relation to disabled children's experiences of services it has been argued that we need to develop processes that balance adult and child expectations and offer opportunities for dialogue, negotiation and change (Davis and Watson 2000).

There is hope that the professionals who are currently involved in the diagnosis of ADHD will not disregard the promotion of such a participatory approach. For example, recent policy developments in Scotland have led to the development of a participatory strategy for children and young people's mental health services (http://www.scotland.gov.uk/consultations/health/cypmh-00.asp). Indeed, UK child psychiatrists are thought to place a greater emphasis on social and psychological aspects of child mental health than their US counterparts. Indirectly, this means that they tend to discourage the use of medical diagnoses (Hindley and Kroll 1998). Research within this field has suggested that both biological and contextual factors should be considered when diagnosing ADHD (Cooper 1997).

This suggests that there is hope that we can move the agenda on to a more complex and participatory position that considers the relationship between professionals, policy-makers, drug companies, parents, children and advocacy groups. Recent guidance suggests that diagnosis of ADHD should be:

- Timely;
- Comprehensive;
- Involve *children*, parents and carers and the child's school;
- Include assessment by educational/clinical psychologists and social workers; and
- Take into account cultural factors in the child's environment (NICE 2000; SIGN 2001).

It may take some time for professionals to work out how to include children in processes of diagnosis. It is important that the guidance does not restrict the professionals that can be involved. For example, childhood studies researchers, local authority participation officers, community educators, youth workers and child care specialists have as much (if not more) of a tradition of listening to children as do social workers, teachers and psychologists. If a truly holistic approach is to be adopted then a range of experts on working with children, families and community development must be at the heart of processes that enable children to plan effective solutions in partnership with adults.

The need to develop processes of dialogue, planning and partnership brings into question the use of medication as a solution to ADHD. In addition to the short- and long-term dangers of prescribing drugs to children, the effect of medication for ADHD is such that children and young people become very susceptible to adult suggestion and very compliant with adult direction (Sing 2002). This means that the drugs prevent children from participating openly in discussions. It is difficult to see how the use of such overbearing chemical solutions can form the basis for a progressive approach to the complex phenomenon that is ADHD.

## Conclusion

This chapter has linked concerns over the diagnosis of ADHD to theoretical perspectives in education, disability and childhood studies. Arguments over the causes of ADHD have been related to medical and social models of disability, discussions concerning parents' morality and social control, changes in the structure of society and the development of managerialism and inclusion in the education systems of the UK. A comparison of different theoretical approaches has suggested that both medical and social perspectives on ADHD have their faults. By comparing different theoretical perspectives and ideas in childhood, disability and educational studies it has been possible to highlight the potential for the development of a progressive holistic approach to ADHD that gives equal weight to the opinions of adults, children and young people. It has been concluded that at the centre of this approach should be a recognition of the ability of children and young people to identify solutions to their own life problems.

## Bibliography

Abberley, P. (1987) 'The Concept of Oppression and the Development of a Social Theory of Disability'. *Disability, Handicap and Society*, 21: 5–19.

Adams, J., Swain, J. and Clark, J. (2000) '"What's So Special?" Teachers' Models and their Realisation in Practice in Segregated Schools'. *Disability and Society*, 15(2): 233–246.

Ainscow, M. (1992) 'Doing the Right Things: Seeing Special Needs as a School Improvement Issue'. In Fairbairn, G. and Fairbairn, S. (eds) *Integrating Special Children: Some Ethical Issues*. Aldershot: Avebury.

Alderson, P. (1993) *Children's Consent To Surgery*. Buckingham: Open University Press.

Alderson, P. (1995) *Listening to Children: Children Ethics and Social Research*. Buckingham: Barnardo's.

Alderson, P. (2000) *Young Children's Rights: Exploring Beliefs, Principle and Practice*. London: Jessica Kingsley.

Alderson, P. and Goodey, C. (1999) *Enabling Education: Experiences in Special and Ordinary Schools*. London: Tufnell Press.

American Psychiatric Association (1994) *Diagnostic and Statistical Manual of Mental Disorders* (4th ed.). Washington, DC: American Psychiatric Association.

Archard, D. (1993) *Children: Rights and Childhood*. London: Routledge.

Armstrong, D. and Galloway, D. (1994) 'Special Educational Needs and Problem Behaviour; Making Policy in the Classroom'. In Riddell, S. and Brown, S. (eds) *Special Educational Needs Policy in the 1990s: Warnock in the Market Place*. London: Routledge.

Avery, D. (1999) 'Talking "Tragedy": Identity Issues in the Parental Story of Disability'. In Corker, M. and French, S. (eds) *Disability Discourse*. Buckingham: Open University Press.

Baldwin, S. and Cooper, P. (2000) 'How Should ADHD be Treated? Head to Head'. *The Psychologist*, 13(12): 598–602.

Barnes, C. (1991) *Disabled People In Britain And Discrimination: A Case For Anti-Discrimination Legislation*. London: Hurst/BCODP.

Barnes, C., Mercer, G. and Shakespeare, T. (1999) *Exploring Disability: A Sociological Introduction*. London: Polity Press.

Beck, U. (1992) *Risk Society: Towards a New Modernity*. London: Sage.

Beresford, B. (1997) *Personal Accounts: Involving Disabled Children in Research*. York: Social Policy Research Unit.

Berger, P. L. and Berger, B. (1991) 'Becoming a Member of Society – Socialisation'. In Waksler, F. (ed.) *Studying the Social Worlds of Children, Sociological Readings*. London: Falmer.

Bondi, L. (1991) 'Choice and Diversity in School Education'. *Comparative Education*, 27: 125–134.

BPS (1996) *Attention Deficit Hyperactivity Disorder (ADHD). A Psychological Response to an Evolving Concept*. Leicester: British Psychological Society.

BPS (2000) *Attention Deficit/Hyperactivity Disorder: Guidelines and Principles for Successful Multi-agency Working*. Leicester: British Psychological Society.

Bricher, G. (2001) '"If you want to know about it just ask." Exploring Disabled Teenagers' Experiences of Health and Health Care'. Ph.D. unpublished, University of South Australia.

Brown, P. (1990) 'Education and the Ideology of Parentocracy'. *British Journal of Sociology of Education*, 11: 65–85.

Brynner, J. (2001) 'Childhood Risk and Protective Factors in Social Exclusion'. *Children and Society*, 14: 285–301.

Campbell, J. and Oliver, M. (1996). *Disability Politics. Understanding Our Past, Changing Our Future*. London: Routledge.

Clark, C., Dyson, A., Millward, A. and Skidmore, D. (1997) *New Directions in Special Needs Schooling: Innovations in Mainstream Schools*. London: Cassell.

Cockburn, T. (1998) 'Children and Citizenship in Britain'. *Childhood*, 5(1): 99–118.

Coleman, J. (1998) 'Social Capital, Human Capital, and Investment in Youth'. In Petersen, A. and Mortimer, J. (eds) *Youth Unemployment and Society*. Cambridge, MA: Harvard University Press.

Coles, B. (2000) *Joined-Up Youth Research, Policy and Practice: A New Agenda for Change*. Leicester: Youth Work Press.

Conrad, P. and Potter, D. (2000) 'From Hyperactive Children to ADHD Adults: Observations on the Expansion of Medical Categories'. *Social Problems*, 47(4): 559–583.

Cooper, J. (ed.) (2000) *Law, Rights and Disability*. London: Jessica Kingsley.

Cooper, P. (1997) 'Biology Behaviour and Education: AD/HD and the Bio-psychosocial Perspective'. *Educational and Child Psychology*, 14(1): 31–38.

Cooper, P. and Ideus, K. (1995) 'Is Attention Deficit Disorder a Trojan Horse?' *Support for Learning*, 10: 29–34.

Cooper, P. and Ideus, K. (1996) *Attention Deficit Disorder: A Practical Guide For Teachers*. London: David Fulton.

Cooper, P. and Shea, T. (2000) 'ADHD from the Inside: An Empirical Study of Young People's Perceptions of the Experience of ADHD'. In Cooper, P. and Bilton, K. (eds) *ADHD: Research, Practice and Opinion*. London: Whurr.

Cooper, P., Maras, P., Norwich, B., Lovey, J., Rollock, N. and Szpakowski, J. (1999) 'Attributions of Attentional and Activity Problems'. Paper presented at BERA Annual Conference, September 1999.

Corker, M. (1999) 'They Don't Know What They Don't Know – Disability Research as an "Emancipatory" Site of Learning'. Sites of Learning Conference, University of Hull, September.

Corker, M. and Davis, J. M. (2000) 'Disabled Children – (Still) Invisible under the Law'. In Cooper, J. (ed.) *Law, Rights and Disability*. London: Jessica Kingsley.

Corker, M., and Davis, J. M. (2001) 'Portrait of Callum: The Disabling of a Childhood'. In Edwards, R. (ed.) *Children, Home and School: Autonomy, Connection or Regulation*. London: Falmer Press.

Corker, M. and Shakespeare, T. (2002) 'Mapping the Terrain'. In Corker, M. and Shakespeare, T. (eds) *Disability and Postmodernity*. London: Continuum.

Corsaro, W. A. (1997) *The Sociology of Childhood*. Thousand Oaks, CA: Pine Forge.

Dale, R. (1989) *The State and Education Policy*. Oxford: Oxford University Press.

Davis, J. M. (1998) 'Understanding The Meanings of Children: A Reflexive Process'. *Children and Society*, 12(5): 325–335.

Davis, J. M. (2000) 'Disability Studies as Ethnographic Research and Text: Can We Represent Cultural Diversity Whilst Promoting Social Change?' *Disability and Society*, 15(2): 191–206.

Davis, J. M. (forthcoming) 'Changing childhoods and social inclusion'. In Davis, J. M., Hill, M., Tisdall, K. and Prout, A. (eds) *Participation For What? Children, Young People And Social Inclusion*. Bristol: Policy Press.

Davis, J. M. and Watson, N. (2000) 'Disabled Children's Rights in Everyday Life: Problematising Notions of Competency and Promoting Self-Empowerment'. *International Journal of Children's Rights*, 8: 211–228.

Davis, J. M. and Watson, N. (2001) 'Where Are the Children's Experiences? Analysing Social and Cultural Exclusion in "Special" and "Mainstream" Schools'. *Disability and Society*, 16(5): 671–687.

Davis, J. M. and Watson, N. (2002) 'Countering Stereotypes of Disability: Disabled Children and Resistance'. In Corker, M. and Shakespeare, T. (eds) *Disability and Postmodernity*. London: Continuum.

Davis, J. M., Watson, N. and Cunningham-Burley, S. (2000) 'Learning the Lives of Disabled Children: Developing a Reflexive Approach'. In Christiensen, P. and James, A. (eds) *Research With Children*. London: Falmer.

Department of Health (2002) *Children's Task Force*. London: HMSO (www.doh.gov.uk/childrenstaskforce).

Easen, P., Atkins, M. and Dyson, A. (2000) 'Inter-professional Collaboration and Conceptualisations of Practice'. *Children and Society*, 14: 355–367.

Finkelstein, V. (1993) 'Disability: A Social Challenge or an Administrative Responsibility'. In Swain, J., Finkelstein, V., French, S. and Oliver, M. (eds) *Disabling Barriers – Enabling Environments*. London: Sage.

Finn, J. (2001) 'Text and Turbulence; Representing Adolescence as Pathology in the Human Services'. *Childhood*, 8(2): 167–192.

Fischer, M., Barkley, R. A., Fletcher, K. E., and Smallish, L. (1993). 'The Adolescent Outcome of Hyperactive Children: Predictors of Psychiatric, Academic, Social and Emotional Adjustment'. *Journal of the American Academy of Child and Adolescent Psychiatry*, 32: 324–332.

Foley, P., Roche, J. and Tucker, S. (2001) *Children in Society: Contemporary Theory, Policy and Practice*. Basingstoke: Open University Press/Palgrave.

Franklin, B. (ed.) (2002) *The New Handbook of Children's Rights*. London: Routledge.

Gilmore, A., Best, L. and Milne, R. (1998) 'Methylphenidate in Children with Hyperactivity'. *DEC Report 78*. Bristol: South and West Research and Development Directorate.

Glass, N. (1999) 'Development of the Sure Start Programme'. *Children and Society*, 13: 258–264.

Grant, W. (2000) *Pressure Groups and British Politics*. Basingstoke: Macmillan Press.

Griffin, C. (2001) 'Imagining New Narratives of Youth'. *Childhood*, 8(2): 147–166.

Hargreaves, A. (1989) *Curriculum and Assessment Reform*. Oxford: Oxford University Press.

Heiman, R. (2001) 'The Ironic Contradictions in the Discourse of Generation X, or How "Slackers" are Saving Capitalism'. *Childhood* 8(2): 274–293.

Hindley, P. and Kroll, L. (1998) 'Theoretical and Epidemiological Aspects of Attention Deficit and Overactivity in Deaf Children'. *Journal of Deaf Studies and Deaf Education*, 3(1): 64–72.

Hinshaw, S. P. (1994) *Attention Deficits and Hyperactivity in Children*. Thousand Oaks, CA: Sage.

James, A., Jenks, C. and Prout, A. (1998) *Theorising Childhood*. Cambridge: Polity Press.

Jenks, C. (1996) 'The Postmodern Child'. In Brannen, J. and O'Brian, M. (eds) *Children in Families*. London: Falmer.

Lawton, D. (1989) *Education, Culture and the National Curriculum*. London: Hodder and Stoughton.

Lee, N. (2001) 'The Extensions of Childhood: Technologies, Children and Independence'. In Hutchby, I. and Moran-Ellis, J. (eds) *Children, Technology and Culture: The Impact of Technologies in Children's Everyday Lives*. London: Falmer.

Levitas, R. (1998) *The Inclusive Society*. London: Palgrave/Macmillan.

Linton, S. (1998) *Claiming Disability: Knowledge and Identity*. New York: New York University Press.

Lloyd, G. and Norris, C. (1999) 'Including ADHD?' *Disability and Society*, 14: 505–517.

McCubbin, M. and Cohen, D. (1999) 'Empirical, Ethical and Political Perspectives on the Use of Methylphenidate'. *Ethical Human Sciences and Services*, 1(1): 81–101.

Males, M. (1999) *Framing Youth: Ten Myths About the Next Generation*. Monroe, ME: Common Courage.

Maloney, W. A., Jordan, G. and McLaughlin, A. M. (1994) 'Interest Groups and Public Policy: The Insider/Outsider Model Revisited'. *Journal of Public Policy*, 14(1): 17–38.

Marsh, D. (1998) 'The Development of the Policy Network Approach'. In Marsh, D. (ed.) *Comparing Policy Networks*. Buckingham: Open University Press: 3–17.

Marsh, D. and Smith, M. (2000) 'Understanding Policy Networks: Towards a Dialectical Approach'. *Political Studies*, 48: 4–21.

Marshall, K. (1997) *Children's Rights in the Balance: The Participation–Protection Debate*. Edinburgh: Stationery Office.

Mayall, B. (1996) *Children's Health and the Social Order*. Buckingham: Open University Press.

Mayall, B. (1998) 'Towards A Sociology of Child Health'. *Sociology of Health and Illness*, 20: 269–288.

Mayall, B. (2000) 'Conversations with Children: Working with Generational Issues'. In Christensen, P. and James, A. (eds) *Conducting Research With Children*, London: Falmer.

Merril, C. and Tymms, P. B. (2001) 'Inattention, Hyperactivity and Impulsiveness: Their Impact on Academic Achievement and Progress'. *British Journal of Educational Psychology*, 71: 43–56.

Mills, R. (2000) 'Perspectives of Childhood'. In Mills, J. and Mills, R. (eds) *Childhood Studies: A Reader in Perspectives of Childhood*. London: Routledge.

Morrow, V. (1999) 'Conceptualising Social Capital in Relation to the Well-Being of Children and Young People: A Critical Review'. *The Sociological Review*, 47(4): 744–765.

Morrow, V. and Richards, M. (1996) 'The Ethics of Social Research with Children: An Overview'. *Children and Society*, 10: 28–40.

Munn, P. (2000) 'Can Schools Make Scotland a More Inclusive Society?' *Scottish Affairs*, 33: 116–131.

Murray, C. (1990) *The Emerging British Underclass*. London: IEA.

NICE – National Institute for Clinical Excellence (2000). *Guidance on the Use of Methylphenidate for Attention Deficit/Hyperactivity Disorder (ADHD) in Childhood*. London: NHS NICE. Technology Appraisal Guidance – No. 13.

Norris, C. and Lloyd, G. (2000) 'Parents, Professionals and ADHD – What the Papers Say'. *European Journal of Special Needs Education*, 15(2): 123–137.

Oliver, M. (1990) *The Politics of Disablement*. Basingstoke: Macmillan.

Orford, E. (1998) 'Commentary: Diagnosis Needs Tightening'. *British Medical Journal*, 316: 1594–1596.

Parsons, T. and Bales, R. F. (1955) *Family Socialisation and the Interactive Process*. New York: The Free Press.

Pinkerton, J. (2001) 'Developing Partnership Practice'. In Foley, P., Roche, J. and Tucker, S. (eds) *Children in Society: Contemporary Theory, Policy and Practice*. Basingstoke: Open University Press/Palgrave.

Postman, N. (1982) *The Disappearance of Childhood*. New York: Random House.

Pribilsky, J. (2001) 'Nervios and Modern Childhood'. *Childhood*, 8(2): 251–273.

Priestly, M. (1998) 'Childhood Disability and Disabled Childhoods: Agendas for Research'. *Childhood*, 5(2): 207–223.

Prout, A. (2000) 'Childhood Bodies: Constructing Agency and Hybridity'. In Prout, A. (ed.) *The Body Childhood and Society*. Basingstoke: Macmillan Press.

Pupavac, V. (2001) 'Misanthropy Without Borders. The International Children's Rights Regime'. *Disasters*, 25(2): 95–112.

Putnam, R., Leonardi, R. and Nanetti, R. (1993) *Making Democracy Work: Civic Traditions in Modern Italy*. Princeton, NJ: Princeton University Press.

Qvortrup, J. (1994) 'Childhood Matters: An Introduction'. In Qvortrup, J. *et al.* (eds) *Childhood Matters: Social Theory, Politics and Practice*. Aldershot: Avebury.

Qvortrup, J. (2000) 'Macroanalysis of Childhood'. In Christensen, P. and James, A. (eds) *Conducting Research With Children*. London: Falmer.

Rhodes, R. A. W. (1981) *Control and Power in Central–Local Government Relationships*. Farnborough: Gower.

Rhodes, R. A. W. (1997) *Understanding Governance*. Buckingham: Open University Press.

Riddell, S. (1996) 'Theorising Special Educational Need in a Changing Political Climate'. In Barton, L. (ed.) *Disability and Society: Emerging Issues and Insights*. Harlow: Addison Wesley Longman.

Robinson, I. and Delahooke, A. (2001) 'Fabricating Friendships'. In Hutchby, I. and Moran-Ellis, J. (eds) *Children, Technology and Culture: The Impact of Technologies in Children's Everyday Lives*. London: Falmer.

Robinson, J. (1997) 'Listening To Disabled Youth'. *Child Right*, 140: 546–547.

Rowley, D. (1992) 'Creating a Desirable Future for People with Significant Learning Difficulties'. In Fairbairn, G. and Fairbairn, S. (eds) *Integrating Special Children: Some Ethical Issues*. Aldershot: Avebury.

Safer, D., Zito, J. and Fine, E. (1996) 'Increased Methylphenidate Usage for Attention Deficit Hyperactivity Disorder in the 1990s'. *Pediatrics*, 98: 1084–1088.

Scraton, P. (ed.) (1997) *Childhood In Crisis*. London: UCL Press.

Searight, H. R. and McLaren, A. L. (1998) 'Attention Deficit Hyperactivity Disorder: The Medicalisation of Misbehaviour'. *Journal of Clinical Psychology in Medical Settings*, 5(4): 467–495.

Shakespeare, T. and Watson, N. (1998) 'Theoretical Perspectives on Research with Disabled Children'. In Robinson, C. and Stalker, K. (eds) *Growing Up with Disability*. London: Jessica Kingsley.

Shamgar-Handelman, L. (1994) 'To Whom Does Childhood Belong?' In Qvortrup, J. (ed.) *Childhood Matters: Social Theory, Practices and Politics*. Ashgate: Avebury.

SIGN (2001) *Attention Deficit and Hyperkinetic Disorders in Children and Young People*. Sign Publication No. 52, Scottish Intercollegiate Guidelines Network.

Singh, I. (2002) 'Bad Boys, Good Mothers and the "Miracle" of Ritalin'. *Science in Context*, 15(4): 577–603.

Slee, R. (1995) *Changing Theories and Practices of Discipline*. London: Falmer Press.

Slee, R. (1996a) 'Clauses on Conditionality: The Reasonable Accommodation of Language'. In Barton, L. (ed.) *Disability and Society: Emerging Issues and Insights*. Harlow: Addison Wesley Longman.

Slee, R. (1996b) 'Inclusive Schooling in Australia? Not Yet!' *Cambridge Journal of Education*, 26(1): 9–32.

Slee, R. (1997) 'Imported or Important Theory? Sociological Interrogations of Disablement and Special Education'. *British Journal of Sociology of Education*, 18(3): 407–419.

Stalker, K. and Robinson, C. (1998) *Growing Up with Disability*. London: Jessica Kingsley.

Stanton-Rogers, W. (2001a) 'Constructing Childhood – Contrasting Child Concern'. In Foly, P., Roche, J. and Tucker, S. (eds) *Children in Society*. Basingstoke: Open University Press.

Stanton-Rogers, W. (2001b) 'Theories of Child Development'. In Foly, P., Roche, J. and Tucker, S. (eds) *Children in Society*. Basingstoke: Open University Press.

Szreter, S. (1999) 'A New Political Economy for New Labour: The Importance of Social Capital'. *Renewal*, 7(1): 30–44.

UPIAS/Disability Alliance (1976) *Fundamental Principles of Disability*. Methuen: London. http://www.leeds.ac.uk/disability-studies/archiveuk/UPIAS/UPIAS.pdf.

Utting, D. (2001) 'Made to Measure: Evaluating Community Initiatives for Children'. *Children and Society*, 15(1): 1–54.

Waksler, F. C. (1991) 'Beyond Socialisation'. In Waksler, F. C. (ed.) *Studying the Social Worlds of Children: Sociological Readings*. London: Falmer.

Ward, H. and Skuse, T. (2001) 'Performance Targets and Stability of Placements for Children Long Looked After Away from Home'. *Children and Society*, 15: 333–346.

Webb, R. and Vulliamy, G. (2001) 'Joining Up the Solutions: The Rhetoric and Practice of Inter-agency Co-operation'. *Children and Society*, 15: 315–332.

Williams, C., Wright, B. and Partridge, I. (1999) 'Attention Deficit Disorder – A Review'. *British Journal of General Practice*, 49(44): 563–571.

Wilson, L. M. (2002) *Attention Deficit/Hyperactivity Disorder and Indicators of Social Deprivation in Primary Schools in Bath and North-East Somerset*. London: Disability Rights Commission.

Woodhead, M. and Faulkner, D. (2000) 'Subjects, Objects or Participants? Dilemmas of Psychological Research with Children'. In Christensen, P. and James, A. (eds) *Research With Children*. London: Falmer.

World Health Organization (1992) *International Classification of Diseases* (10th edn). Geneva: WHO.

Wrong, D. H. (1961) 'The Oversocialised Concept of Man in Modern Sociology'. *American Sociological Review*, 26: 183–193.

Zametkin, A. and Liotta, W. (1998) 'The Neurobiology of Attention-Deficit/Hyperactivity Disorder'. *Journal of Clinical Psychiatry*, 59(7): 17–23.

Zametkin, A. and Ernst, M. (1999) 'Problems in the Management of Attention-Deficit–Hyperactivity Disorder'. *New England Journal of Medicine*, 340(1): 40–46.

# Chapter 4

# ADHD as the new 'feeblemindedness' of American Indian children

*David Walker*

The white people are civilized; they have everything and go to school, too. They learn how to read and write so they can read newspaper.

The yellow people they half civilized, some of them know to read and write, and some know how to take care of themself.

The red people they big savages; they don't know nothing.

(Essay written by American Indian boy at Hampton Institute in 1890, quoted in Adams 1995: 148)

The fact that one meets this type (feebleminded individuals) with such frequency among Indians, Mexicans, and Negroes suggests quite forcibly that the whole question of racial differences in mental traits will have to be taken up anew and by experimental methods. Children of this group should be segregated in special classes and be given instruction which is concrete and practical. They cannot master, but they can be made efficient workers, able to look out for themselves. There is no possibility of convincing society that they should not be allowed to reproduce, although from a eugenic point of view they constitute a grave problem because of the unusually prolific breeding. . . .

(Dr Lewis Terman 1916, quoted in Stoskepf 1999)

Oh! ADHD! That's what I am?!

(Native client reviewing health chart at Indian Health Service Clinic in 2003)

The 14 Confederated Tribes of the Yakama Nation[1] are situated on 1.3 million acres of the plateau region of central Washington in the Pacific Northwest of the United States. This close-knit confederation of family bands speaking several dialects of Sahaptin were forced together into a single entity by the Treaty of 1855, grudgingly signed 'in friendship only' by but a few of their actual representatives at the time. Their close family relations were pushed in other geographic directions along the Columbia River and became the Oregon tribes of the Umatilla and Warm Springs Indians. They have lived there for at least 12,000 years.

## Psychiatric diagnosis as a source of Native American oppression

The label Attention Deficit Hyperactivity Disorder (ADHD) was introduced by the surrounding EuroAmerican culture in the late 1980s through treaty-guaranteed health care clinics. The ADHD diagnosis has been applied since to Native[2] youth and adults with no examination of its intercultural utility or validity. To assess the impact of this modern psychiatric label on the children of Yakama Nation, one must first understand how similar labels have been applied freely across cultural boundaries since the inception of the mental health movement in the United States at the turn of the twentieth century.

The most famous 'first' psychiatric observation of American Indians came from Dr Charles Lillybridge of Virginia who attended to Cherokees from 1837 to 1839 as they were forced into refugee camps prior to removal from their ancestral lands via the disastrous Trail of Tears. Lillybridge contended that, despite conditions of extreme stress impinging upon the 20,000 persons under his care, he 'never saw or heard of a case of insanity among them' (Hurd *et al.* 1916: 49). By the late 1890s, however, new ideas about Indian insanity had emerged. The 16 inmates held at the Hiawatha Asylum for Insane Indians in Canton, South Dakota in 1904, including 10 men and 6 women,[3] carried such diagnoses as 'acute melancholia,' 'chronic melancholia,' and 'chronic mania,' as well as epilepsy, dementia, and 'feeblemindedness' (Saxman 1999).

With hindsight, it would be difficult to deny that these labels obfuscated the actual situations of these individuals. Oppressed and despairing over their imprisonment, they had been recast as mentally ill. Their emotional state was not attributed to their wounded spirits, their rage over being chained to bed frames, or their grief over being held far away from their families. The frequent, mournful songs emanating from the rooms and halls of the Asylum likely were spiritual preparations for death (Yellow Bird 2002).

By the mid-1920s, many of the men among now almost 100 inmates at the Asylum were American Indian combat veterans of World War I suffering from 'shell shock' (Lincoln County History Committee 1985). The same mental health movement that had screened American Indians into front-line combat now held them involuntarily for the stress reactions resulting from that exposure. Asylum inmates not exposed to combat may have attempted to resist the 'power of the reservation agent, who could simply declare one insane and have one shipped off' (Yellow Bird 2002: 4). Until its closure in 1933 – after the 'discovery' that most of its inmates were 'sane' – no one left Hiawatha Insane Asylum alive. Its history illustrates how psychiatric models and their labels bound the hands and feet and silenced the protests of these ancestors. Native Americans should be wary, then, of any alleged 'science' that might attempt to repeat the past, especially in relation to the trust they hold on behalf of their sacred children.

## Eugenics, mental hygiene, and oppression in American Indian education

Mental hygiene, which we now call 'mental health,' evolved partly out of the pseudoscience of eugenics, a race purification movement founded by British scientist Sir Francis Galton, a cousin of Charles Darwin, who felt that '[t]he nature of American Indians appears to contain the minimum affectionate and social qualities compatible with the continuance of their race' (1865: 14). Efforts were made to establish American Indian inferiority scientifically and to 'rescue' Indian children from their allegedly brutish existence by forced removal and adoption into white homes throughout the first half of the twentieth century (Emmerich 1998). Organized attacks on Indian motherhood were so effective that between one quarter and one half of all American Indian children lived in institutions, foster care, or adoptions through the 1940s. Promotion of sterilization, including the coercion of mothers by health care providers, continued through the 1970s at the Indian Health Service (IHS) (Torpy 2000) and may continue to occur subtly in some provider interactions today.

Establishing American Indian inferiority hinged upon the use of psychological measurement. Eugenics research institutions at Cold Spring Harbor, Maine brought 'Karl Pearson's biometrical studies to the attention of American geneticists' (Selden 1999: 5) and his statistical genius in mapping the Gaussian or bell-shaped curve inspired early American psychologists to seek an active role in 'race science' (Gelb *et al.* 1986). Early psychologists were drawn to validate the 'feebleminded' label applied to Indian children. Demonstrating their presumed inferiority, especially of those who remained steadfastly unassimilated, i.e. 'full bloods,' helped establish the merits of psychology before scientific academia of the time. Twenty of the 25 studies of psychological tests and measures of American Indians reviewed by Texas psychologist Thomas Garth (1931) for his book, *Race Psychology*, supported such claims.

One of Garth's own studies (1919) sought to support the cultural evolutionist claim of Indians' 'primitive' status, by measuring their 'continuous mental performance' on an attention task as being superior to that of 'whites' and 'Negroes.' This same task appears to have been a forerunner to the popular Continuous Performance Task (CPT) utilized by so many modern day American educational and clinical psychologists for ADHD diagnosis. The modern version of the CPT, mentioned first in 1956 by Rosvold and colleagues, has become 'one of the most widely studied laboratory measures of vigilance or attention span with the ADHD population,' according to leading ADHD proponent, Dr Russell Barkley (1990). This CPT 'ancestor' supported a positive stereotype of superior reaction time, while the modern CPT supports the negative stereotype of the 'ADHD American Indian child.'

Psychology's sister field of psychiatry made its own eugenics claims as to the dominance of biology and racial inheritance in human behavior at the turn of the twentieth century. At the Third International Congress of Eugenics, held in

New York in 1932, Nazi psychiatrist Ernst Rudin chaired the Committee on Race Psychiatry. Paul Popenoe, a board member of the American Eugenics Society, praised Hitler for placing 'his hopes of biological regeneration solidly on the application of biological principles of human society' (in Kuhl 1994: 36). At the close of World War II, however, Rudin's import of American social policies was linked to rationalizing the savagery of German psychiatry during the Holocaust and eugenics fell out of favor. Pre-War eugenics philosophies were not so much erased as recast into a softer rhetoric of benevolence:

> It is accepted that mentally deficient children need special attention in the educational process, and special classes are set up for them. These special classes are adjusted according to the grade of deficiency, but the general trend is to lessen the amount of academic work the child is called upon to do and increase the manual part of learning, further increasing this trend as the child becomes older until he is learning the rudiments of some trade or skill in which he can work after the school years.
>
> (Oberholzer 1949: 330)

Thus, lowered expectations, classification, and segregation of allegedly 'racially inferior' children survived World War II. American Indian children remain the most underrepresented ethnic group at US colleges and universities (Stein 1999). Currently, intelligence tests may or may not be used by educational and clinical psychologists making ADHD diagnoses for 'special education status' in public or Bureau of Indian Affairs-administered schools but such testing is required in order to carry over the 'accommodations' related to such status to sitting for pre-entry examinations like the Scholastic Achievement Test or for college entry itself:

> . . . tests that are selected by the evaluator should be technically accurate, reliable, valid, and standardized on the appropriate norm group.
>
> (Educational Testing Service 1999)

Although 'there have been more than 600 published research papers, conceptual papers, and agency reports that have tried to assess the utilization and relevance of ability testing with Native Americans and Alaska natives,' reliable and valid tests do not yet exist. Currently available tests 'themselves grew from and are heavily embedded in the dominant culture' and 'are geared toward a population that has had different experiences than those of Native American children' (Nicolosi and Stavrou 2000: 3). The paucity of normative research notwithstanding, the continued use of misrepresentative and flawed psychological and educational testing on behalf of ADHD 'special education status' promotes a conclusion to outsiders, including colleges and universities, that ADHD *exists* conceptually in Native American communities for which it is culturally invalid.

The validity of the ADHD label for American Indian children, like that of 'feebleminded,' is supported by the pseudo-objectivity of psychological tests and highly subjective 'behavior scales' (Conners 2004), leading to the continued segregation of Indian children, lowering expectations regarding their academic potential, deepening a self-concept of inferiority, and encouraging parents and caretakers to put them on stimulant drugs.

## Diagnosing intergenerational trauma, grief and oppression as ADHD

American Indian children have been labeled 'deviant' in some manner by EuroAmerican culture for hundreds of years. From their inception in 1875, boarding schools sought to move these children from their 'primitiveness' into modern EuroAmerican civilization by depicting their culture as immoral and corrupt, and their own selves as ignorant and incompetent.

The severe approach of 'kill the Indian but save the man' at the Carlisle Indian School in Pennsylvania was invented by Captain Henry Pratt, a former warden of the military prison at Fort Marion, Florida. Arapaho, Cheyenne, Kiowa, and Apache prisoners of war were subjected to his ideas while a warden, the 'effectiveness' of which caught the attention of early Indian educators and missionaries (Noriega 1992; Child 1998). Pratt's method soon dominated thousands of kidnapped, coerced, or even voluntarily enrolled students in similar schools throughout the US. By 1902, 25 federally operated schools existed, including Fort Simcoe Boarding School near White Swan in the Yakama Nation and Chemawa in western Oregon. By 1943, there were 18 non-reservation boarding schools, 31 reservation boarding schools, and 216 day schools 'educating' 35,000 Indian children and youth (Noriega 1992). Pratt's philosophies also permeated public day schools (Noriega 1992; Churchill 1997) at the reservation train junctions at Wapato and Toppenish, Washington (Heuterman 1995). From 1890 to 1940, 50 to 70 percent of each successive generation of American Indian children was subjected to boarding school (Thompson 1978; US Surgeon General 2001).

Often forcibly removed to settings far from their own families and homes, the sacred hair of newly enrolled children was quickly sheared. Children were dressed in burlap smocks or uniforms that they often had to make themselves. They might be beaten severely for speaking their own language and were compelled to pray to a Christian God. Their days of adventuring, exploration, and gentle hands-on learning from an elder back home were suddenly and shockingly converted into a rigid sunup to sundown routine of military drilling and training for manual labor or domestic servitude. At Chemawa, for example, drilling in uniforms and high-top boots began at dawn. Not a few children spent summers on 'outings,' serving as free labor to local farmers and storeowners, perhaps not visiting their relations for any sizeable period of time for the whole of their childhood (Noriega 1992). Many children became despondent and physically ill. American Indian boarding schools are unusual academic institutions in having their own dedicated cemeteries.

These children were at continual risk of physical and sexual abuse from those charged with their care (Brookings Institution 1971). Workers could, if they chose, violate them with relative impunity (National Resource Center on Child Sexual Abuse 1990). From the time of war and invasion that established Fort Simcoe in 1855 – a time during which, according to Relander (1956), young women were forced to perform sexual favors for US soldiers while their men looked on, held at gunpoint – the potential rape of Yakama girls was a chronic danger. Up through the 1950s and 1960s, elders continued to warn Yakama girls not to walk the main roads of their own reservation alone for fear of possible attack (Wilkins 2004, personal communication).

The unique boarding school experience of each bereft and institutionally reared Native American child brought the trauma of a cumulative social catastrophe to subsequent generations, infiltrating communities with corrupted family patterns that continue to the present. Bonds were broken as were hearts, languages lost, positive traditional Indian parenting and family behaviors damaged or destroyed. Oppression from the outside gradually came to be reenacted by community members upon one another. Domestic violence, physical and sexual abuse, hopelessness, and powerlessness emerged alongside their medicaments and facilitators – the alcohol and drugs that proliferate across numerous communities today – to maim the very identity of Native Americans.

While boarding schools exacted their heavy toll, several states enacted laws that allowed school administrators to exclude minority children, negating Indians from enrollment in public education. The public school typecast for American Indians equated them with disease and dirt. For example, the California Political Code Section 662 of 1924 stated: 'The governing body of school districts shall have the power to exclude children of filthy and vicious habits, or children suffering from contagious or infectious diseases, and also to establish separate schools for Indian children, and for children of Chinese, Japanese, or Mongolian parentage' (quoted in Huff 1997: 5).

It would be a grave mistake, however, to focus only upon the damage of current and past indignity. Yakama Nation's cultural survival against continual assaults upon its way of life was achieved by community efforts at resistance. Surviving beliefs, spiritual practices, language forms, subsistence styles, art, and practical methods of living have been preserved among the Yakama against nearly insurmountable odds. A Yakama elder (Wilkins 2004, personal communication) tells of asking her caretaker grandmother why she had been raised separately from her siblings, who grew up with her mother and father. Her grandmother told her that years before her birth the elders had come together, concerned about the impositions and actions of outsiders in attempting to destroy their culture. They agreed to each choose a grandchild to raise themselves 'in the old ways.' Among many other teachings, she was taught to speak the Wenatshapum dialect of the Yakama language fluently by her grandmother and did not know English when she was enrolled in public school at White Swan at about 6 years old in the 1940s. She recalled the pain of being ridiculed by the white teacher before her peers at the time as 'ignorant and backwards.' Today, she remains one of a group of dwindling but highly valued fluent speakers and teachers at Yakama Nation, fully legitimizing the efforts of her ancestors.

## Culturally preferred learning styles diagnosed as ADHD

The ADHD label recasts active, exploratory, hands-on Yakama child learners as brain-diseased and genetically inferior. Observing interactions between caretakers and children at Yakama Nation, one is struck by how often learning occurs through modeling and activity rather than words alone. A child raised in Yakama tradition appears to be expected not to interrupt or question what has been said, while interactive questioning and commentary by students is one of the most supported of EuroAmerican didactic styles. If the traditional Yakama child fails to follow a verbal instruction, he or she would expect to be shown the right way to undertake a task or verbally corrected rather than expected to have to ask questions beforehand. Charles and Costantino (2000) remark:

> Research in the area of cultural difference theory suggests that many American Indian students in the public schools experience a discontinuity between learning styles they come to school with and the learning styles that are supported and rewarded in typical US classrooms.
>
> (Charles and Costantino 2000: 4)

For American Indian students, such is only the beginning of the culture conflict in moving between two separate worlds. Some students, particularly on a reservation, have been observed to develop an *oppositional identity* in which learning the standard language and behavior practices of the public school is seen as a threat to one's own cultural identity. To be called an 'apple' means one is 'red on the outside and white on the inside.' To be academically successful may be desirable but to behave as a 'non-Indian' to achieve such success may be completely undesirable. For example, a depressed young man reported felt pleased after achieving a 99 percent score on a trigonometry examination. When visiting relatives asked him how he was doing academically, he sheepishly reported his strong scores. An uncle abruptly observed, 'Huh, I'll bet you think you're better than the rest of us now.' His grades and school motivation then dropped substantially.

The *oppositional identity* phenomenon is a powerful counter-explanation to any so-called etiology of ADHD for American Indian children – their overt resistance to the imposition of teaching approaches and learning styles felt as culturally undesirable or foreign may result in and of itself in their being diagnosed as ADHD and sent to a special education classroom. Once again, these children are left to internalize a stereotype of their own inferiority – and the continuous onslaught of such experiences develops increasing alienation, doubt, and self-hatred – a process Freire (1998) described as the 'internalization' of oppression.

Caught between overt oppression and forced assimilation seen in boarding and public schools and the mental hygiene eugenics movement disguised in the garb of benevolence, American Indian children could never hope to succeed. Their own learning style like their beautiful culture and its values has seldom been appreciated or integrated into the classroom curriculum. With trauma and dysfunction as an added burden for some children, no wonder their 'attention' might wander.

## Fetal alcohol syndrome: tragic reality and new stereotype

Pre- and post-natal alcohol and drug exposure has also taken its toll upon children in American Indian communities. Over the last 20 years, clinical neuropsychologists have made progress toward understanding the lifelong effects of such exposure (Streissguth *et al.* 1999). They have also invented the diagnostic terms of 'Fetal Alcohol Syndrome' (FAS), 'Fetal Alcohol Effected' (FAE) and, more recently, 'Fetal Alcohol Spectrum Disorder' (FASD). FASD is a complex neurodevelopmental disorder that involves a multidisciplinary assessment of growth, central nervous system dysfunction, and craniofacial abnormalities (Moore and Green 2004). Diagnosis of the less severe 'FAE end' of the fetal alcohol 'spectrum' often depends upon neuropsychological testing, including the same kinds of ability tests with intercultural validity problems that are used to diagnose ADHD.

For example, Streissguth and colleagues (2004) examined the potential contribution of fetal alcohol exposure to adverse psychosocial experiences, claiming that the 'lifetime prevalence of adverse life outcomes . . . documents more specifically the poor prognosis that has been suggested in previous studies [of FAS]' (2004: 234). They state that 'psychological testing . . . [reveals] the mean Arithmetic standard scores are 2/3 of a standard deviation below mean IQ scores' which 'suggests a functional deficit in problem solving' (ibid.: 235). The procedure in this University of Washington study, where 104, or 25 percent of, FAS or FAE diagnosed subjects from across the Pacific Northwest were described as Native American, relied heavily on the Wechsler series tests. Yet these tests are 'not generally recommended' (ibid.: 5) in professional practice guidelines published by the Washington State Association of School Psychologists (2000) due to cultural biases. Furthermore, discussion of the various psychosocial problems identified – 'inappropriate sexual behavior,' 'disrupted school experience,' 'trouble with the law,' 'confinements,' and 'drug and alcohol problems' – failed to mention the context of either socio-historical or contemporary oppression of Native Americans. Instead, the history of intergenerational trauma and grief remains invisible and irrelevant, biased IQ findings and the psychosocial problems of fetal alcohol exposed Native American children are melded together, and their situation is attributed to deviant, unfit Indian mothers in a manner reminiscent of the eugenics movement.

The reported prevalence of FAS among American Indians ranges from 1.3 to 10.3 per 1,000 (May 1991) compared to 1 to 5 per 1,000 in the general US population (Harwood *et al.* 1985). These prevalence rates show considerable overlap between populations, while the statistics on alcohol addiction across Indian communities vary widely. For example, 60 percent of Navajos report abstaining from alcohol entirely, while 80 percent of Utes and Ojibwes report using alcohol (May 1991). Taylor (2000) has demonstrated that, when findings are combined across Native American communities, the proportion of those who consume alcohol to those who do not in both Indian and non-Indian communities is about equal.

Without disputing the consensus that fetal alcohol exposure is an important challenge for some Native American communities, to what extent are the current prevalence rates for FASD affected by the artifact of flawed methodology and inappropriate psychological tests? Lack of critical analysis allows LaDue *et al.* (1999) to specify a bridge between FAS and ADHD:

> Associated with this primary condition [FAS], there may be comorbidity or co-occurring health conditions, as well as secondary conditions. For example, attention deficit hyperactivity disorder (ADHD) is often associated with FAS. It is a distinct disability that may co-occur with FAS but is not necessarily caused by FAS.
>
> (LaDue *et al.* 1999: 8)

Describing the behavioral problems resulting from FAS as being 'often associated' with ADHD hampers closer scrutiny of the latter category's cultural validity when applied to Native Americans, while lending credibility to the dubious brain science of ADHD (Galves and Walker 2003; Leo and Cohen 2003). Instead, a more accurate understanding of the behavioral effects of brain injury resulting from alcohol exposure would seem to entirely refute ADHD's explanatory value and, instead, call into question the labeling of toxin-exposed Native children with ADHD.

Flawed Native American FASD diagnosis and its alleged links to the pseudo-neurology of ADHD survive intact in current research, supporting a new stereotype tied to that of the 'drunken Indian,' the 'firewater myth,' and the flawed genetic 'science' of American Indian alcohol addiction (McTighe 1996). Some local Yakama observers have even been overheard to remark: 'We're all FAS or FAE.' The most pessimistic interpretation of FASD prevalence rates would suggest such an idea to be false for 99 percent of the American Indian population. Unfortunately, this new stereotype, predicated upon the same misuse of psychological tests, may be even more damaging to communities than fetal alcohol exposure itself.

The brain injury of children from substance exposure is a criminal act in the law and order code at Yakama Nation. Beyond individual culpability, however, the crime has its roots in the aggressive introduction of alcohol by EuroAmericans to Yakama people, despite their repeated protests for 150 years that such trade on their reservation is a violation of Article 9 of the Treaty of 1855. To date, there is no particular penalty for the misapplication of psychological tests or psychiatric labels in a manner that deleteriously affects the future of a people.

## Psychiatric eugenics embedded in the contemporary language of ADHD

Within the most recent US National Institute of Mental Health web-brochure (NIMH 2004), it is contended that 'there is little compelling evidence at this time that ADHD can arise purely from social factors or child-rearing methods. Most substantiated causes appear to fall within the realm of neurobiology and genetics.' These statements exhibit masterful double-speak. Humans are born with con- stitutional and temperamental differences that affect activity level and tolerance for stimulation and no credible observer would contend that behavior could be based 'purely' on social factors. But numerous studies in developmental and clinical psychology and anthropology have just as clearly refuted the notion that social factors are unimportant in the development of the kinds of child (and now adult) behaviors that have come to be called ADHD (Galves and Walker 2003).

It is also interesting that this statement contends that causes of ADHD can be 'substantiated' while at the same time be 'apparent.' Deceptive language has a painful relevance to the community history of many Native Americans, who have valiantly sustained at least 566 separate federally recognized cultures and often do not share a 'biopsychiatric' view of self. For one thing, the ADHD label and its conceptual basis are highly foreign to the general cultural psychology of American Indians (Duran and Duran 1995). Contemporary Western psychiatric diagnosis seems intent on mimicking the fashionable 'evidence-based' approach in US public health while obscuring its roots in eugenics pseudoscience and jargon. Fortunately, concerted efforts by ADHD proponents to develop international consensus about diagnosis have been met with critical opposition, particularly in relation to cultural variations in systems of meaning:

> Not only is it completely counter to the spirit and practice of science to cease questioning the validity of ADHD as proposed by the consensus statement [i.e. Barkley *et al.* 2002], there is an ethical and moral responsibility to do so. History teaches us again and again that one generation's most cherished therapeutic ideas and practices, especially when applied to the powerless, are repudiated in the next but not without leaving countless victims in their wake.
>
> (Timimi *et al.* 2004: 59)

In the NIMH web-brochure, a brief history of ADHD is offered that depicts the detection of the disorder as harking back to the early 1800s. Actually, the contem- porary definition for ADHD was established and evolved very recently – during the 1980s – alongside many other new psychiatric labels developed with the same level of scientific sophistication 'as you and I might choose a restaurant,' according to one DSM-III-R Task Force member (Caplan 1995). For this reason, psychiatric diagnostic labels like ADHD are and should continue to be questioned and debated.

NIMH neurobiological and genetic explanations for ADHD have an important cultural and historical meaning for American Indians. The NIMH web-brochure writers try to fortify their deceptive spin on the history of ADHD by rolling back across the generations to 1902 when 'Sir George F. Still published a series of lectures to the Royal College of Physicians in England in which he described a group of impulsive children with significant behavioral problems, caused by genetic dysfunction and not by poor child rearing – children who today would be easily recognized as having ADHD.' The same Sir George Still also claimed 'there is a link between "morbid defect of moral control" in children and diseases such as brain tumor, epilepsy, and meningitis' (Meinsma 1998). Still was speaking to the mainstream of his day – the international eugenics movement.

There is no directly analogous word for 'mental' in the *Yakama Nation Practical Dictionary* (Beavert 1985) and, despite numerous attempts, a Yakama elder could not be located who knows of an equivalent word for 'insane' or 'mentally ill.' Elder and language expert Levina Wilkins (2004) indicated that such concepts do not exist in the Yakama language. There is a word for 'crazy,' *at'ilpi*, but this appears to mean 'a funny or amusing manner' or 'reckless behavior' as opposed to the 'disturbed or disturbing' connotation of the word in English.

There is also a word for 'retarded,' *ayay'yesh*. It is used to describe stupid ideas.

## Contemporary indoctrination of the ADHD concept

As has been mentioned, the current language of ADHD is stored in the lexicon of 'mental illness,' the *Diagnostic and Statistical Manual of Mental Disorders-IV (DSM)*, a living document, revised every few years and published by the American Psychiatric Association (2000). Using the neurology and biology metaphor, the NIMH dismisses other causes and, by default, seeks to fund and substantiate a claim that seems rooted in eugenics – that the ADHD descriptor within the DSM applies as well to American Indian children and is not better explained by a US cultural legacy of oppression, genocide, and destruction, nor in the failures of US public education to respond to their variant cultural learning styles (Charles and Costantino 2000).

It is convenient to see ADHD as a *brain disease* without acknowledging the impact of mental health eugenics on American Indian children. American Indian children can then be viewed as eligible for stimulant medication 'treatment' dispensed at Indian Health Service clinics. At the Yakama Nation in 2005, prescribed stimulant medication has a street value of $10 for 4 tablets. Its abundant availability is the result of a 75 percent probability that, on his or her first visit to the Yakama Indian Health Clinic for behavioral problems, a child will be diagnosed ADHD and prescribed stimulants.[4]

Spero Manson, editor of *American Indian and Alaska Native Mental Health Quarterly (AIANMHQ)*, and his students have undertaken a great deal of psychiatric-based research in over 40 Indian Country communities through the American Indian and Alaska Native Programs at Colorado Health Sciences University, including a 15-year research portfolio in excess of $42 million that draws upon government, private, and tribal sources (AIANP 2002). The primary funding source for this collaboration is the NIMH.

The earliest mention of ADHD in online editions of *AIANMHQ* appears in a description of an Ojibwe family with a child having a 'history of Attention Deficit Hyperactivity Disorder (ADHD) like behavior . . .' (Mohatt and Varvin 1998: 90). The authors offer no critical assessment of their own statement. By 2004, however, researchers had derived data calling the ADHD concept into question in Indian Country. Simmons *et al.* (2004) noted that a primary finding in their multi-community survey of serious emotional disturbances (SED):

> was the sentiment that the available definitions of SED did not incorporate traditional American Indian and Alaska Native perspectives. For example, the existing SED definitions are deficit- rather than strength-based, fail to emphasize the important family and community contexts of emotional and behavioral difficulties, and fail to note that some of these difficulties may be part of an individual's and family's life path.
>
> (Simmons *et al.* 2004: 61)

These recent observations are nonetheless absent from comments on many psychiatric labels operationalized for research in *AIANMHQ*. Researchers in Indian Country continue to neglect critical analysis of the history of American mental health eugenics and the 'pathologizing' of Native American culture and reactions to cultural oppression.

Practitioners in so-called transcultural psychiatry have critiqued one of their own assumptions – that psychiatric 'illness' exists universally (Kleinman and Good 1985). This is because psychiatry is a culturally based system of understanding human beings predicated on predominantly EuroAmerican values and beliefs. Still, European and American psychiatrists do not always agree on the exact meanings of their own terminology.

Manson *et al.*'s (1985) paper, 'The Depressive Experience in American Indian Communities: A Challenge for Psychiatric Theory and Diagnosis,' from the edited book, *Culture and Depression: Studies in the Anthropology and Cross-Cultural Psychiatry of Affect and Disorder* (Kleinman and Good 1985), reveals what happens when psychiatric categories are translated indiscriminately. Despite the book's promising title and a seemingly solid method of Hopi lexical analysis with regard to the concept of 'depression,' Manson *et al.* characterize Hopi depression as a problem within the individual rather than as individual and group human behaviors occurring as resistance to cultural oppression. The behavioral descriptors utilized for a Hopi-attuned concept of 'depression' were completely devoid of the Hopi research subject's learning and experience in relation to historical family disruption by federal authorities via forced boarding school attendance, land theft and relocation, or other forms of cultural subversion, oppression, racism, as well as the class position of impoverishment, and the like. In this and similar research designs, such intergenerational family experiences are again made invisible. The researchers undertook this study under grant 1-RO1-MH33280 from the NIMH. When publications from ADHD research in Indian Country do appear, they should be reviewed carefully for similar biases.

EuroAmerican psychiatric nomenclature like the DSM serves the values of EuroAmerican culture, particularly in relation to emotional behavior. Anthropologist Catherine Lutz (1985) indicates that EuroAmerican culture has a highly *individualistic* approach to emotion:

> The 'essence' of both thought and emotion is to be found within the boundaries of the person; they are features of individuals rather than of situations, relationships, or moral positions. Thus, they are construed as psychological phenomena. Although social, historical, and interpersonal processes are seen as *correlated* with these psychic events, thought and emotion are taken to be the property of individuals, that is, they are located in individual minds.
>
> (Lutz 1985: 77)

Lilith Finkler (1993) has also noted:

> Psychiatrists, typically content to focus on the individual, rarely acknowledge the impact of residential schools, the systematic removal of Native children from their families and their placement into white adoptive homes. Broken treaties, the mass sterilization of Native women, the outlawing of spiritual practices all remain invisible in the medical understanding of human behavior.
>
> (Quoted in Caplan 1995: 280)

DSM concepts like ADHD are akin to a 'restricted code' (Bernstein 1971), a term which refers to a sub-language accessible only to members of a certain class. Restricted codes can be utilized to form exclusionary boundaries and dominance over other classes. This sub-language excludes the typical Native American patient or client, as well as members of the dominant EuroAmerican culture, and even practitioners themselves who are not always certain what is meant exactly by DSM terminology. In this sense, the language of the ADHD label represents colonialism – an attempt to colonize the mind of Yakama people with concepts about themselves and their children quite foreign to their culture.

A word from this restricted code, this 'borrowed language' of English, has entered the Yakama Nation community. The word 'ADHD' describes children who won't settle in the *'pushtin* [white man] classroom,' who have classroom behaviors that result in phone calls to overwhelmed caretakers and grandmothers, who are chronically agitated, perhaps due to exposure to sexual and physical violence that has been passed down through generations in their families, or who may be neglected or exposed to toxins due to the infection of substance abuse introduced from outside their community. Among them are also many children with no such problems at all – raised in the unique and beautiful remnant traditions of the Yakama Nation community and in distinct learning situations that reflect the strength of cultural survival and resistance. Of course, their learning styles are a poor fit with schools they are compelled to fit into.

Many of these children are starting to call themselves 'ADHD.'

## Notes

1   The 14 Confederated Tribes and Bands of the Yakama Nation include the Yakama, Palouse, Pisquose, Wenatshapam, Kliquet, Kow-was-say-yee, Liaywas, Skinpah, Wishram, Shyiks, Ochechotes, Ka-milt-pah, Satus, Seacap, and the Klickitat. Note that there are actually 15 listed here – some elders contend that there are other unaccounted bands within this confederation.

2   There are over 550 separate and distinct federally recognized American Indian and Alaska Native communities in the US and likely 100 tribal communities and entities deprived of 'recognition' status. Terms such as 'American Indian,' 'Indian,' 'Native,' and 'Native American' are used interchangeably in this chapter and denote a shared *political* rather than specific cultural identity.

3   The tribal affiliations of these patients were Cherokee, Comanche, Osage, Pawnee, Mission Indian of California, Winnebago, Shoshone, Chippewa, and Sioux.

4   From 2000 to 2004, the author served as the only clinical psychologist associated with the Yakama Indian Health Service. During that time, he undertook several personal analyses of diagnostic patterns for ADHD within the clinic and interviewed numerous Native American youth clients and client families with regard to their experiences. The statements are based upon his own analyses undertaken in 2002 and are not intended to represent the official position of the Indian Health Service or the United States government.

## Bibliography

Adams, D. (1995) *Education for Extinction: American Indians and the boarding school experience.* Lawrence, KS: University Press of Kansas.

AIANP (2002) 'Spero Manson, Ph.D., biography.' Division of American Indian and Alaska Native Programs, University of Colorado Health Sciences Center. Online. Available HTTP: <www.uchsc.edu/sm/psych/dept/faculty/manson_s.htm> (accessed 4 March 2005).

American Psychiatric Association (2000) *Diagnostic and Statistical Manual of Mental Disorders, Text Revision, DSM-IV-TR.* Washington, DC: Author.

Barkley, R. (1990) *Attention Deficit Hyperactivity Disorder: A handbook for diagnosis and treatment.* New York: Guilford Press.

Barkley, R. *et al.* (2002) 'International Consensus Statement on ADHD.' *Clinical Child and Family Psychology Review,* 5: 89–111.

Beavert, V. (1985) *Yakama Language Practical Dictionary.* Self-published. Available from the Yakama Nation Tribal Library, Toppenish, Washington, USA.

Bernstein, B. (1971) *Class, Codes and Control, Volume 1.* London: Routledge and Kegan Paul.

Brookings Institution (1971) *The Problem of Indian Administration.* Institute for Government Research. New York: Johnson Reprint.

Caplan, P. (1995) *They Say You're Crazy: How the world's most powerful psychiatrists decide who's normal.* Philadelphia, PA: Perseus Books.

Charles, J. and Costantino, M. (2000) 'Reading and the Native American learner: Research report.' Olympia, Washington: Office of Superintendent of Public Instruction. Online.

Available HTTP: <www.evergreen.edu/ecei/projects/home.htm> (accessed 2 April 2005).

Child, B. (1998) *Boarding School Seasons: American Indian families, 1900–1940*. Lincoln, NE: University of Nebraska Press.

Churchill, W. (1997) *A Little Matter of Genocide*. San Francisco, CA: City Lights Books.

Conners, C. K. (2004) 'Validation of ADHD rating scales.' *Journal of the American Academy of Child and Adolescent Psychiatry*, 43(10): 1190–1191.

Duran, E. and Duran, B. (1995) *Native American Postcolonial Psychology*. Syracuse, NY: State University of New York Press.

Educational Testing Service. Office of Disability Policy (June, 1999) *Policy Statement for Documentation of ADHD in Adolescents and Adults*. Princeton, NJ: Author.

Emmerich, L. (1998) 'Genocide or family planning? Indian Health Service policy in the 1960s and 1970s.' *Inside*, 28(6). Online. Available HTTP: <www.csuchico.edu/pub/inside/archive/98_10_22/genocide.html> (accessed 4 March 2005).

Freire, P. (1998) *Pedagogy of the Oppressed*. New York: Continuum Publishing Company.

Galton, F. (1865) 'Hereditary talent and character.' *Macmillan's Magazine*, 12: 318–327.

Galves, A. and Walker, D. (2003, September) 'Debunking the science behind ADHD as a "brain disorder," Coalition report, 3–9. Online. Available HTTP: <www.thenationalcoalition.org/CoalitionReport7-03.pdf> (accessed 4 March 2005).

Garth, T. (1919) 'Racial differences in mental fatigue.' *Journal of Applied Psychology*, 4: 235–244.

Garth, T. (1931) *Race Psychology: A study of racial mental differences*. New York: McGraw-Hill.

Gelb, S., Allen, G., Futterman, A. and Mehler, B. (1986) 'Rewriting mental testing history: The view from American Psychologist.' *Sage Race Relations Abstracts*, 11(2): 18–31.

Guthrie, R. (1976) *Even the Rats were White*. New York: Harper and Row.

Harwood, H., Napolitano, D., Kristiansen, P. and Collins, J. (1984) *Economic Costs to Society of Alcohol and Drug Abuse and Mental Illness: 1980*. Research Triangle Park, NC: Research Triangle Institute.

Harwood, H. *et al.* (1985) 'Fetal alcohol syndrome.' *Alcohol Topics in Brief*, National Institute on Alcohol Abuse and Alcoholism (NIAAA), April 1985.

Heuterman, T. (1995) *The Burning Horse: The Japanese–American experience in the Yakima Valley*. Cheney, WA: Eastern Washington University Press.

Huff, D. (1997) *To Live Heroically: Institutional racism and American Indian education*. Syracuse, NY: State University of New York Press.

Hunter, W. and Sommermeir, E. (1922) 'The relation of degree of Indian blood to score on the Otis Intelligence test.' *Journal of Contemporary Psychology*, 2: 257–277.

Hurd, H., Drewry, W., Dewey, R., Pilgrim, C., Blumer, G. A. and Burgess, T. J. W. (1916) *The Institutional Care of the Insane in the United States and Canada*. Baltimore, MD: Johns Hopkins Press.

Kleinman, K. and Good, B. (eds.) (1985) *Culture and Depression: Studies in the anthropology and cross-cultural psychiatry of affect and disorder*. Berkeley, CA: University of California Press.

Kuhl, S. (1994) *The Nazi Connection: Eugenics, American racism, and German National Socialism*. New York: Oxford University Press.

LaDue, R., Schact, R., Tanner-Halverson, P. and McGowan, M. (1999) *Fetal Alcohol Syndrome: A training manual to aid in vocational rehaiblitation and other non-medical services*. Report of the Institute for Human Development, Northern Arizona University, University Affiliated Program, American Indian Rehabilitation and Training Center, P.O. Box 5630, Flagstaff, AZ.

Leo, J. and Cohen, D. (2003) 'Broken brains or flawed studies: A critical review of ADHD neuroimaging research.' *Journal of Mind and Behavior*, 24(1): 29–56.

Levine, B. (2001) *Commonsense Rebellion: Debunking psychiatry, confronting society.* New York: Continuum.

Lincoln County History Committee (1985) *The History of Lincoln County, South Dakota.* Freeman, SD: Pine Hill Press.

Lutz, C. (1985) 'Depression and translation of emotional worlds.' In Kleinman, K. and Good, B. (eds.) *Culture and Depression: Studies in the anthropology and cross-cultural psychiatry of affect and disorder.* Berkeley, CA: University of California Press: 63–100.

May, P. A. (1991) 'Fetal alcohol effects among North American Indians: Evidence and implications for society.' *Alcohol Health and Research World*, 15(3): 239–248.

May, P. (1994) 'The epidemiology of alcohol abuse among American Indians: The mythical and real properties.' *American Indian Culture and Research Journal*, 18: 121–143.

May, P., Hymbaugh, K., Aase, J. and Samet, J. (1983) 'Epidemiology of fetal alcohol syndrome among American Indians of the Southwest.' *Social Biology*, 30: 374–387.

McTighe, S. (1996) 'Debunking the firewater myth.' *Minority Science Report*, 2(1): 1–4.

Meinsma, R. (1998) 'A brief history of mental health therapy.' Online. Available HTTP: <http://home.earthlink.net/~openedbook/History.mental.therapy.html> (accessed 4 March 2005).

Mohatt, G. and Varvin, S. (1998) 'Looking for 'a good doctor': A cultural formulation of the treatment of a First Nations woman using Western and First Nations method.' *American Indian and Alaska Native Mental Health Journal*, 8(2): 83–103.

Moore, T. and Green, M. (2004) 'Fetal alcohol spectrum disorder (FASD): A need for closer examination by the criminal justice system.' *Criminal Reports*, 19(1): 99–108.

National Institute of Mental Health (2004) 'Attention deficit hyperactivity disorder.' Online. Available HTTP: <www.nimh.nih.gov/publicat/adhd.cfm> (accessed 4 March 2005).

National Resource Center on Child Sexual Abuse (1990) *Enhancing Child Sexual Abuse Services to Minority Cultures.* Huntsville, AL: Author.

Nicolosi, E. and Stavrou, E. (2000) 'IQ tests and their fairness for Native American students.' *School Psychologist*, 54: 58–79. Online. Available HTTP:<www.indiana.edu/~div16/iq_tests_and_their_fairness.htm> (accessed 4 March 2005).

Noriega, J. (1992) 'American Indian education in the United States: Indoctrination for subordination to colonialism.' In Jaimes, M. A. (ed.) *The State of Native America: Genocide, colonization and resistance.* Boston, MA: South End Press: 371–402.

Oberholzer, E. (1949) *Psychology: A text-book of mental science*, trans. Lemkau, P. and Kronenberg, B. Pittsburgh, PA: University of Pittsburgh Press.

Relander, C. (1956) *Drummers and Dreamers.* Caldwell, ID: Caxton Printers.

Rosvold, H., Mirsky, A., Sarason, I., Bransome, E. and Beck, L. (1956) 'A continuous performance test of brain injury.' *Journal of Consulting Psychology*, 20: 343–350.

Saxman, M. (1999) 'The Canton Asylum for Insane Indians.' *Cultural Resource Management*, 9: 40–43.

Selden, S. (1999) *Inheriting Shame: The story of eugenics and racism in America.* New York: Teachers College Press.

Simmons, T., Novins, D. and Allen, J. (2004) 'Words have power: (Re)-defining serious emotional disturbance for American Indian and Alaska Native children and their families.' *American Indian and Alaska Native Mental Health Journal*, 11(2): 59–64.

Stein, W. J. (1999) *Tribal Colleges: 1968–1998.* Charleston, WV: ERIC Clearinghouse on Rural and Small Schools (ED 427 913).

Stoskepf, A. (1999) 'The forgotten history of eugenics,' *Rethinking Schools,* 13(3). Online. Available HTTP:<www.rethinkingschools.org/archive/13_03/eugenic.shtml> (accessed 4 March 2005).

Streissguth, A., Barr, H., Bookstein, P., Sampson, P. and Carmichael-Olsen, H. (1999) 'The long-term neurocognitive consequences of prenatal alcohol exposure: A 14-year study.' *Psychological Science,* 10(3): 186–190.

Streissguth, A., Bookstein, P., Barr, H., Sampson, P., O'Malley, K. and Young, J. (2004) 'Risk factors for adverse life outcomes in fetal alcohol syndrome and fetal alcohol effects.' *Journal of Developmental and Behavioral Pediatrics,* 25(4): 228–238.

Taylor, M. (2000) 'The influence of self-efficacy on alcohol use among American Indians.' *Cultural Diversity and Ethnic Minority Psychology,* 6(2): 152–167.

Thompson, T. (ed.) (1978) *The Schooling of Native America.* Washington, DC: American Association of Colleges for Teacher Education.

Timimi, S. and 33 Coendorsers (2004) 'A critique of the International Consensus Statement on ADHD.' *Clinical Child and Family Psychology Review,* 7: 59–63.

Torpy, S. (2000) 'Native American women and coerced sterilization: On the Trail of Tears in the 1970s.' *American Indian Culture and Research Journal,* 24(2): 1–22.

United States Surgeon General (2001) 'Mental health care for American Indians and Alaska Natives.' In *Mental Health: Culture, race, and ethnicity.* Department of Health and Human Services: US Public Health Service. Internet edition.

Washington State Association of School Psychologists (2000) 'Professional practice standards guidelines in evaluation and identification of students from bilingual or culturally diverse backgrounds.' Online. Available HTTP: <www.wsasp.org/home.html> (accessed 4 March 2005).

Wilkins, L. (2004) Personal communication from an enrolled member, Yakama Nation elder and cultural specialist.

Yellow Bird, P. (2002) 'Wild Indians: Native perspectives on the Hiawatha Asylum for Insane Indians.' Online. Available HTTP: <www.mindfreedom.org/pdf/wildindians.pdf> (accessed 4 March 2005).

# Chapter 5

# A brief philosophical examination of ADHD

*Gordon Tait*

Concerns have been raised over ADHD from within a range of different disciplines, concerns which are not only voiced from within the hard sciences themselves, but also from within the social sciences. This chapter will add the discipline of philosophy to that number, arguing that an analysis of two traditionally philosophical topics – namely 'truth' and 'free will' – allows us a new and unsettling perspective on conduct disorders like ADHD. More specifically, it will be argued that ADHD not only fails to meet its own ontological and epistemological standards as an 'objective' pathology, but it also constitutes one more element in what has already become a significant undermining of a crucial component of social life: moral responsibility.

A pupil in Wisconsin was one of three who vandalised two elementary schools causing $40,000 worth of damage. His school sought to expel him, along with the two others who caused the damage. During the hearing into his actions, his mother raised the possibility that he might have ADHD, and soon acquired a private psychologist who concurred with this appraisal, even though the school district's psychologist disagreed. Once again, the matter ended up in court, with the student winning his case and avoiding expulsion as a 'disabled' student – unlike his two co-vandals who only escaped expulsion by withdrawing from the school. As the school district attorney pointed out, the admission of such *post hoc* diagnoses is both 'disturbing and mysterious', and adversely affects the schools' ability to discipline not only students with disabilities, but also those who may then choose to claim them (Zirkel 2001).

There is nothing particularly shocking or extreme about this case. Schools are vandalised every day, and children are diagnosed with ADHD every day – thousands of children. However, two issues emerge from this incident that are of interest to the philosopher. This first concerns the notion of truth. It seems apparent from this case that significant disagreement exists over precisely who might be considered to have ADHD, as there was certainly no agreement between the two psychologists involved here. Furthermore, it would not have been too difficult to produce yet another expert to argue that the entire dispute was moot, since there are no reasonable grounds for believing that ADHD exists at all.

The second issue concerns the notion of moral responsibility. At school, children learn to make appropriate, sanctioned decisions on the assumption that they will be held accountable for transgressions. Governance is thus ultimately founded upon self-governance, and in turn, self-governance itself is founded upon a number of crucial assumptions, the most significant of which is the belief that we all have the capacity to make free choices, and that we can be held accountable for those choices. The obvious conclusion to be drawn from the above incident is that a student who has been diagnosed with ADHD is not to be held as responsible for their actions as a student who has not been so diagnosed. The question here is how this issue impacts upon the traditional philosophical understanding of free will?

These two issues – truth and free will – will be addressed in turn. The intention here is to examine not only the ontological and epistemological status of the truth-claims made by proponents of ADHD, but also to address the possible consequences of adopting an understanding of the relationship between free will and moral responsibility that has some very significant implications for the way we educate our children.

## ADHD and truth

Attention Deficit Hyperactivity Disorder (ADHD), which is primarily a theory concerning the misbehaviour of children, has yet to reach the status of 'established truth', in spite of what its advocates may claim. Debates continue not only within the pages of learned journals, but also in the popular media, where various treatments and protocols of diagnosis are discussed alongside the arguments of those who refuse to recognise the disorder at all. Leaving aside those who think that the disorder may exist, but that it has been wildly over-diagnosed, as well as those who regard it as a fraud perpetrated by the drug companies, or those who think that ADHD advocates are just plain wrong, having erroneously extrapolated the data to produce an unsupportable outcome, this chapter will examine two other theories concerning ADHD.

The first theory consists of ADHD's true believers. There is now a huge literature on various aspects of the disorder (its aetiology, its central characteristics, different methodologies for intervention) written from within any number of different disciplines (medicine, neurobiology, psychology, biochemistry, pedagogy, jurisprudence, to name but a few). These knowledges largely take ADHD to be an objective truth, an aberration of the human mind finally uncovered by the keen eye of contemporary science.

An alternative, second theory questions the objective validity of ADHD, contending instead that the advent of such disorders is best understood in terms of differentiating forms of government. That is, by the sub-division of the population into an exponentially increasing number of categories, it becomes possible to regulate conduct to an ever-finer degree. This does not just include the most obvious external manifestations of docility and discipline (Foucault 1977), but with the rise of the psy-disciplines, also the smallest workings of the human mind (Rose 1990). ADHD is therefore best understood not as an isolated issue, a single bounded natural category/truth to be identified and rectified, but rather as one of over three hundred (at latest count) categories/truths of childhood difference (Whitefield 1999), each with its own specific characteristics, forms of intervention, and prognosis. This position has been discussed at length elsewhere (Tait 2001).

This raises an interesting question. Are those with an interest in ADHD logically compelled to pick one of the theories and say, 'This is the truth. All those who do not agree with this position are wrong,' or is it possible for two seemingly mutually exclusive theories both to be true? What is being suggested here is that it is possible that the heart of this problem lies not with the disease entity ADHD in itself, but rather in precisely what we mean when we say that something is true. At the risk of over-simplification, philosophers have been divided into two main camps over the issue of truth: *realism* and *anti-realism*.

## Realism

According to the realist position, it should make no difference as to who conducts an investigation into the nature of the world, the truth will always be the same, regardless of how different they may be or how different their domain assumptions. A logical extension of this position is that all systems of knowledge – philosophical, religious, aesthetic, and in particular, scientific – should be directed towards the uncovering of this truth. According to this model, ADHD therefore is a fact of human genetics, accessible to researchers irrespective of their background, and existing whether we choose to acknowledge it or not. To put this assertion another way: the statement 'ADHD is a real disorder' is true because it corresponds to an external reality. This example provides the theoretical underpinning for the realist position on truth, that is, something is true if it corresponds to the facts. This is called correspondence theory.

The central appeal of correspondence theory is its self-evidence, in that it seems to support a basic human perception as to the nature of truth. Furthermore, since it rules out human interpretive agency from the process, it objectively delineates the true from the false, thereby further adding to its apparent clarity and utility. However, a number of philosophers have also noted that significant problems exist when attempting to gain objective knowledge about a mind-independent reality, from our own sense data. As Christian notes, correspondence theory:

> compares a concept with a set of sensations – the sensations we use when we go about inferring what exists in the real world. Therefore, we are checking a subjective concept with a subjective set of sensations. If they match to some tolerable degree, then we call the concept true; if they don't, we call it false. This is not really a happy condition to live with, but given our present knowledge of the cognitive processes, the predicament seems inescapable. It looks as thought . . . we can never be certain of anything.
>
> (Christian 1981: 193–194)

Therefore, according to the logic of correspondence theory, Theory 1 regards ADHD as true because a mental concept – the notion of a disorder called ADHD dealing with hyperactive conduct – matches with sets of sense data gathered from the real world, data involving the observation and measurement of hyperactive children. It is therefore concluded that ADHD exists in that real world. A problem arises when it is pointed out that there is always a possibility that more than one mental concept can fit the relevant data, thereby producing more than one truth. For example: Theory 2 argues that a set of mental concepts – the notion of social governance through the proliferation of categories of difference, such as ADHD – also matches with sets of sense data gathered from the real world. At this point, logic would suggest that the existence of more than one truth for a single reality must prove to be either a fatal flaw for one of the truths (i.e. either Theory 1 or Theory 2), or if not, for the entire realist position on truth itself.

Employing the correspondence theory to check the truth of Theory 1 presents a number of difficulties. ADHD is not a physical object that can be held up for public scrutiny and compared to the subjective concept of the disorder. Rather it is an amalgam of various types of data – statistical, observational, behavioural, pharmacological, experiential, educational – which have been assembled in a piece-meal fashion to the point where their combined presence is deemed to correspond to the existence of an objective disorder. It is a brave realist who makes the ontological leap of saying that one *is* the other.

Using the correspondence theory with Theory 2 is also fraught with problems. Social governance is comprised of, and is operationalised through, an almost infinite number of bits of information – in this case, largely historical, statistical, administrative, cultural, medical, and legal – all of which combine within a given theoretical framework to produce a particular truth. This truth positions ADHD, not as an objective fact of nature, but rather as a governmental product formed in a given historical and medical context, along with a myriad of other new behaviour disorders which also have their genesis within the wider processes of differentiating government. Claiming a correspondence between this version of ADHD (i.e. the statement 'ADHD is a product of social governance') and objective reality is a complex and piecemeal process, but arguably no less so than that associated with taking ADHD at face value.

In summary, the correspondence truth test appears incapable of providing definitive proof of the truth of either Theory 1 or Theory 2, although there appears to be less dispute over the latter than the former from within the communities of people responsible for their respective formulations. However, this lack of certainty should not be regarded as a fatal shortcoming to either theory, since the fact is that most science struggles in similar ways with correspondence theory, although there does seem to be an irony in the fact that those researchers who adopt a realist understanding of ADHD, and who advocate a direct correspondence between the mental concept and the physical reality, are probably able to use the correspondence test least of all to make their case effectively.

## Anti-realism

In contrast to the realist position on truth (a position based upon the belief that there exist indisputable facts about a singular reality), the anti-realist position argues that facts themselves necessarily reflect particular points of view. The central animating assumption is that it is impossible to describe an ontological fact in the absence of a conceptual framework. Lynch (1998) characterises this position as being founded upon the postulation that, 'There is no scheme-neutral way of making a report about the world. It would be a mistake to search for the scheme that tells it like it 'really' is – there is no such thing' (1998: 23). Putnam (1981) argues that in the absence of a 'God's Eye' point of view – which many would argue is the unspoken prerequisite of realism – all that can remain are various interpretations of how the world is.

ADHD provides an effective example of this reasoning. As has been discussed, the realist approach to truth leads to the conclusion that it is a fact about reality that either ADHD exists, or it does not exist. This absolute knowledge, either for or against, is ascertainable via approximations to the 'God's Eye' point of view. To put it another way, science may not be 'God's Eye', but it gets close to it, and will get ever closer. In contrast, the anti-realist would argue that such a viewpoint is not just unobtainable, but in fact an illusion which both inflates the boundaries of what can be regarded as true, as well as fundamentally distorts the nature of truth itself. Therefore, claims about the existence of ADHD can never be made with absolute certainty; however, it is possible to say that they appear to be true within the logical parameters of particular types of knowledge. According to Lynch (1998), this latter position is based upon what he refers to as *metaphysical pluralism*. This is the belief that reality is tolerant of more than one description of its nature. Reality does not come 'ready made and complete' as realists would have us believe, but rather is shaped by our own interpretations of it.

Anti-realist theories of truth (of the epistemic variety) come in two main forms. The first is pragmatic theory. Pragmatism is normally associated with the work of William James (1911), and follows the logic that theorising – whether about truth, or anything else for that matter – is a pointless activity in and of itself. The only relevance that theorising can have is when it is converted into the solution of concrete intellectual problems. A philosopher must ask, what is the practical worth of any particular claim? That is, what difference would it make if a set of claims were believed to be either true or false? If the answer is 'none whatsoever', then the issue should be of no philosophical interest. The sequela of this domain assumption is that the only reason we have for asserting that something is true, is if *it works*. If an explanation can be translated into a verifiable and predictable outcome – an observable effect – then that explanation is true, if not, then the explanation is either false, or irrelevant, or both. Thus, James rejects, *a priori*, the realist notion that truth is a property independent of human intentionality.

Once again, ADHD can provide an effective example. If the question of the ontological existence of ADHD is put to one side (as irrelevant and/or unknowable) then, according to pragmatism, the truth of the disorder is determined by some of the questions outlined by James above, focusing solely upon what ADHD actually does, or attempts to do: that is, improve the educational opportunities of difficult, disruptive, and marginal students. As has been discussed, some of the principal questions to ask regarding ADHD would include, 'What is the value of this particular truth in people's lives?' as well as the definitive pragmatic question of, 'Does this truth *work*?' Within the logic of Theory 1, given that ADHD was originally formulated around the educational needs of a particular kind of at-risk student, there is little doubt that it aims to make a concrete contribution to the educational and emotional wellbeing of a specific category of child. Similarly, since the truth of ADHD is be determined by whether the category *works*, it can be argued that the disorder provides a straightforward *workable* explanation as to why seemingly otherwise healthy and normal children are incapable of behaving well in class. In addition, it could be argued that the apparent success of Ritalin in treating the behavioural outcomes of the disorder adds credence to ADHD's claim to truth. That is, since Ritalin works as a treatment, it can be argued that ADHD works as an explanation.

A pragmatic test of truth also appears to work for Theory 2, the governmental understanding of ADHD, in that it works as an explanation of why so many new disorders are appearing, and at such an incredible rate, and why previously untapped areas of human conduct are being opened up to pathologisation. That is, excessive shyness, unpopularity, vagueness, impulsiveness or loneliness, to name but a few, are all now likely to be explained in terms of a disorder, at which point the organs of intervention and regulation will be put in place, and normalisation will commence – more often than not pharmacologically. This depiction of ADHD also works in that it explains why such disorders seem to be discovered almost exclusively in areas where they pose a threat to effective social and educational management.

In addition to pragmatic theory, there is another anti-realist, epistemic approach to the notion of truth: coherence theory. This theory evolved as an attempt to sidestep the metaphysics of correspondence theory. That is, since we can never know whether a statement corresponds to external reality, all that can be said is that the statement coheres with a given set of already accepted beliefs. Generally, things we believe to be true form part of a huge, interrelated matrix. The truth of a statement is therefore assessed by how well it fits into that matrix – if it dovetails well with the ideas in the matrix, it is regarded as true, if not, it is regarded as false.

The coherence theory of truth would appear to work in Theory 1's favour. The notion of ADHD appears to mesh in easily with any number of other sets of accepted beliefs within the truth matrix. Taking just two of these: first, ADHD is based upon the premise that some kind of minor brain dysfunction results in unwelcome social behaviour, behaviour which had previously been categorised as simply as naughtiness/inattentiveness. This reappraisal coheres readily with a wide range of other accepted truths concerning the relationship between specific mental problems and undesirable forms of conduct, two examples being bipolar disorder and depressive behaviour, schizophrenia and paranoid behaviour. A second set of truths with which ADHD coheres involves the belief that, as part of pushing back the boundaries of ignorance, science is finally discovering the real workings of the human mind by uncovering more and more mental disorders. ADHD fits snugly into this triumphalist and teleological understanding of the psychological sciences, and coheres with, and adds to, the validity of all the other new disorders. One problem here is that there are problems of circularity within this logic. Comparing a statement with a broader set of beliefs is problematic when that broader set of beliefs turns out to be false or unsupportable. That is, it is circular to argue that ADHD is true because it coheres with the logic underpinning an enormous set of other newly discovered childhood disorders, when the validity of their existence is likewise, in part, premised upon the existence of ADHD. That said, there are any number of other knowledges with which ADHD coheres, and through which it gains its validity.

Theory 2's governmental understanding of ADHD also fits neatly into the truth matrix comprised of accepted historical beliefs and interpretations. Even those theoretical positions which place greater emphasis on other issues, such as the role of political power, or the distribution of wealth, would most likely concur with the central premise that categories of difference have a pivotal role to play in the management of the modern population. This understanding of ADHD also dovetails into the widely accepted belief that social governance is becoming more and more densely layered, and that the web of governmental intelligibility is becoming ever more finely meshed, as reflected in the aforementioned fact that the number of these categories/disorders appears to be increasing exponentially.

To summarise the three approaches to truth, as applied to Theory 1 and Theory 2: advocates of the disorder can argue that ADHD can make a solid claim to veracity when applying pragmatic and coherence theories of truth, but the case is somewhat weaker when applying correspondence theory. Likewise, the nature of evidence required to support Theory 2 makes the application of the correspondence theory *a priori* problematic, but the theory seems to survive well under pragmatic and coherence theory.

Having covered the necessary theoretical and empirical ground, it is now possible to address the two questions set out earlier: first, can Theory 1 and Theory 2 both be true? Can ADHD be both a real disorder *and* the product of social governance? If a realist position on truth is adopted, then the answer is probably not, although a limited number of philosophers would disagree (see Lynch 1998). Instead, it is more likely that the choice would have to be made between the two truths – Theory 1 and Theory 2 – and the less convincing one rejected. This might seem a relatively easy decision with ADHD, since even the scientific community is unsure of its status.

In contrast, if an anti-realist position on truth is adopted, there does not seem to be the same kind of epistemological problem; both theories can be true, and the social scientists and psychologists can stop squabbling with each other. That is, each theory can function as a truth within its own contextual framework, a situation founded in the pluralist logic that reality is not fixed and complete, and that facts can only ever reflect given points of view. The problem here is that advocates of ADHD are generally making a scientific claim to ontological truth, to truth as understood in realist terms, and hence the anti-realist position is not readily open to them.

Thus, it is probably fair to say that, first, ADHD has not made its case within a realist understanding of truth, and second, if it adopts an anti-realist understanding of truth, it is in danger of undercutting the foundations of its own argument. In which case, Theory 1 appears to have a long way to go before making an effective and convincing claim for truth.

## ADHD, free will and moral responsibility

This chapter will now move on to the second set of concerns raised by the case of the pupil in Wisconsin mentioned in the introduction, those of free will and moral responsibility. The question of whether we have free will is one of the oldest in philosophy, speaking, as it does, to the very foundations of what it means to be a rational and autonomous living entity. The fundamental problem hinges upon the apparent irreconcilable tension between the sure and certain knowledge that each of us makes all manner of decisions on a daily basis, choices based upon nothing but our own volition, and the equally sure and certain knowledge that we are part of a material universe, and hence subject to the same physical laws as any other form of matter, laws which preclude us from magically producing causation out of thin air. The debate has primarily, but not solely, been between those who believe that we have free will – libertarians – and those who believe that we do not – determinists.

## Free will: libertarianism vs. determinism

The libertarian position needs little explanation, in that it confirms some fundamental assumptions that most of us take for granted. That is, we assume that our decisions somehow have their origins within us; we assume that although we are subject to external influences, the final choice is ours; and we assume that if valid choices do exist, then *post facto*, we could always have acted otherwise.

Determinism is somewhat less obvious. To explain this concept, David Hume (1984) famously used the example of balls on a billiard table, noting that the balls themselves are not able to choose where to roll, as their movements are simply the inevitable (and calculable) outcome of other events. This logic was applied to the human mind by the nineteenth-century mathematician Laplace, amongst others, with the following speculation: suppose there exists a super-intelligent being that knows the location of every atom in the universe, along with every force acting upon those atoms, and the laws of motion which governs the movement of those atoms, then that being would be able to predict each and every event in the universe from that moment onward with absolute accuracy. These predictions would not just involve macro-events, like the movement of planets, but also micro-events, such as those that occur in our heads. That is, given our brains are made of matter, just like planets, the same causative laws necessarily apply, and ultimately the atoms in our brains follow the same rules as balls on a billiard table, with their movements being equally determined. What each person says, does and thinks could then theoretically be foretold millions of years in advance (Shipka and Minto 1996). Unless we are to believe that there is something about human brains that gives them an ability to make atoms swerve off their preordained path, there is no other logical alternative to this position. Indeed, most commentators would agree that if we adopt a materialist understanding of the universe and the human mind, a determinist position on free will is almost impossible to rebut – and consequently, it would follow that the sensation of free will which we all possess, and hence freedom itself, is simply a conditioned response. As John Searle states in 'Freedom of the Will':

> . . . for reasons I don't really understand, evolution has given us a form of experience of voluntary action where the experience of freedom, that is to say, the experience of the sense of alternative possibilities, is built into the very structure of conscious, voluntary human behaviour.
>
> (Searle 1994: 774)

In this sense, Searle is contending that the experience of freedom of the will is, in some ways, analogous to Kant's arguments about the 'hard-wiring' of the perception of space and time into the human mind. Voluntarism similarly becomes a primary component of consciousness, a component which not only determines how we perceive the world, but also how we are able to perceive ourselves. In the final analysis though, whether we base our analysis on libertarian or determinist presuppositions, the most significant issue is not really whether we have free will at all – even though this is hardly trivial in the grand scheme of things – rather, the critical issue is what all of this has to say about the notion of moral responsibility.

## Are we morally responsible?

If we are totally determined creatures, whether we realise it or not – as most philosophers would contend – then can we be held morally accountable for our actions? The Scottish philosopher David Hume made what is probably the most famous attempt to answer this question in *An Enquiry Concerning Human Understanding* in 1748. As a compatibilist (i.e. one who believes that we can be both determined and morally responsible), Hume sees no necessary contradiction between the notions of liberty of action and causal necessity. The logic of his argument is centred around the belief that such long-standing philosophical problems can most often be explained in terms of linguistic ambiguity. In this particular case, the focus falls upon precisely what is meant by 'liberty'.

Throughout this debate, liberty has generally been placed in binary opposition to determinism. If we act freely, then we cannot possibly be determined; if we are determined, we cannot possibly regard our actions as being free, and of course, we cannot possibly be held accountable for our actions. In contrast with this position, Hume argues that liberty actually means the power to make choices based solely upon the determinations of our will. After all, the opposite of necessity is actually chance, and this has nothing to do with being free. Hence, according to Hume, liberty should be placed in opposition, not to determinism, but rather to constraint. Therefore, we act freely if we are untrammelled in our choices. As Calvin Pinchin states:

> Thus we are offered a compatibilist account asserting no inconsistency between the concepts of liberty and necessity. A human action can be necessary in the sense that it is the inevitable outcome of causes. It can also be free in the sense that it is not subject to constraints.
>
> (Pinchin 1990: 117)

Even though compatiblism is undoubtedly the dominant position within the debate, it is not without its critics. More often than not, these critics are grouped together under the umbrella of incompatibilism, even though often the only thing they have in common is their status as 'other' – that is, both libertarian and determinist positions have been categorised as incompatibilist.

The most common and obvious incompatibilist position is generally referred to as 'hard determinism'. This involves the assertion that our conduct is determined, but also a refusal to accept that this state of affairs is compatible with moral responsibility. The implications of this conclusion are either that we abandon holding citizens accountable for their conduct altogether, or we hold them accountable, even if we know this is not really the case. John Hospers (1994) adopts a psychoanalytic approach to the issue, arguing that our conscious mind – the '*sanctum sanctorum* of freedom', and the only parts of our 'selves' which can logically be held accountable for anything – is not the driving force behind our choices or our conduct. Rather, the unconscious mind is ultimately responsible for how we act, or, as Hospers puts it: 'the unconscious is the master of every fate and the captain of every soul' (1994: 758). While not suggesting abandoning the notion of moral responsibility entirely, he does indicate that it has no intellectual or ethical foundation. Significantly for this chapter, he goes on to state that psychiatry has begun the process of coming to terms with the implications of non-conscious factors of human conduct in ways that philosophy has not. Precisely what this might mean will be addressed later, since presumably disorders such as ADHD would be included within this assertion.

Another approach in opposition to compatibilism (this time a libertarian approach) begins its analysis, not with hard determinism's refusal to accept that causal necessity and moral responsibility can co-exist, but rather with the premise that because being totally determined is unthinkable to us, we *must* have free will, therefore we can also be held morally responsible for our actions. In his essay 'The Nature of Responsibility', Morris Ginsberg (1968: 345) makes precisely this point. He asks whether anyone seriously doubts that we have the minimum level of freedom necessary to be held morally accountable, as we make judgements every day which involve weighing the consequences of given acts and the relative worth of available alternatives. Ginsberg also notes that the steadily increasing focus on the criminal conduct of young people has played a significant role in reconfiguring the debate around varying *degrees* of responsibility, particularly in children. The key to this process, apparently, is a greater understanding not only of types of conduct/crime as they relate to particular mental conditions, but also a greater understanding of the mental conditions themselves (Ginsberg 1968).

Once again, this analysis speaks through a very familiar understanding of the relationship between science and the 'discovery', rather than the production, of truth – an understanding that supports Theory 1 of ADHD, as opposed to Theory 2, as outlined in the previous discussions on truth. In spite of three decades of postmodern thought, scientific knowledge, and psychological knowledge in particular, is still most frequently presented as objective, benevolent and teleological, slowly uncovering the facts of the natural world, with the individual researchers merely perceptive but neutral observers to whom these truths are passed. History is thus presented in triumphalist terms: the heroic unmasking of the hidden realities of nature, the shedding of light into the mysteries of the human body and mind, and the identification and control of independent disease entities.

There are a number of issues here: first, disorders such as ADHD are premised upon explanations of human action, founded not in the reasoned conduct of responsible agents, but rather in terms of causal necessity. Children diagnosed with ADHD are more than likely to have any action that fits into the lexicon of symptoms associated with the disorder explained as being a *function* of that disorder. So, children diagnosed with ADHD who fidget, fidget because of that disorder. Children without ADHD who fidget, presumably make the free and voluntary decisions to do so, and hence become liable to punishment.

Second, greater and greater numbers of school children are being diagnosed as suffering from particular forms of behaviour disorder. Children with special needs, once rare in classrooms, are now commonplace. That schools should be equipped to deal with difference is not in question. Of course they should. Rather, the point is that the discipline of psychology appears to be engaged in the ongoing and accelerating process of *creating* difference. And in the case of behaviour disorders, as more categories are 'discovered', more and more students will no longer be held fully accountable for their actions. On the one hand, this has the potential to make the situation very difficult. As the number of students claiming the status of disability continues to increase, and as each disorder has different levels of associated accountability, schools may not only find themselves in the situation of being unable to hold an increasing section of the school population liable for their conduct, as the example at the beginning of this chapter demonstrates. On the other hand, it has the potential to make the situation much easier – at least for the highly stressed teacher – but only if we are prepared to leave our ethics at the school gate. The vast majority of behaviour disorders, including ADHD, appear to be treated pharmacologically. So, to put it another way, teaching life will be easier because disruptive students, quiet students, or generally different students, will be drugged into normalcy and passivity.

Finally, until fairly recently the issue of free will and moral responsibility had generally involved debates between philosophers, physicists and jurists. If the solution to this conundrum were to be found anywhere, history suggested it would come from one of these disciplines. However, psychology appears to be in the process of outflanking them all, providing increasing numbers of hard determinist explanations for what was once regarded as voluntary conduct. Hard determinism, a previously unthinkable option, is slowly becoming mainstream. However, under-standing ADHD through the lens of Theory 2, as opposed to Theory 1, may at least allow some room for scepticism over the veracity of the ongoing psy-based erosion of moral responsibility. Indeed, it could perhaps even act as a starting point for some alternative non-pathologising strategies of childhood regulation and education.

## Conclusion

Given the pressures to pathologise those many students now produced as different, it is not surprising that questions are being asked about the veracity of the burgeoning array of medical and psychological categories into which such children are being placed. As has been discussed here, this is not to say that these categories are false, but also the truth of ADHD is still a long way from being made within the scientific community itself. There appears to be little firm agreement on almost any aspect of the disorder: its prevalence, its symptoms, its consequences, its treatment, its boundaries, its aetiology, its longevity, or its constituency. Ontological and epistemological concerns aside, these significant shortcomings regarding ADHD render all truth claims as both contingent and provisional.

In addition to this set of concerns, there appears to exist a widespread belief – mostly spread widely by psychologists – that the psychological sciences are in the process of uncovering the essential truths of the human mind. This is, however, only one interpretation of psychology's history and function. As has been argued when discussing Theory 2 of ADHD (which this chapter regards as currently the more convincing of the two alternatives), Nikolas Rose (1985) has described an entirely different function, that of a crucial cog in the machinery of governmental intervention and regulation. The rise of the psy-disciplines denote the emergence of a new rationale of government targeting human individuality, with the conduct of citizens now to be directed by investigating, interpreting and modifying their mental capacities and predispositions. Fundamental to this process is the need to categorise, to break the population down into smaller and smaller manageable units, because with each new category, each new behaviour disorder, each new *pathology*, comes new possibilities of governance. Contemporary pupils are no longer simply too lively, they are now suffering from Attention Deficit Hyperactivity Disorder or Oppositional Defiance Disorder, or Conduct Disorder. Pupils are no longer simply quiet or shy, they are reclassified as suffering from Generalised Social Phobia, or Selective Mutism, or Avoidant Personality Disorder. Pupils are no longer simply unpopular or obnoxious, they are reclassified as Borderline Personality Disorder, or Antisocial Personality Disorder. However, in each instance, the new possibility of governance comes at a specific cost: the further erosion of individual responsibility. As previously mentioned, if this involved just one or two disorders, this may not be an issue. However, the exponential increase of such disorders has significant implications for our ability to hold people accountable for their actions. Hard determinism is here, and this fact needs to be the subject of far wider discussion than is currently the case.

## References

Christian, J. (1981) *Philosophy: An introduction to the art of wondering*. New York: Holt, Rinehart and Winston.

Foucault, M. (1977) *Discipline and Punish: The birth of the prison*. Harmondsworth: Penguin.

Ginsberg, M. (1968) 'The Nature of Responsibility'. In *Essays in Sociology and Social Philosophy*. Harmondsworth: Penguin: 342–361.

Hospers, J. (1994) 'Human Beings as Controlled Puppets'. In Samuel Stumpf (ed.) *Philosophy: History and problems (5th edition)*. New York: McGraw-Hill: 746–751.

Hume, D. (1984) *Treatise of Human Nature*. London: Penguin.

James, W. (1975) *The Meaning of Truth, 1911*. Cambridge, MA: Harvard University Press.

Lynch, M. (1998) *Truth in Context: An essay on truth and objectivity*. Cambridge: Bradford.

Pinchin, C. (1990) *Issues in Philosophy*. London: Macmillan.

Putnam, H. (1981) *Reason, Truth and History*. Cambridge: Cambridge University Press.

Rose, N. (1985) *The Psychological Complex: Psychology, politics and society in England 1869–1939*. London: Routledge and Kegan Paul.

Rose, N. (1990) *Governing the Soul: The shaping of the private self*. London: Routledge.

Searle, J. (1994) 'Freedom of the Will'. In Samuel Stumpf (ed.) *Philosophy: History and problems (5th edition)*. New York: McGraw-Hill: 766–774.

Shipka, T. and Minto, A. (eds.) (1996) *Philosophy: Paradox and discovery*. McGraw Hill: New York.

Tait, G. (2001) 'Pathologising Difference, Governing Personality'. *Asia-Pacific Journal of Teacher Education*, 29(1): 93–102.

Whitefield, P. (1999) 'Disordered Behaviour and Fuzzy Categories'. *Education Links*, 59: 22–25.

Zirkel, P. (2001) 'Courtside – Manifest Determination?' *Phi Delta Kappan*, 82(6): 478–479.

# Chapter 6

# Inclusion and exclusion in school

## Experiences of children labelled 'ADHD' in South Africa

*Nithi Muthukrishna*

This chapter explores the exclusionary and inclusionary factors that impact the lives of three children labelled as ADHD in South Africa. The aim of this qualitative study was to listen to the voices of the children and their mothers in order to ascertain the meanings of schooling experiences. Three mothers and their sons were participants in the study. In-depth interviews were conducted with participants. In the case of the children, the interviews included various participatory data collection techniques, including time lines, and diamond-ranking activities.

Results in this study suggest that all three children experienced various exclusionary pressures in schools that were context dependent. Hegemonic influences emanate from the power of the biological/medical and learner deficit systemic barriers to learning and participation in education, such as negative attitudes from teachers; power imbalances between parents and professionals; inappropriate teaching methodologies; stigmatisation of children who experience difficulties learning; lack of parental recognition and support. The narratives of the children and their mothers revealed that schooling contexts that were more inclusive had an ethos that valued all learners irrespective of diversity, affirmed and supported the parents, engaged in curriculum differentiation, and strove to minimise discriminatory practices. The question to be asked is: How can all public schools become more inclusive, and how can education systems ensure that schools are committed to addressing systemic barriers to learning and participation embedded in their cultures and curriculum?

In July 2001, the Ministry of Education in South Africa published White Paper 6 which is entitled, 'Special Needs Education: Building an Inclusive Education and Training System' (Department of Education 2001). This policy document marked the culmination of a policy process begun in 1996 with the appointment by the Minister of the National Commission on Special Needs in Education and Training (NCSNET) and the National Committee on Education Support Services (NCESS). These two bodies in their terms of reference had the task of investigating and making recommendations on all aspects of 'special needs' and support services in education and training in South Africa. A Report, 'Quality Education for All: Overcoming barriers to learning and development' was presented to the Minister in November 1997 (Department of Education 1997).

Both the Report of NCSNET and NCESS and Education White Paper 6 reflect a 'paradigm shift' in special education in South Africa. Muthukrishna and Schoeman (2000) explain that this entails a shift from a 'learner deficit view and psycho-medical view of special needs . . . to a systemic one' (2000: 331). The Education White Paper recognises that there are many learners in the education system who *experience barriers to learning* because of the inability of the education and training system to accommodate their diverse learning needs. Key barriers in the South African context that result in a large number of children and adults being vulnerable to learning breakdown and sustained exclusion include: problems in the provision and organisation of education; socio-economic barriers; factors that place learners at risk such as high levels of violence and crime, and the HIV/AIDS epidemic; substance abuse; negative and harmful attitudes towards difference in society; an inflexible curriculum including inappropriate teaching methodologies; problems with language and communication; inaccessible and unsafe built environment; inappropriate and inadequate provision of support services to schools, parents, care-givers, families and communities; lack of enabling and protective legislation; disability; inadequate teacher development; and lack of parental recognition and involvement. White Paper 6 locates the 'problem' with the system, and suggests that a broad range of learning needs exist in the learner population at any point in time and learning breakdown or exclusion occurs when these needs are not met. White Paper 6 stresses the urgent need to move away from the categorisation and labelling of learners to a recognition that a range of needs exist in the learner population. Addressing barriers to learning requires a change in the nature and structure of this system, and a focus on identifying and minimising them. Howell (2003) explains that this paradigm shift involves a shift in the way in which we understand why particular learners continue to experience learning difficulties in the classroom or to be excluded from the system as a whole.

White Paper 6 calls for the building of an inclusive education and training system. Inclusion is defined as

- Acknowledging that all children and youth can learn and that all children and youth need support
- Enabling education structures, systems and learning methodologies to meet the needs of all children
- Acknowledging and respecting difference in children, whether due to age, gender, ethnicity, language, class, disability, HIV status, or other infectious diseases
- Broader than formal schooling, and acknowledging that learning occurs in the home, the community, and within formal and informal contexts
- Changing attitudes, behaviour, teaching methods, curricula, and environment to meet the needs of all learners
- Maximising the participation of all learners in the culture and curriculum of educational institutions and uncovering and minimising barriers to learning.

(Department of Education 2001: 6–7)

White Paper 6 is located within the principles and values of the Constitutional framework of South Africa, and therefore, embedded in it is a rights discourse. The policy is seen to be about ensuring that *all* learners are able to exercise their right to basic education.

In the context of policy change in South Africa since 1994, the aim of the study presented in this chapter was to explore exclusionary factors (or barriers to learning and development) and inclusionary factors that impact the lives of three learners labelled as ADHD. The aim was to listen to the generally excluded voices of these learners and their mothers, and document their schooling experiences. It was hoped that data gathered would have implications for ways to make schools more responsive to the needs of these learners.

Little is known about ADHD on the African continent. Research by Meyer (1998) suggests that ADHD is the most prevalent child psychiatric disorder in South Africa. The Hyperactivity/Attention Deficit Support Group of South Africa (2004) estimates that 10 per cent of all South African children may have characteristics associated with ADHD. However, there are no official statistics available on the prevalence in South Africa. There have been concerns in South Africa that Ritalin may be over-prescribed in private and public schools that serve advantaged and affluent communities (*Mail and Guardian*, June 1999). It has not been possible to locate any in-depth qualitative studies that explore the voices of children and their mothers on the schooling experiences of children labelled as ADHD.

## The study

Three children and their mothers were participants in this study. The children were selected through purposive sampling in that children who were on Ritalin at some stage in their lives were included in the study. Since the children would be required to reflect on their schooling experiences, it was decided to limit the study to children who were at the adolescent stage of development. Pseudonyms are used to protect the identity of the children and the schools.

Christo is a 12-year-old white Afrikaans-speaking boy in grade 6. For the past year, he has been attending Parkhaven special school approximately 10 km from his home. He travels to and from school by the school bus. He spent the first three years of schooling at the Central Primary School, in his neighbourhood within walking distance from his home. He then transferred to the Learning Together Remedial School in the city about 20 km from his home. He travelled to this school with a teacher who lives in his neighbourhood. After spending two and a half years at this school, he had to leave as it is a short-term placement facility. Children who leave either go back to a mainstream setting or to a special school. Christo was transferred to the Parkhaven Special School that caters for children, from grade one to matriculation, labelled learning-disabled.

Dashan is a 15-year-old South African Indian boy and is currently in grade 10 at high school approximately 5 km from his home. He began his schooling at a public school in his neighbourhood. In grade 2, his parents transferred him to a more well-resourced school, the Hillfield Primary School, in a neighbouring suburb. This school was a 'white' school under the apartheid era. Currently, it is a public school but the school governing body has a high level of autonomy so that on decentralised levels they may determine the policy and nature of the school, such as, for example, school fees, securing better learning resources than other public schools, and additional teachers. Class size is generally smaller than in the majority of public schools because of the employment of teachers paid by the governing body from the higher school fees. The school may be considered a semi-private school. In grade 4, Dashan's parents made the decision to place him back at an ordinary public school. He is now at public high school close to his home.

Samuel is 11 years old, and in grade 5. He is South African Indian. Samuel started school at a semi-private school in a suburb about 10 km from his home. His parents placed him at the school largely because it was a better-resourced school, of the type that Dashan attended. From grade 3, he was transferred to a remedial unit in a mainstream school approximately 20 km from his home.

In the case of all three children, parents were informed that there was a 'problem' in the first year at primary school. The 'problem' was identified by the class teachers, and children were referred to private psychologists for assessment. The outcome was a 'diagnosis', and the label 'ADHD' was applied. The children were subsequently placed on Ritalin. The three children have experienced very disrupted schooling – changing schools three and four times in their schooling careers.

The children were interviewed individually through semi-structured interviews. Assurance was given that all information would be treated with utmost confidentiality, and that their identities would be kept anonymous. The interviews were tape-recorded, and later transcribed. The children and their mothers had no problems with the use of a tape recorder, and understood that the purpose was to obtain accurate accounts of their narratives. Interviews lasted from approximately one to one and half hours. All three children were able to maintain interest and concentration throughout the interviews. The research approach applied with the children recognised the importance of active involvement of the children in the research in line with the methodological shift in recent years from approaches which view children as 'objects' of concern to methods that view children as active constructors of meaning (James and Prout 1997; O'Kane 2000). Certain participatory activities were used with the children during the interviews, namely, time line, diamond-ranking activities, and a pots and beans activity.

In the time line activity, the child discussed and recorded key events that had had an impact on his life from his earliest memories of schooling. In the pots and beans activity, adapted from O'Kane (2000), the child gave his views about the things he liked most and least about school and schooling. The child had to label the pots indicating things most liked and least liked, for example, sport, maths; and decide how many beans each pot most and least deserved. This was followed by a discussion on why a particular pot had more beans than another. The diamond-ranking activity, also adapted from O'Kane (2000), aimed to explore what the child would change about school and schooling, and what he would not change. The researcher wrote the statements from the child on small rectangular cards and the child had to place each card on a diamond-shaped figure drawn on a board, with the thing he would like changed the most at the apex of the diamond (for example, my teachers) and the least at the bottom (for example, my friends). The placement of the cards was then discussed with the researcher in order to obtain a glimpse of the meanings children construct about their schools and schooling experiences.

In all cases, only the mothers were available for participation in the study. Semi-structured interviews were used. The broad question asked was: 'What has been your experience of your child's schooling from the pre-school years?' This question opened the discussion, and responses were then probed to obtain a more complete picture of the social context in which mothers and their children were experiencing ADHD.

## Findings

The primary objective in this chapter is to allow mothers' and children's own narratives to inform an understanding of how the label ADHD impacts on their experiences of diagnosis, drug treatment and schooling. The study is grounded in a psychosocial theoretical approach (Sameroff 1975, 1991), focusing on the role of context in the experience of ADHD. The approach focuses on how individual-context transactions influence the course of development differently at various critical periods in the life cycle. Donald *et al.* (2002) explain that at any one point in time, a child has existing psychological capacities (whether behavioural, cognitive, emotional, social) that are the product of earlier transactions. The child brings these existing capacities to her current situation and context. Thus, her current transactions are shaped not only by these capacities but by her present context and the particular period in her life cycle.

In the following sections, the findings in the study are presented according to the main themes that emerged across the data sets obtained from the mothers and the children.

## Coming to know

The children were diagnosed with ADHD at primary school, and placed on Ritalin treatment. Two of the mothers regretted that they did not 'come to know' earlier in their children's schooling lives.

Samuel's mother suspected that her son was having difficulty 'picking up the skills' at nursery school, although his developmental milestones were normal. She indicated her concerns to the grade 1 teacher but was told that he would develop with time, and that she should not be too concerned. However, when Samuel was in grade 3, the teacher said, 'I think there is a problem with this child'. Samuel is not hyperactive, according to his mother, but the teacher indicated that he had problems concentrating in class. She was advised by the teacher to 'get him assessed'. The process resulted in assessments by a private psychologist who found 'a bit of a lag' and suggested that Samuel be placed in a remedial unit at a mainstream school for two years. The parents were referred to a medical doctor who placed him on Ritalin.

Christo's mother explained that when her son was 6 the preschool teacher told her that Christo was not emotionally ready to go to school. He had always been a very clingy child from birth, and she felt that he would get over that once at a mainstream school. She explains:

> Christo started his primary school at a school near home. He had just turned 6, and every time when I used to fetch him in the afternoon, I would ask, 'How is Christo doing?', the teacher would say, 'He is doing fine . . . no problem.' There were 30 in class. When I used to say, 'Could I look at my child's books', the answer was, 'No, no it is not school policy'. I used to help Christo with homework and never understand why my child could not learn to read simple words such as 'the', 'was' – there was reversal of letters. I was not trained in any field. I am a housewife. (Christo's mother)

This continued, then in grade 2 the school informed her that there was something wrong with her child:

> The class teacher asked me to take him to a paediatrician to put him on Ritalin. We had to have an EEG done. After extensive testing, they found from the EEGs that he had petitmal – he was epileptic. They put him on Epilum and because nobody at that stage knew that he was allergic to an ingredient in the medication . . . my child came out in terrible big hives. They took him off the Epilum and put him on Ritalin, and told me that he was ADHD. (Christo's mother)

Dashan's mother only knew that the problem was serious two weeks after he was placed at the Hillfield Primary School. She explains:

> The teacher said, 'I think you should look into this', she said she suspects . . . she also said that he doesn't concentrate. This is the first time we heard this . . . that he does not concentrate. The teacher said that in every class you will get two or three children who have this problem . . . unfortunately Dashan has this problem. She said we will have to take him to a psychologist to have tests. She told me she suspects he has ADHD and that normally these children go on Ritalin. It was the first time I heard of Ritalin. I did not know how good or bad it was at that time . . . we just went with what we were told to do – we were so ignorant. (Dashan's mother)

The mothers' narratives suggest that they are all sceptical about their son's diagnosis and the Ritalin treatment. A concern that emerges is that teachers and professionals tend to explain or diagnose ADHD with a kind of biological, reductionist simplicity, and that they have not engaged with the complexities embedded in the label. The dynamic and complex interaction between individual and social context argued in research is absent from the dialogues of parents with teachers and professionals (Lloyd and Norris 1999).

## Facing troubling choices

According to the three mothers, as parents they were faced with troubling choices throughout their children's schooling. Two of the mothers clearly indicated a sense of powerlessness, lack of knowledge, and a sense that they had no control over events in their children's lives. All three stated that as parents they had to constantly make decisions relating to their child's education. Major choices had to be made around issues of change of school, obtaining extra tuition and remedial help, taking their children for various assessments, finding alternate schools, placement on medication, and Ritalin dosage.

> He found that the dosage was not helping – so he put him on the long-acting, slow-release capsules. It's long acting . . . and the half a dose to jump start him in the morning. Last term the teacher wanted him to go onto a stronger dose. I spoke to the doctor, and said that I was not happy with this child going on anything stronger. He said OK we will cut off both the tablets just give him one. He is going to cut off the other two. There is another new tablet he is going to place him on . . . also Ritalin . . . aim is to cut off the other two. He will place him on it to see if he can swing him back into improving his concentration. The teacher wanted to know should I not be giving it to him at home. I said no . . . at home I can manage with him. I don't want him to be even more subdued. (Samuel's mother)

Christo's mother explains that she had no idea where to turn when she realised that her child was having a very difficult schooling experience at the Central Primary School.

> I told the principal, how I felt about the school. Christo was told he was stupid, you're useless, look the child was made fun of, told you are lazy, you are disruptive, you are lazy, you are just a waste of time, why don't you just get out of my class . . . he was six, seven and eight years. I told the principal that it was obvious they wanted Christo out of the school. The principal responded 'Well, Mrs C. you have to do what you have to do' when I informed him that I had decided to remove Christo from the school. Christo was a non-reader and non-writer when he left

that school in grade 3. He was very good in maths. I moved him to Learning Together Remedial School after the intervention of a friend and neighbour. I never heard of this school before – it is about 20 km from where we live. Anyway, nobody tells you anything – what choices do we have as parents? (Christo's mother)

Christo's mother explained that she had similar difficult choices to make when he had to leave the Learning Together Remedial School after two and a half years there as this is a short-term placement centre:

The choice was mainstream or special school. We were told that Christo would not cope in mainstream – I still wonder about this. But we had no real choice. We were told that the Eastwood School for the Cerebral Palsied was a possibility but we felt that it is not exactly the place for Christo. The teachers at Learning Together said he is such a bright little chap . . . to put him in a class of children with CP children . . . would destroy him – he is very sensitive. Besides Eastwood only goes up to grade 7 – then you sit with the problem. Where to from there? (Christo's mother)

The parents decided to place Christo at Parkhaven, a special school for children with learning disabilities. The school does go up to matriculation but the curriculum does not suit Christo's interests. He would like to go to a Technical College that offers technical subjects. Christo is very artistically inclined. According to the mother, it seems Christo may have to move again in grade 8.

## Conflicting meanings

The responses of all mothers suggested that they felt they were taking risks regarding their children's schooling, and this was linked to the fact that they always met with conflicting suggestions and meanings relating to their children's schooling from teachers and professionals.

Dashan's mother explained how they were given so many conflicting suggestions about the best placement for their child and about his medication, and they never knew whether they were making the right decisions.

At first, all we were told is that he needed to see the private speech therapist contracted to the school, then extra remedial help . . . and he will be fine . . . so we took him to a private remedial centre near the school, then we were told that he belongs to the school for cerebral palsied children. We were told that Dashan should spend a week at the CP school where he would be assessed by the speech therapist, occupational therapist, remedial teachers, psychologists, class teacher etc. – and at the end of the week they will decide if Dashan can stay there.

Now we were getting confused but because we had handed this whole thing to the school, we decided to go with what they say. We felt he did not fit in – there were children who were CP. I mean there is nothing wrong. But the thing is we felt that Darshan did not fit there. We were very confused at this stage. At the end of the week, we had to speak to the school psychologist. She said, 'look Dashan does not belong here . . . there is nothing wrong with him'. She suggested . . . he needs some extra lessons . . . remedial tuition . . . maybe twice a week. So put him back into his school . . . then after a few weeks, his teacher then said put in a remedial unit at a primary school in another suburb. Then my husband was fuming. He said that we are doing damage to this child. (Dashan's mother)

There were also conflicting messages about Ritalin and its effects. In grade 2 and 3, the teachers were very happy with Dashan on medication. But before the end of grade 3, the teacher told the parents that their child is not ready to go to grade 4, and that he needs to repeat grade 3. The parents agreed, although they felt that unsure of whether they were making the right decision. The mother explains:

It really affected Dashan. Children teased him . . . even in high school they still tease him. They remembered him . . . I feel this wrecked up his whole life. It really affected him. We always tell him that he did not fail . . . he just repeated the year. But they teased him and call him failure and everything. (Dashan's mother)

The year Dashan repeated grade 3 was perfect, according to his mother, as he seemed to know all the work expected of him. The teacher told the parents that he was her favourite child. Dashan progressed to grade 4. In the first term, the teacher informed the mother that Dashan would fail grade 4. The mother recalls how devastated she was:

We did all that the school wanted . . . placed him on Ritalin and this is what we were faced with. That evening I had to tell my husband . . . he told me . . . you know what, that school is full of nonsense . . . it has been nonsense from day one. He said we put up with too much of their nonsense. Ritalin and this school and that. Even when he is on Ritalin . . . he still has to repeat . . . what is the point of it all. (Dashan's mother)

Dashan also recounts his parent's frustration:

What happened . . . the teacher told my parents that I would fail in the first term. My father was angry – how can you know in the first term that I will fail? I remember my parents kept me at home – it was two weeks before the end of term. I did not write the exams . . . they told my parents I had to go on Ritalin. My parents kept me at home for the rest of the term about two weeks and then I went to another primary school, Endeavour Primary School. (Dashan)

The mother stated that Dashan's schooling has been without major problems from the time he enrolled at Endeavour Primary School to his transition to high school.

## Being on Ritalin

The narratives of the mothers and their children suggest the following scenario. The children were described by teachers as having either poor attention skills, poor concentration, displaying disruptive behaviour, or making poor progress academically. Parents are advised to take the child to the 'experts', namely, psychologists, medical specialists, then a diagnosis is made. The child is then placed on Ritalin. The outcome of such a scenario as pointed out by Hill and Castro (2002) is that it serves the purposes of all adults involved. The question to ask is: What about the child? Has anyone engaged with the complexity of the child's problem? It has been well documented that ADHD is a pervasive disorder that can present in many different and complex ways.

Two of the mothers explain their experiences of Ritalin:

When we pick him up you can see he has a headache . . . the tiredness is there . . . he is very subdued and quiet . . . he won't talk like normal – normally he will chat with you all the time. And THAT [mother's emphasis] is what upsets me. I get very, very upset. I hope that this year he is going to finish with it . . . and I will put him back into mainstream. (Samuel's mother)

Ritalin does not seem to be an effective treatment for Christo. He gets very tearful and angry . . . he has bursts of anger. He does not eat, no appetite whatsoever. Even Learning Together School felt that Ritalin was not working for Christo. Since the 4th of Dec. to today 21 Jan. – he has not touched his Asthma pump once. I think the reason is he has not been on Ritalin for the whole holiday. He has been such a happy child – with a good appetite. He would come in after playing with his friends, and say, 'Mum, what's to eat?' Now that he is back on Ritalin and that school has started, the problems begin again. He was angry and tearful the first day when he got home. He had these headaches again. (Christo's mother)

Two children stated that they 'hated' Ritalin. In one of the participatory exercises, they indicated that their medication is what they would change about their lives. They felt that their parents were powerless in decisions about their medication. When Christo was asked whether he had discussed his feelings about his medication with his parents, he responded:

> Yes, my mum is trying to get me to get me off it . . . but the school thinks it's the best thing in the world. Every single . . . almost everyone takes Ritalin . . . even though they don't need it and hate it. Everybody hates it . . . not a single person likes it. It gives them headaches . . . you are not hungry . . . so you can't eat. Makes me grumpy. When I get home all I want to do is sit down. Then my father says go and change and that makes me angry. Some days, my teacher forgets to give it to me . . . so I don't take it . . . and I won't remind her about it because I hate it . . . I actually concentrate better. (Christo)

The power and control of the experts, namely teachers, doctors and other professionals, emerges in these narratives. The voices of parents and the children themselves are not heard. A more crucial concern when examining the narratives is the underlying view of teachers and professionals that Ritalin is the answer to the learning problem. The fact that Ritalin cannot compensate for good teaching methodologies to meet the needs of these learners is not understood. The medical/learner deficit view as opposed to a systemic view of learning difficulty is entrenched in certain schools. This was also a finding of the National Commission on Special Needs in Education and Training and the National Committee on Education Support Services (Department of Education 1997).

## Exclusion and inclusion in school

The nature of the schooling experiences of the children depended largely on context, that is, the ethos and values upheld by particular settings. Schools (irrespective of whether they were mainstream or special schools) that reflected an ethos and culture of valuing diversity, including and supporting parents, commitment to quality education for all learners, and affirming all learners, were supportive environments for the three children. It was clear from the narratives that in certain schools children experienced tremendous exclusionary pressures such as stigmatisation, negative attitudes, inappropriate teaching methodologies, lack of commitment to quality education for all, failure to respond to diversity in the learner population, lack of parental recognition and support.

Christo's mother explains how she felt excluded at the neighbourhood primary school which her son attended, and the negative experiences her son had in his early years of schooling:

> It so happened, I was unaware that for the first six months of that child's first year that Christo never really attended school. He would go to school, he would be received and he would be sent out. Until one of the other little children from his class came to me, and said to me that

Christo has been very naughty. He is not allowed in our class, he was kicked out long time ago. When Christo came home, I questioned him and he would button up. It took me a year, he was very frightened he was threatened, to find out what was going on. At the age of 6 . . . a whole day's worth of work, Maths, English whatever it was . . . he would do in the principal's office. The principal or nobody would not check if the child understood the work. Then at the end of the day, the principal would put a line through the work and draw sad faces with tears. This neglect of my child carried on for two and half years. (Christo's mother)

In our conversation, Christo questioned his classroom experience at the primary where he began his schooling:

That school sucks . . . my teacher hated me . . . she sent me out of the class everyday . . . and then she expects me to do well. I had to stand outside the classroom . . . she didn't like me. I never, ever got a star. Why did I never ever get a star? (Christo)

In the diamond-ranking exercise, Christo was asked what makes learning easy at his present school, Parkhaven Remedial School. His response was 'nothing'. When asked what made learning hard, his answer was 'my teacher'.

The vignette below is in response to a diamond-ranking exercise done with the researcher (interviewer):

I: Which subject do you like best?
N: I do not like any of them – it's a dumb school I want to get out of the school – but my mother thinks it's the most wonderful school.
I: What are hard about your subjects?
N: They not hard . . . in fact, they just boring. My teacher treats us like we are babies . . . I mean she's like . . . she thinks we are so young . . . she has to explain things word for word even if it's the most simple thing.
  She does not leave you to do your work . . . she keeps on explaining the whole way through . . . she does not give you peace of mind. She explains the same thing over and over again. We have her for all the subjects . . . Yuk! But she says the same thing 20 times – so many times that you just get irritated and you don't want to hear it. Like she's explained something and she says the same exact words again . . . like we are dumb.
I: What makes learning easy?
N: The work is on the easy side . . . but the way the teachers make it . . . they make it boring. They way they explain . . . they explain over and over again . . . like we're babies. THEY [child's emphasis] make it boring . . . the work is boring and easy.

Christo, speaking of his experience at the remedial school he currently attends, said:

> My reading is OK, but only if I am interested in it. My teachers want me to read the most boring stuff in the world . . . then I can't read. I can read about skate magazines etc. It gives you tips about skating, lot of interesting stuff. (Christo)

However, the narratives revealed that all children and their mothers did experience certain inclusive settings and inclusionary teaching practice.

Samuel is finding learning at the remedial unit less difficult, and he suggests it is because there are just 13 children in the class and the teacher is able to provide more individual attention. He did not find the transition to the remedial unit in the new school difficult because one of his friends was also placed there:

> At the primary school, I found mostly spelling hard – the hard parts of words. Now my spelling is easier – the teacher teaches us and helps us with the hard parts . . . she just helps us a lot to understand it better. We have 13 children in our class, and the teacher can pay more attention. All the children in my class are my friends – all of us are boys. I am happy here and there is nothing I feel I want to change. The books are good – they have adequate books. The teachers are nice and kind. They help us if we have difficulty with our work. My teacher handed out a special effort badge to us – I wear it. (Samuel)

Christo commented that there is a teacher at his current school with whom he can relate:

> There is one nice teacher at my present school (Parkhaven Special School) . . . she teaches the grade fours. You can talk to her like a friend. Like say, if I feel I want to hit someone and that he . . . that person has done a lot of bad things to me . . . she will understand . . . She helps us sort out our problems because if the teachers come and try to sort out our problems, it will never get sorted out . . . it gets worse and worse and eventually if a fight does happen, it will be a lot worse. That's what teachers don't understand. They think they must sort everything out. They should let the people sort out for themselves. They act like they can sort everything out. (Christo)

Litner (2003) argues that children labelled ADHD as with any other children need help to learn how to make decisions and take responsibility for choices they make and their outcomes, as the long-term goal is to make children more self-reliant.

Christo's mother explains her experience at the Learning Together School:

It is the most wonderful school. I have nothing but praise for the teachers. The teachers have got pure dedication, they have got compassion – they care for and love every single child . . . no matter how bright or how weak. The children could go for a drink of water. The children are not allowed to make fun of each other. They have slogans all over the place saying I won't push anybody, I won't bully, I am here to help somebody. When any child had an epileptic fit, the children were trained what to do to assist the teacher. The children were permanently there for the children. It did not matter if it was day or night or holiday. (Christo's mother)

Commenting on the teaching methodologies she observed:

The teaching was very much on my child's level. If Christo was reading at a 9-year-old level, then they would put him in a 9-year-old group for reading. They would have volunteer mothers come in and read with them because the teacher did not have all that much time . . . she had about 17 in the class. Why can the regular schools not use these methods? What is so hard? Can they not care for all children no matter who and what the child is? If a child has a gap, like times tables . . . try to work on the gaps even if it means placing him with children at that level for certain times in the week or day. I am prepared to volunteer my help. (Christo's mother)

She elaborated on the support to parents:

The support to parents was wonderful . . . there were always meetings . . . to tell us about any latest information . . . on diets, Ritalin. I was never ever called in to see the headmistress to listen to complaints and insinuations about my child – as the previous primary school had given me. What I loved about the school . . . it is that they were helpful and very, very supportive of us, the parents. They were never too busy to listen to me. (Christo's mother)

Christo's mother also felt that the school brought out the best in her son:

THEY informed ME [mother's emphasis] that Christo had an artistic flair. They actually said that he is a 'graphic designer in the making'. I never knew this. He has got an eye for colour. He is so good . . . he understands graphs, he understands lines. Last year, at Parkhaven, he got a distinction for natural sciences and tech. He is very good with geography. He can remember photographically a map – he can draw a blank map, colour it in, and put the names of the countries. He has drawn some stunning artwork. He did beautifully for Geography. He did very well last year. (Christo's mother)

Dashan's mother has a very high regard for the teachers at Endeavour Primary School, an ordinary public school with limited resources and low school fees. She recounts what she was told by Dashan's teacher when she went to the school to enrol her child for the first time:

> I told his teacher everything. His teacher said, 'please don't put him on that medication. None of our children are taking that tablet. Don't put him on any medication . . . we are teachers we know how to deal with him.' She said that all children are active in different ways . . . 'we don't have a problem'. You know something, the teachers at that school never heard of Ritalin. He passed every year grade 4 to 7. We were pleased that without Ritalin his aggregate used to be around 55–58 – but he used to battle to be get 60. The teachers did tell me that Dashan does have the problem of talking too much in class to a point where they get irritated and shout at him. (Dashan's mother)

Dashan is now in grade 10 at a high school close to his neighbourhood. There were no problems with transition to high school. He seems very motivated to do well despite the fact that the high school environment may be experienced as very complex for many children labelled ADHD (Litner 2003). At the end of 2004, Dashan passed grade 9 with an aggregate of 60 per cent. His mother explains that 'he seems to better in the learning subjects as he obtains As and Bs in History and Geography (HSS), and Life Orientation'. His parents send him for private tuition twice a week in Maths, English and Physics. Dashan indicated that he would like to become an engineer and has chosen his subjects accordingly. The mother explained that the high school is an ordinary public school and that it is one of the high-achieving schools in the region. The matriculation results at the school are very good, and one of the students was amongst the top 20 students in the province in the 2004 matriculation exams. She finds it a very caring school, and Dashan is extremely happy at the school. He tries very hard to improve his grades.

## 'Talking to the birds'

It has been documented that children labelled ADHD are often rejected by their peers, that they have few friends and low self-esteem (e.g. Weiss and Hechtman 1993; Whalen and Henker 1999) However, with the heterogeneity among children labelled ADHD, some children find socialisation easier than others.

His mother mentioned that Dashan recently told her that he had no friends at Hillfield Primary School, and no one at the school identified this as a problem for him:

> During the breaks at the primary school, he used to play with the birds and talk to them. They used to sit on the trees and he will go to them . . . and they will fly away to another tree . . . and he will run to that tree

... the whole break time. The teacher never told me that he had no friends ... she never take notice I think. (Dashan's mother)

Dashan appears to have good friends in high school who, in fact, motivate him to commit to his studies:

I like to play soccer with my friends at Dolphin grounds. I spend breaks with them. Sometimes there is too much to learn. My friends taught me how to learn. I asked them how to learn. They said start a couple months before exams ... start studying ... and go over things many times. They taught me how to study when there is a lot to learn. So two weeks before an exam I start studying ... I got it from them. (Dashan)

It is interesting that Dashan is able to engage in self-monitoring and self-regulation with the support of his friends. ADHD literature suggests that teenagers begin high school with serious delays in self-regulation skills, weak self-discipline, and difficulties in reflecting on their own behaviour and actions (Barkley 1997; Litner 2003).

When probed about what were good experiences in his school, Christo responded,

What do I like about school. OK ... I like mainly my friends ... I have a whole bunch of them. I am seriously popular. I am only here for a year [referring to Parkhaven Remedial School] ... everyone likes me. They like the fact that we will stand up for each other ... 'cause like the respect is mutual. (Christo)

Christo's mum recounted how the teachers at the Learning Together Remedial School one day told her:

Do you know how helpful your child is? They could not get over this little boy. They all said to me what a helpful little child you've got here. You know if a child is sad or if a child is crying, Christo would go and be the first to say 'never mind' 'don't worry', and he will sit next to the kid the whole day. And if some one is new in the middle of the year, Christo will leave his friends, and say I am going to make this new child welcome, and he will be with the new child the whole day. The teachers commended Christo for that. (Christo's mother)

Litner (2003) suggests that successful socialisation depends on the mixture of individual, family, school, and peer group characteristics.

## 'He must have REALLY irritated her'

There is extensive literature on the compelling link between ADHD characteristics in children and problems with behaviour (Fredrick and Olmi 1994; Saunders and Chambers 1996; Barkley 1996, 1997; Whalen and Henker 1998; Merrell and Boelter 2001). The children have difficulty responding appropriately to others in social situations, for example, in their ability to participate, co-operate and communicate with peers; they ask too many questions at inappropriate times, and are considered to have difficulty adapting their behaviour to accommodate the requirements of a shifting social climate. Two mothers reported that their children presented behaviour problems, and in primary school were a challenge to teachers and to them as parents:

> He did have behaviour problems as a child . . . Talked all the time and was very active – could not sit still . . . on the move all the time . . . At times, we had to tell him to just 'shut up' for a while. I remember, at Hillfield School, after two weeks, the teacher said he is irritating her . . . I remember she said she wants to MURDER [her emphasis] him. I know he must have really irritated her for her to say that to me as his mother. While she is teaching him . . . he will go to the front and write on the board. Then he will talk in class. In junior primary, they sit in groups of six. He was always disturbing the other children . . . kicking them under the table until they start crying. When the teacher came, he would deny that he did anything. We tried to speak to him, and deny him certain privileges . . . never really worked.

Christo's mother explains that there were numerous complaints from the teachers at Central Primary School about his behaviour:

> I moved him from this school. I did not want my child to be a gardener. I also personally had seen my child during the day . . . one day I was walking up to the shops and I saw this little boy . . . on the sports field . . . I thought but that looks like Christo – so I went up onto the sports field and there was Christo pulling out weeds. I said, 'Christo, what are you doing?' He replied, 'My teacher said I have to pull out weeds . . . and the principal said I must pull out weeds.' He never told me this was going on . . . he was very frightened. I was getting one letter after another. Always Christo is disruptive, we are going to give him detention – because he was not behaving. He was permanently in detention. In his school reports, I would see that his social skills ranked very low. (Christo's mother)

However, the parents received no help to deal with the challenging behaviours. The impression given to them was that Ritalin was the answer to the problem, but this was not the case. Litner (2003) points out that children labelled ADHD become hypersensitive to criticism, as their difficulties have become the focus of negative attention, complaints and punitive actions. In addition to this, they have been struggling with self-esteem issues. All children who have behaviour problems need systematic, closely monitored interventions to help them self-manage their problem behaviours. Such interventions should be planned in a collaborative way, and should involve partnerships between the children and teachers, peers, parents. Parker (1999) suggests the need to identify a few distinct areas for goal-setting based on problem spots that the child has acknowledged, and an action plan. The narratives of the mothers and the children point to the need for teacher professional development in this area.

## Conclusion

The voices of the mothers and their children presented in this chapter highlight the complexity of ADHD within the cultural politics of schools and schooling in South Africa. There is evidence that there are teachers and professionals within the system who have embraced psycho-medical discourses that entrench various discursive practices. These practices result in exclusionary pressures. It is clear that all three children have been pathologised and labelled, and researchers over the years have questioned whether this is the most useful way of meeting their needs (Ballard 1995; Lloyd and Norris 1999). The narratives of the mothers and their children reflect familiar themes in literature on inclusion and exclusion in schools, including parents' struggles for choice and empowerment; human rights and social justice for children irrespective of diversity; the power of professionals in educational decision-making; power and control in schools; and the need for a political critique of social values, structures and practices in schools that place exclusionary pressures on learners (for example, Booth and Ainscow 1998; Armstrong *et al.* 2000; Corbett and Slee 2000; Balagopalan 2003; Sayeed 2003).

## References

Armstrong, D., Armstrong, F. and Barton, L. (2000) 'Introduction'. In Armstrong, D., Armstrong, F. and Barton, L. (eds) *Inclusive Education: Policy, contexts and comparative perspectives*. London: David Fulton: 1–11.

Balagopalan, S. (2003) '"These children are slow": Some experience of inclusion, formal schooling, and the Advasi child'. *Perspectives in Education*, 2(3): 13–25.

Ballard, K. (1995) 'Inclusion, paradigms: Power and participation'. In Clark, C., Dyson, A. and Millward, A. (eds) *Towards Inclusive Schools?*. London: David Fulton: 1–14.

Barkley, R.A. (1996) 'Attention-deficit/hyperactivity disorder'. In Mash, E.J. and Barkley, R.A. (eds) *Child Psychopathology*. New York: Guilford Press: 71–126.

Barkley, R.A. (1997) *ADHD and the Nature of Self-control*. New York: Guilford Press.

Booth, T. and Ainscow, M. (1998) *From Them to Us: An international study of inclusion in education*. London: Routledge.

Corbett, J. and Slee, R. (2000) 'An international conversation on inclusive education'. In

Armstrong, D., Armstrong, F. and Barton, L. (eds) *Inclusive Education: Policy, contexts and comparative perspectives*. London: David Fulton: 133–146.

Department of Education (1997) 'Quality education for all: Overcoming barriers to learning and development'. Report of the National Commission on Special Needs in Education and Training (NCSNET) and the National Commission on Education Support Services (NCESS). Pretoria: Department of Education.

Department of Education (July 2001) *Education White Paper 6: Special Education: Building an inclusive education and training system*. Pretoria: Department of Education.

Donald, D., Lazarus, S. and Lolwana, P. (2002) *Educational Psychology in Social Context*. Cape Town: Oxford University Press Southern Africa.

Fredrick, B.P. and Olmi, D.J. (1994) 'Children with attention-deficit/hyperactivity: A review of literature on social skills deficits'. *Psychology in Schools*, 31: 288–295.

Hill, R.W., and Castro, E. (2002) *Getting Rid of Ritalin*. Charlotteville, VA: Hampton Roads Publishing Company.

Howell, C. (2003) 'A Critical Analysis of White Paper 6.' Unpublished manuscript. Cape Town: Education Policy Unit, University of Western Cape.

Hyperactive/Attention Deficit Disorder Support Group of South Africa (2004) Untitled document. http://www.mutiman.co.za/H/hyper.html. accessed November 2003.

James, A. and Prout, A. (1997) *Constructing and Reconstructing Childhood*. Basingstoke: Falmer Press.

Litner, B. (2003) 'Teens with ADHD: The challenge of high school'. *Child and Youth Care Forum*, 32(3): 137–158.

Lloyd, G. and Norris, C. (1999) 'Including ADHD?' *Disability and Society*, 14(4): 505–517.

*Mail and Guardian* (June 1999) 'Ritalin Kids: Doped to wake up or shut up'.

Merrell, K.W. and Boelter, E. (2001) 'An investigation of relationships between social behaviour and ADHD in children and youth'. *Journal of Emotional and Behavioral Disorders*, 9(4): 35–58.

Meyer, A. (1998) 'Attention deficit/hyperactivity disorder among North Sotho speaking primary school children in South Africa: Prevalence and sex ratios'. *Journal of Psychology in Africa*, 8: 186–195.

Muthukrishna, N. and Schoeman, M. (2000) 'From "Special Needs" to "Quality Education for All": A participatory problem-centred approach to policy development in South Africa'. *International Journal of Inclusive Education*, 4(4): 315–336.

O'Kane, C. (2000) 'The development of participatory techniques'. In Christensen, P. and James, A. (eds) *Research with Children*. London: Falmer Press: 136–159.

Parker, H. (1999) *Put Yourself in Their Shoes*. Plantation, FL: Impact Publications.

Sameroff, A. (1975) 'Transactional models in early social relations'. *Human Development*, 18: 65–79.

Sameroff, A. (1991) 'The social context of development'. In Wood, M., Light, P. and Carr, R. (eds) *Becoming a Person*. London: Routledge: 167–189.

Saunders, B. and Chambers, S.M. (1996) 'A review of literature on attention-deficit/hyperactivity disorder in children: Peer interactions and collaborative learning'. *Psychology in Schools*, 33: 333–340.

Sayeed, Y. (2003) 'Educational inclusion and exclusion: Key debates and issues'. *Perspectives in Education*, 2(3): 1–12.

Weiss, G. and Hechtman, L. (1993) *Hyperactive Children Grown Up*. Second edition. New York: Guilford Press.

Whalen, C.K. and Henker, B. (1998) 'Attention-deficit/hyperactivity disorder'. In Ollendick, T.H. and Hersen, M. (eds) *Handbook of Child Psychopathology*. New York: Plenum: 63–81.

# Chapter 7

# 'ADHD' and parenting styles

*Üstün Öngel*

It has been widely accepted that so-called Attention Deficit and Hyperactivity Disorder (ADHD) is biologically and neurologically determined and has nothing to do with parenting styles, poor parenting or difficult family environment. While this scientifically unsupported claim has been primarily promoted by psychiatrists, psychologists have not hesitated to jump on to the bandwagon either. As comprehensively outlined in a letter from eleven American psychologists to the American Psychological Association (APA) on May 15, 2003, following the APA's distribution of the ADHD brochure in which ADHD was presented as a biological and neurological disorder that has no connection whatsoever with family environment: 'this is disenfranchisement of our particular perspective on ADHD from our own professional organization' (Galves *et al.* 2003: 19).

This is sheer politics. Not science, just politics. Basically there are two factors underlying this politics. One is the obvious combined power of the pharmaceutical industry together with the institution of psychiatry, the other is the untouchable 'sacred' family. Not only for ADHD, this is true for any known psychological suffering. Take for example Bateson *et al.*'s (1956) 50-year-old 'double-bind' theory on schizophrenia. As comprehensively documented in Koopmans' review (1997), it has never been truly scientifically refuted, yet the institution of psychiatry not only continues to ignore it, it also holds a belief that schizophrenia is a 'brain disorder'.

This is simply not true. Neither schizophrenia nor ADHD nor any psychological suffering is a brain disorder. Even the diagnosis of ADHD is far from being valid, as promoters of neuro-biological aetiology have confessed: 'Because of the inability to demonstrate consistent neurobiological differences between hyperactive children and normal controls, the validity of the hyperactivity syndrome remains controversial' (National Center for Biotechnology Information 2004). There is not a single research study to date that has clearly verified that any psychological suffering is a brain disorder. No objective biological finding, no objective brain mapping. Findings that show an association between 'abnormal behaviour' and brain do not conclusively prove that there is a causal relationship between the two. It is widely known that an association between two entities does not mean that there is a causal relation between them. Yet as seen in one of the most publicized studies (Zametkin *et al.* 1990), very poor findings derived from adults were promoted in and out of psychiatric circles as proving that 'the biological evidence for ADHD is found'. Besides, these poor findings have not been replicated even by Zametkin himself (Zametkin *et al.* 1993) in a study with adolescents (on the web site of the National Center for Biotechnology which is mentioned above, Zametkin *et al.*'s 1990 study is listed, but not the 1993 study).

While these biological and neurological claims are far from being scientifically verified, psycho-social explanations for ADHD and for any psychological suffering have been convincingly presented in the psychological literature. Yet the majority of psychologists together with almost all psychiatrists are willingly choosing to accept the bio-neurological explanations.

As listed in the letter to the APA (Galves *et al.* 2003) the scientific evidence demonstrates that ADHD is significantly associated with poor parenting, difficult family environments and inhumane and oppressive school and community environments. Here I propose to re-list a few of the characteristics of parenting and family environments that have an association with the behavioural characteristics of ADHD, with some additions of my own.

- Family instability, differences in pressure for achievement in the family, provision for early learning, disciplinary practices, interest in the child's schooling, negative and pessimistic perception by parents of the child's academic and intellectual competencies accompanied by decreased expectation levels and decreased desire to participate with the child in learning activities (Lambert and Hartsough 1984).
- Mothers' use of criticism and general malaise in parenting (Goodman and Stevenson 1989).
- Father's hypercritical and destructive attitude, inconsistent, impatient and pressuring parenting approach and mothers who are judged to be emotionally disturbed (Thomas and Chess 1977).
- A negative, critical and commanding style of child management (Campbell 1990).
- Parental distress, hostility and marital discord (Cameron 1977).
- Parents who use aggressive behaviour, indiscriminate aversiveness and submissiveness or acquiescence toward their children during management encounters (Patterson 1982).
- Experiences of high levels of stress in parenting and feelings of lower self-esteem (Goldstein and Goldstein 1998).
- Mothers who were critical of their difficult babies during infancy and showed lack of affection for them continued to be disapproving and tended to use severe penalties for disobedience during the primary school years and assessed their children's intelligence as low (Ross and Ross 1982).
- Overinvolved parenting style is associated with the child's decreased perception of control over events (Hudson and Rapee 2001).
- Conflictual and negative parental behaviour directed specifically at the child (Reiss *et al.* 1995).

- Evidence suggests that the presence of ADHD in children is associated to varying degrees with disturbances in family and marital functioning, disrupted parent–child relationships, specific patterns of parental cognitions about child behaviour and reduced parenting self-efficacy, and increased levels of parenting stress and parental psychopathology, particularly when ADHD is comorbid with conduct problems (Johnston and Mash 2001).
- Low self-esteem in mothers, low parenting efficacy in fathers, and fathers' attributions of noncompliance to their ADHD child's insufficient effort and bad mood, mothers' external locus of control (Hoza *et al.* 2000).

## Attachment and trauma

There are two areas of research – *attachment and trauma* – that have shown the impact of early familial experience on the traits characteristic of ADHD, and one area of research – *parenting styles* – that have successfully shown how powerful the parenting styles could be in producing and overcoming the problems related to ADHD.

It has been documented that there is a significant relationship between the quality of parent–child relationships in the first months of life, the quality of attachment at one year of age and the school performance, sociability, levels of anxiety and even general health of children in primary and secondary school (Bowlby 1988; Cummings and Cicchetti 1990; Crittenden 1992; Goldberg *et al.* 1995; Holmes 1995). Indeed the behaviours that are used to diagnose ADHD can be seen as the natural and understandable reaction of an insecure child to a stressful situation (Erdman 1998; Clarke *et al.* 2002).

On the other hand, research studies on trauma suggest that traumatic experiences early in life have a great impact on the ability of victims to adjust their emotions (van der Kolk *et al.* 1996; Herman 2000). Trauma victims almost always display impulsiveness, high activation, or exactly the opposite, very low activation. *These are precisely the behaviours that are used to diagnose ADHD.*

It is also known that the serious effects of trauma are transmitted across generations, as seen in children of Holocaust survivors (Rowland-Klein and Dunlop 1998), which by itself can be seen as a refutation of highly promoted genetic transmission of many psychological disturbances. Furthermore, Deutsch *et al.* (1982) found that adopted children are much more likely to be diagnosed with ADHD than non-adopted children. This is quite understandable in view of the fact that all adopted children have suffered the trauma of being taken away from their birth mothers and that most of them were raised by over-protective/permissive adoptive mothers (parents).

## Parenting styles

Baumrind's (1967) authoritative research study on parenting styles is one strong tool in the understanding of developmental problems in a spectrum, and indeed of problems related to so-called ADHD. Although the study was not designed to look into the ADHD syndrome (ADHD was not popular at all in the 1960s), it includes almost every feature of ADHD.

Before looking at the details of Baumrind's parenting styles model and how inadvertently it explains the ADHD syndrome, it is worth mentioning the methodological strength of the model. It has been repeatedly emphasized that a true diagnosis of ADHD should be done by careful observation of children's behaviours both at home and at school (and also preferably at a neutral location and not just at the doctor's office). However, we all know that only a few psychiatrists and psychologists are in conformity with this basic principle: whereas in Baumrind's research study, not only the children but also the parents were observed at home and at school.

Based on fourteen weeks of observations, Baumrind identified three groups of children who differed considerably in their behaviour:

1   Energetic-friendly children (self-reliant, self-controlled, cooperative with adults, purposive);
2   Conflicted-irritable children (aimless, easily annoyed, lack of self-control, lack of self-reliance);
3   Impulsive-aggressive children (aimless, lack of self-control, lack of self-reliance).

Baumrind then interviewed the parents of these children and observed them interacting with their children. She found three distinctive patterns of parenting which were associated with the three groups of children as follows (see Table 7.1):

Authoritative parenting → Energetic-friendly child
Authoritarian parenting → Conflicting-irritable child
Permissive parenting → Impulsive-aggressive child

*Table 7.1* Parenting styles and children's behaviour

| Parental type | Children's behaviour |
| --- | --- |
| *Permissive-indulgent parent* | *Impulsive-aggressive children* |
| • Rules not enforced | • Resistive, non-compliant to adults * |
| • Rules not clearly communicated | • Low in self-reliance * |
| • Yields to coercion, whining, nagging, crying by the child | • Low in achievement orientation * |
| • Inconsistent discipline | • Lacking in self-control * |
| • Few demands or expectations for mature, independent behaviour | • Aggressive * |
| • Ignores or accepts bad behaviour | • *Impulsive* ** |
| • Hides impatience, anger, and annoyance | • Quick to anger but fast to recover cheerful mood * |
| • Moderate warmth | • *Aimless, low in goal-directed activities* ** |
| • Glorification of importance of free expression of impulses and desires | • Domineering ** |

*Table 7.1* continued

| Authoritarian parent | Conflicted-irritable children |
|---|---|
| • Rigid enforcement rules<br>• Confronts and punishes bad behaviour<br>• Shows anger and displeasure<br>• Rules not clearly explained<br>• View of child as dominated by uncontrolled antisocial impulses<br>• Child's desires and opinions not considered or solicited<br>• Persistent in enforcement of rules in the face of oppositions and coercion<br>• Harsh, punitive discipline<br>• Low in warmth and positive involvement<br>• No cultural events or mutual activities planned<br>• No educational demands or standards | • Fearful, apprehensive *<br>• Moody, unhappy *<br>• Easily annoyed *<br>• Passively hostile and guileful *<br>• Vulnerable to stress *<br>• Alternates between aggressive unfriendly behaviour and sulky withdrawal *<br>• *Aimless* ** |

| Authoritative parent | Energetic-friendly children |
|---|---|
| • Firm enforcement rules<br>• Does not yield to child coercion<br>• Confronts disobedient child<br>• Shows displeasure and annoyance in response to child's bad behaviour<br>• Shows pleasure and support of child's constructive behaviour<br>• Rules clearly communicated<br>• Alternatives offered<br>• Considers child's wishes and solicits child's opinions<br>• Warm, involved, responsive<br>• Expects mature, independent behaviour appropriate for the child's age<br>• Cultural events and joint activities planned<br>• Educational standards set and enforced | • Self-reliant<br>• *Self-controlled*<br>• High energy level ✔<br>• Cheerful<br>• *Friendly relations with peers*<br>• Copes well with stress<br>• *Interest and curiosity in novel situations*<br>• *Co-operative with adults*<br>• Tractable<br>• *Purposive*<br>• *Achievement-oriented* |

Source: From Baumrind 1967: 43–88.

Note: Please see text for an explanation of the use of italics and asterisks in this table.

The characteristics of the authoritarian, permissive, and authoritative approaches to discipline were summarized by Baumrind (1978) as follows:

1   *The authoritative parent* attempts to direct the child's activities in a rational issue oriented manner. He or she encourages verbal give and take, shares with the child the reasoning behind parental policy, and solicits the child's objections when the child refuses to conform. Both autonomous self-will and discipline conformity are valued. Therefore, this parent exerts firm control when the young child disobeys, but does not hem the child in with restrictions. The authoritative parent enforces the adult perspective, but recognizes the child's individual interests and special ways. Such a parent affirms the child's present qualities, but also sets standards for future conduct, using reason as well as power and shaping by regimen and reinforcement to achieve parental objectives.

2   *The authoritarian parent* values obedience as a virtue and favors punitive, forceful measures to curb self-will at points where the child's actions or beliefs conflict with what the parents thinks is right. The authoritarian parent believes in keeping the child in a subordinate role and in restricting his autonomy, and does not encourage verbal give and take, believing that the child should accept a parent's word for what is right. Authoritarian parents may be very concerned and protective or they may be neglecting.

3   *The permissive prototype* of adult control requires the parent to behave in an affirmative, acceptant, and benign manner towards the child's impulses and actions. The permissive parent sees him- or herself as resource for the child to use as he wishes but not as an active agent responsible for shaping and altering the child's ongoing and future behaviour. The immediate aim of the ideologically aware permissive parent is to free the child from restraint as much as is consistent with survival. Some permissive parents are very protective and loving, while others are self involved and offer freedom as a way of evading responsibility for the child's development.

(Baumrind 1978)

What are the results of these models of discipline for preschool children? As can be seen in Table 7.1, it appears that authoritative parents are most effective in *controlling undesirable behaviour* while authoritarian parents tend to have children who are *fearful, unhappy, less assertive* and *aimless*. Children of authoritative parents are more likely to be *self-reliant, explorative, self-controlled, friendly, cheerful* and *cooperative* while children of permissive parents tended to be the *least self-controlled, self-reliant* and *explorative* of all the three groups.

Surprisingly, many of the behaviours of permissive-indulgent parents' and authoritarian parents' children are exactly the same behaviours characteristic to ADHD. The behaviours with two stars in Table 7.1 are exactly the same as ADHD behaviours. The ones with one star are also similar to ADHD behaviours, but to a lesser degree. Moreover, the children of permissive parents are identified as 'impulsive' children, exactly the same as in ADHD's 'hyperactivity-*impulsiveness*' category.

Being 'aimless', as highlighted in *italics* in Table 7.1, seems to be the common characteristic of children of both permissive and authoritarian parents. Indeed, ADHD children who are diagnosed with a checklist that has no scientific validity suffer from primarily 'being aimless' (they act with no specific purpose) not from 'HYPER-activity'. One of the distinct characteristics of children of authoritative parents is 'high energy level' (as highlighted with '✔' in Table 7.1) which is desirable. He or she is 'energetic' and 'purposive' at the same time. As a consequence, the problem DOES NOT lie in 'high activity level', but in 'aimless' activity. It is highly likely that looking only for 'high activity level' is the main reason that 86 per cent of 375 rural North Carolina Appalachian children who, 'experts' decided, needed to start taking medication did not fulfil the criteria for ADHD (Angold *et al.* 2000). Note that 29 per cent of these children had no ADHD symptoms at all before onset of medication.

## Implications

Baumrind's parenting styles model not only explains how parenting styles are undoubtedly associated with the behaviours characteristic of ADHD (regarding the aetiology of ADHD), it also shows ways to overcome these problems related to ADHD (regarding the remedy).

As highlighted in *italics* in Table 7.1, most of the behavioural patterns that energetic-friendly children display are exactly the opposite of the behaviours characteristic of ADHD-diagnosed children. ADHD-diagnosed children do have problems with their peers, whereas energetic-friendly children don't; ADHD children are not cooperative with adults, whereas energetic-friendly children are; ADHD children are aimless, whereas energetic-friendly children are purposive (and have interest and curiosity in novel situations; i.e. 'purposive curiosity', not 'wandering about without any specific purpose' as in ADHD children); ADHD children do lack self-control and self-reliance, whereas energetic-friendly children are self-controlled and self-reliant; ADHD children are not achievement-oriented, energetic-friendly children are.

As a social psychologist, who has turned to be more of a practising psychologist, I propose that the practitioners in the field should focus on how to improve the parenting skills to help the child to develop such behaviours characteristic of the energetic-friendly child.

This should not prove too difficult to implement once the parents free themselves from the 'good parent–bad parent' syndrome.

Figure 7.1 summarizes the basics of being an effective (authoritative) parent. Four dimensions of parenting that clearly help in developing the desired behaviours of children are as follows:

> *Parental control*: consistency in enforcing directives, ability to resist pressure from the child, willingness to exert influence upon the child.

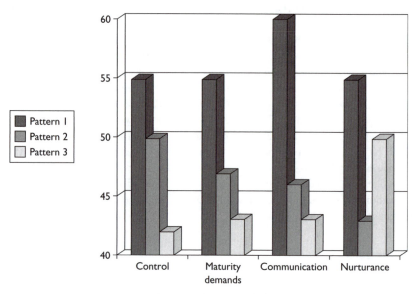

*Figure 7.1* Profile of composited parent dimension scores.
Source: From Baumrind 1967: 73.

*Parental maturity demands*: both the pressures put upon the child to perform at least up to ability in intellectual, social, and emotional spheres (independence training) and flexibility in the choice given the child to make his/her own decisions (independence granting).

*Parent–child communication*: the extent to which the parent uses reason to obtain adaptive behaviour, solicits the child's opinions and feelings, and uses open rather than manipulative techniques of control.

*Parental nurturance*: parental acts and attitudes that express love and are directed at guaranteeing the child's physical and emotional well-being. Nurturance is expressed by warmth and involvement.

(Baumrind 1967: 54–57)

Among the four dimensions, 'communication' seems to be the crucial one. I strongly believe that the simple implementation of 'parental control', as can be seen in 'authoritarian parenting', without improving communication skills will not work. It has been noted that lately some psychiatrists with very poor knowledge in psychology advise parents to use strict control on their ADHD children. However, a strict framework with rules and a behaviouristic approach that relies on a token economy programme (along with poor communication) might make things even worse. It is possible that this same approach is the reason behind the 1999 MTA study suggesting that behaviouristic intervention did not work well with ADHD children. Note that the MTA study was criticized by one of the inspectors of the study (Pelham 1999) not only for its behaviouristic approach, but also for its critical methodological flaws. The study was highly criticized by others, too (e.g. Boyle and Jadad 1999).

Looking at Figure 7.1 again, priority should be given to communication skills. Following that, and supported by my own personal experience with the ADHD children and their parents, I would suggest that maturity demands should be followed by parental control and parental nurturance. Nevertheless, we should bear in mind that all four dimensions should equally be in action at all times.

## Negligence and ignorance

I mentioned in the first paragraph of this chapter the letter to the APA by eleven psychologists which eloquently says 'this is disenfranchisement of our particular perspective on ADHD from our own professional organization' (Galves *et al.* 2003: 19). I would personally add that the APA and most psychologists, by accepting the psychiatric stance, are being negligent and/or ignorant.

Even before Baumrind's (1967) research study on parenting styles, Becker's (1964) research study entitled 'Consequences of Different Kinds of Parental Discipline' clearly demonstrates that children of permissive (detached, indifferent, neglecting and rejecting) parents become *impulsive, goalless*, delinquent, disobedient and aggressive, i.e. all traits characteristic of ADHD. There are also comparatively recent research studies, albeit few, that demonstrate that ADHD behaviours may represent a developmental phenomenon that is largely preventable:

- In Carlson *et al.*'s (1995) prospective, longitudinal research study, 191 firstborn children were followed from infancy to end of sixth grade. They found that for hyperactive children, intrusive and over-stimulating parenting played a prominent role. The authors proposed that development of early parenting skills and social support would play a preventive role.
- Wilson and Wilson (1996), again in a prospective research study, surveyed parents who joined a community parent-training programme and compared the outcomes with no participating parents. The programme taught a nurturing, but structured child-rearing approach, much in the manner of Baumrind's authoritative parenting. When the children were surveyed at ages 4 to 7 years, participants who followed the principles on which the curriculum was based had a substantially lower incidence of DSM-III-R ADHD criteria (5 per cent) than non-participants (16 per cent).
- Further evidence came from another research study done by Stein (1999). Stein has implemented a novel behavioural approach to managing ADHD behaviours and reported encouraging data on the effectiveness of using this approach. Stein's Caregivers Skills Program's (CSP) underlying assumptions are different from the conventional behavioural approach. Stein proposes that ADHD children can be trained to develop those behavioural traits they lack,

and that effective behavioural management relies upon avoiding material reinforcers, incentives or token economy programmes. Reinforcement for appropriate behaviour is stressed, consisting of social reinforcement only. Stein found that eleven of twelve targeted ADHD behaviours improved dramatically or disappeared within four weeks among the 37 children fulfilling DSM-IV criteria for ADHD ages 5 to 11 years. These gains were stable at follow-up one year after intervention.

## Concluding remarks

Last year (in 2004) 84,000 boxes of stimulants were prescribed in Turkey to children diagnosed with ADHD (80 per cent in three big cities, Istanbul, Ankara and Izmir), which approximately equates to 10,000 children with this diagnosis.

Psychological circles in Turkey are acting in line with the APA's approach to the ADHD issue. Psycho-social interventions are non-existent. About two years ago (by the end of 2003), the Turkish Ministry of Education together with psychiatrists and assisting psychologists started a project identifying children with ADHD and then referring them to psychiatry clinics. Reluctantly, I have to say, I was the only psychologist who opposed the project. I had already written many essays on ADHD published in various Turkish newspapers and journals and translated the letter to the APA in full length, and although I could not publish it I have nevertheless distributed it widely by e-mail; and from the moment I learned about the project I did my best to intervene in the process. My solitary intervention and success (if it can be seen as a success) seems to have just slowed down the increase rate of consumption of stimulants (from 11 per cent rise in 2003 to 6 per cent rise in 2004). Yet the project is still in action.

As I have tried to outline in this chapter, we already have powerful psycho-social tools to understand the phenomenon and to produce solutions to the problems related to so-called ADHD. As I will present in detail elsewhere, my research suggests that we can make a major contribution to the solution of the ADHD-type problems *by focusing on parenting styles*, on the basis of Baumrind's (1967) model. The model is also effective with teachers, as brilliantly demonstrated in Wentzel's (2002) study where data were gathered from 452 sixth graders.

Having been highly involved in cross-cultural research, my final remarks would be related to cultural issues both regarding Baumrind's model and the ADHD issue. It has been said, but not confirmed by research, that there is almost no ADHD in Japan. I contacted several Japanese researchers asking for solid evidence for the problem. I have been told that since the problem does not exist in their social context it did not seem necessary to research it. However, I believe that we still need to do cross-cultural research in order to understand the phenomenon in every aspect and to refute bio-neurological claims. Baumrind's model applied to the Chinese culture (Chao 1994, 2001; Chen 1998; Chen *et al.* 1997, 1998, 2000a, 2000b) suggests that despite disparate views presented in these research studies, both perspectives accommodate the notion that parenting patterns may be discussed within Baumrind's parenting styles framework. My own application of Baumrind's model to the Turkish social context will be discussed in detail in a future article.

As I mentioned above, we should focus on how to improve parenting skills in order to help the child to overcome ADHD-type problems. Other than psychiatric neurobiological dominance, there are two major difficulties ahead: one is the negligence and lack of knowledge/ignorance on the part of psychologists, the other is the fragility/sensitivity on the part of parents (mostly mothers). As comprehensively discussed in Singh's (2004) article, in a culture (or rather, cultures) of mother-blame, mothers are desperately trying to do their jobs without the backlash of accusations. Neurobiological explanations and medical interventions serve the purpose of easing their guilt/souls. It is our duty to overcome this problem and include their specific knowledge in our research in order to produce successful results in a short span of time. Once they witness that the approach works almost immediately (to compete with the immediate effect of stimulants), I believe they would not hesitate to proceed with it since the results will be proof of their personal efforts without the help of medication.

## References

Angold, A., Erkanli, A., Egger, E. and Costello, J. (2000) 'Stimulant treatment for children: a community perspective'. *Journal of the American Academy of Child and Adolescent Psychiatry*, 39: 975–994.

Bateson, G., Jackson, D. D., Haley, J. and Weakland, J. (1956) 'Toward a theory of schizophrenia'. *Behavioral Science*, 1: 251–264.

Baumrind, D. (1967) 'Child care practices anteceding three patterns of preschool behaviour'. *Genetic Psychology Monographs*, 75: 43–88.

Baumrind, D. (1978) 'Parental disciplinary patterns and social competence in children'. *Youth and Society*, 9: 239–276.

Becker, W. C. (1964) 'Consequences of different kinds of parental discipline'. In Hoffman, M. L. and Hoffman, L. W. (eds) *Review of Child Development Research*. New York: Russell Sage Foundation: 169–208.

Bowlby, J. (1988) *A Secure Base: Parent–child Attachment and Healthy Human Development*. New York: Basic Books.

Boyle, M. H. and Jadad, A. R. (1999) 'Lessons from large trials: the MTA study as a model for evaluating the treatment of childhood psychiatric disorder'. *Canadian Journal of Psychiatry*, 44: 991–998.

Cameron, J. R. (1977) 'Parental treatment, children's temperament, and the risk of childhood behavioural problems: I. Relationships between parental characteristics and changes in children's temperament over time'. *American Journal of Orthopsychiatry*, 47: 568–576.

Campbell, S. B. (1990) *Behavior Problems in Preschoolers: Clinical and Developmental Issues*. New York: Guilford Press.

Carlson, E. A., Jacobvitz, D. and Stroufe, L. A. (1995) 'A developmental investigation of inattentiveness and hyperactivity'. *Child Development*, 66: 37–54.

Chao, R. K. (1994) 'Beyond parental control and authoritarian parenting style: understanding Chinese parenting through the cultural notion of training'. *Child Development*, 65: 1111–1119.

Chao, R. K. (2001) 'Extending research on the consequences of parenting style for Chinese Americans and European Americans'. *Child Development*, 72: 1832–1843.

Chen, X. (1998) 'The changing Chinese family: resources, parenting practices, and children's social-emotional problems'. In Gielen, U. P. and Comunian, A. L. (eds) *Family and Family Therapy in International Perspective*. Trieste, Italy: Edizioni LINT.

Chen, X., Dong, Q. and Zhou, H. (1997) 'Authoritative and authoritarian parenting practices and social and school performance in Chinese children'. *International Journal of Behavioral Development*, 21: 855–873.

Chen, X., Hastings, P. D., Rubin, K. H., Chen, H., Cen, G. and Stewart, S. L. (1998) 'Child-rearing attitudes and behavioural inhibition in Chinese and Canadian toddlers: a cross-cultural study'. *Developmental Psychology*, 34: 1–10.

Chen, X., Liu, M. and Li, D. (2000) 'Parental warmth, control, and indulgence and their relations to adjustment in Chinese children: a longitudinal study'. *Journal of Family Psychology*, 14: 401–419.

Chen, X., Liu, M., Li, D., Cen, G., Chen, H. and Wang, L. (2000) 'Maternal authoritative and authoritarian attitudes and mother–child interactions and relationships in urban China'. *International Journal of Behavioural Development*, 22: 119–126.

Clarke, L., Ungerer, J. A., Chahaud, K., Johnson, S. and Stiefel, I. (2002) 'Attention deficit hyperactivity disorder is associated with attachment insecurity'. *Clinical Child Psychology and Psychiatry*, 7: 179–198.

Crittenden, P. M. (1992) 'Quality of attachment in the preschool years'. *Development and Psychopathology*, 4: 209–241.

Cummings, E. M. and Cicchetti, D. (1990) 'Toward a transactional model of relations between attachment and depression'. In Greenberg, E. T., Cicchetti, D. and Cummings, E. M. (eds) *Attachment in the Preschool Years: Theory, Research, and Interventions*. Chicago, IL: University of Chicago Press: 339–372.

Deutsch, C. K., Swanson, J. M., Bruell, J. H. and Cantwell, D. V. (1982) 'Over-representation of adoptees in children with attention deficit disorder'. *Behavioural Genetics*, 12: 231–238.

Erdman, P. (1998) 'Conceptualizing ADHD as a contextual response to parental attachment'. *American Journal of Family Therapy*, 26: 177–185.

Galves, A. O., Walker, D., Cohen, D., Schneider, K. J., Greening, T., Karon, B., Dunlap, M., Wetzel, N. A., Friedman, H., Duncan, B. and Johnson, T. (2003) A letter to APA by 11 psychologists. psychrights.org/Articles/replytorubenstein.pdf.

Goldberg, S., Muir, R. and Kerr, J. (eds) (1995) *Attachment Theory: Social, Developmental and Clinical Perspectives*. Hillsdale, NJ: The Analytic Press.

Goldstein, S. and Goldstein, M. (1998) *Managing Attention Deficit-hyperactivity Disorder in Children: A Guide to Practitioners*. New York: John Wiley and Sons.

Goodman, R. and Stevenson, J. (1989) 'A twin study of hyperactivity – II. The aetological role of genes, family relationships and perinatal adversity'. *Journal of Child Psychology and Psychiatry*, 30(5): 691–709.

Herman, J. (2000) *Trauma and Recovery*. New York: Basic Books.

Holmes, J. (1995) '"Something there is that does not love a wall" John Bowlby, attachment theory and psychoanalysis'. In Goldberg, S., Muir, R. and Kerr, J. (eds) *Attachment Theory: Social, Developmental and Clinical Perspectives*. Hillsdale, NJ: The Analytic Press.

Hoza, B., Owens, J. S., Pelham, W. E., Swanson, J. M., Conners, C. K., Hinshaw, S. P., Arnold, L. E. and Kraemer, H. C. (2000) 'Parent cognitions as predictors of child treatment response in attention-deficit/hyperactivity disorder'. *Journal of Abnormal Child Psychology*, 28: 569–583.

Hudson, J. L. and Rapee, R. M. (2001) 'Parent–child interactions and anxiety disorders: an observational study'. *Behaviour Research and Therapy*, 39: 1411–1427.

Johnston, C. and Mash E. J. (2001) 'Families of children with attention-deficit/hyperactivity disorder: review and recommendations for future research'. *Clinical Child and Family Psychology Review*, 4: 183–207.

Koopmans, M. (1997) 'Schizophrenia and the family: double bind theory revisited'. *Dynamical Psychology: An International, Interdisciplinary Journal of Complex Mental Processes*. Retrieved on April 15, 2005, from http://www.goertzel.org/dynapsyc/1997/Koopmans.html.

Lambert, N. M. and Hartsough, C. S. (1984) 'Contribution of predispositional factors to the diagnosis of hyperactivity'. *American Journal of Orthopsychiatry*, 5: 97–109.

MTA Cooperative Group. (1999) 'A 14-month randomized clinical trial of treatment strategies for attention-deficit/hyperactivity disorder. Multimodal treatment study of children with ADHD'. *Archives of General Psychiatry*, 56: 1073–1086.

National Center for Biotechnology Information (2004) 'Hyperactivity of childhood'. Retrieved on 15 February, 2004, from http://www.ncbi.nlm.nih.gov/entrez/dispomim.cgi?id=143465.

Patterson, G. R. (1982) *Coercive Family Process*. Eugene, OR: Castalia.

Pelham, W. E. (1999) 'The NIMH multimodal treatment study for attention-deficit hyper-activity disorder: Just say yes to drugs alone?' *Canadian Journal of Psychiatry*, 44: 981–990.

Reiss, D., Hetherington, E. M., Plomin, R., Howe, G. W., Simmens, S. J., Henderson, S. H., O'Connor, T. J., Bussel, D. A., Anderson, E. R. and Law, T. (1995) 'Genetic questions for environmental studies: differential parenting and psychopathology in adolescence'. *Archives of General Psychiatry*, 52: 925–936.

Ross, D. M. and Ross, S. A. (1982) *Hyperactivity: Current Issues, Research and Theory*. 2nd edn New York: Wiley and Sons.

Rowland-Klein, D. and Dunlop, R. (1998) 'The transmission of trauma across generations: identification with parental trauma in children of Holocaust survivors'. *Australian and New Zealand Journal of Psychiatry*, 32: 358–369.

Singh, I. (2004) 'Doing their jobs: mothering with Ritalin in a culture of mother-blame'. *Social Science and Medicine*, 6: 1193–1205.

Stein, D. B. (1999) 'A medication-free parent management program for children diagnosed as ADHD'. *Ethical Human Sciences and Services*, 1: 61–79.

Thomas, A. and Chess, S. (1977) *Temperament and Development*. New York: Brunner-Mazel.

Van der Kolk, B., McFarlane, A. and Weisaeth, L. (eds) (1996) *Traumatic Stress*. New York: Guilford Press.

Wentzel, K. R. (2002) 'Are effective teachers like good parents? Teaching styles and student adjustment in early adolescence'. *Child Development*, 1: 287–301.

Wilson, D. and Wilson, D. (1996) *Christian Parenting in the Information Age* (Chapter 4). West Jordan, UT: Tricord.

Zametkin, A. J., Nordahl, T. E., Gross, M., King, A. C., Semple, W. E., Rumsey, J., Hamburger, S. and Cohen, R. M. (1990) 'Cerebral glucose metabolism in adults with hyperactivity of childhood onset'. *New England Journal of Medicine*, 323: 1361–1366.

Zametkin, A. J., Liebenauer, L. L., Fitzgerald, G. A., King, A. C., Minkunas, D. V., Herscovitch, P., Yamada, E. M. and Cohen, R. M. (1993) 'Brain metabolism in teenagers with attention-deficit hyperactivity disorder'. *Archives of General Psychiatry*, 50: 333–340.

# Chapter 8

# The Italian saga of ADHD and its treatment

*Maurizio Bonati*

This chapter discusses recent developments in Italy that further promote the diagnosis of ADHD and its treatment by psychotropic medication. It contextualizes this within a description of the Italian health service and the contribution of children's mental health pressure groups.

There is a wide clinical range of mental health conditions, each with different levels of severity, and in which comorbid disorders are often present. Diagnosis can therefore be questionable when symptom threshold for the demarcation between disease and non-disease is driven more by subjectivity than by shared conventional evidence. No psychiatric disorder exists whose pathophysiology has been investigated sufficiently. As a result, no psychiatric disorder has a biological or psychological test that is sufficiently sensitive and specific to contribute alone to the diagnosis.

Although this situation applies to many psychiatric patients, there is a particular concern with children and adolescents, whose disorders are also influenced by development. However, since 1994, the DSM-IV has provided common diagnostic guidelines, and suggestions for better focusing treatments have been available (APA 1994). As a consequence, for many developmental, behavioural, or emotional disorders, including attention deficit/hyperactivity disorders (ADHD), it is necessary to make a clear cut between the eras before and after DSM-IV publication. Such classification systems (taking into also consideration the International Classification of Disease, 10th edition) allow psychiatric disorders such as ADHD to be better defined, considering their complex characteristics and degrees of symptomatology (WHO 1992).

In the 'past era' (before the 1990s), the Italian approach was characterized by an assessment and treatment of 'hyperactivity' based on psychological methods supporting an environmental and social labelling more than an organic view. Concerning such an approach, the anti-psychiatry movement of the late 1970s and early 1980s, particularly active in Italy under the leadership of Franco Basaglia (1968), contributed to supporting more socio-politically oriented attitudes toward mental health management, also involving child and adolescent psychiatry, including hyperactivity. Moreover, it is worth mentioning the fact that Italian psychiatry became autonomous from neurology by law only in 1976 (legge chiave n. 238).

This division of competency in managing mental health disorders was more evident for adult than child and adolescent patients, for whom the longstanding tradition involving a neuropsychiatric approach is still maintained up until today.[1] A less organic view, and, consequently, a less drug-oriented one, characterizes the Italian and European attitudes toward child mental health compared to the American one, for example.

## The Italian health system's framework

The Italian National Health Service, introduced in 1978, provides universal coverage and comprehensive health care free of cost or at a nominal charge at the point of delivery. Care is provided through a network of 196 local health units covering an average of 290,000 people each. One of the most significant features of the system is the gate-keeping function of the general practitioner (family physician). Each Italian resident is required to register with a general practitioner, who is responsible for prescribing drugs and diagnostic procedures and for referring patients to specialists and hospitals. There are about 7,200 general paediatric practitioners (family paediatricians) caring for over 7 million children, the majority of whom are aged under 6 years. Children are assigned to a family paediatrician until they are 6 years old; after this time, the parents can choose to register the child with a general practitioner. Each family paediatrician cares for an average of 850 children, whereas a general practitioner cares for up to 1,800 citizens. Within each local health unit, a child and adolescent mental health service is organized for children less than 18 years old with developmental difficulties and mental disorders. The service's activity is guaranteed by different professionals (mainly psychologists and child psychiatrists) and is carried out in collaboration with other community structures devoted to rehabilitation and to prevention of children's and adolescents' social and behavioural health deterioration.

Although the World Health Report 2001 ranked the Italian health care system second among 191 countries (France was the first) with respect to health status, fairness in financial contribution, and responsiveness to people's expectations of a health care system, the dissatisfaction felt by Italians with respect to the efficiency and quality of their NHS is the highest in Europe. Moreover, tight budgets and the need to restrain rising health care expenditures have led the NHS to undertake several cost-containment measures to encourage cost-conscious behaviour by consumers and providers, accentuating interregional economic and social disparities. In such a context, the Italian mental health care provision for children and adolescents differs widely between and within regions as regards organization, structure and access to public services.

## ADHD's epidemiological profile

According to the levels of prevalence reported in other European countries, and the profile of neuropsychiatric conditions with respect to burden of diseases in

*Table 8.1* Characteristics of Italian epidemiological studies on ADHD using psychological or/and psychiatric diagnostic instruments

| Year | Setting (source of sample) | Population size (n) | Age (yrs) | Sex (F/M) | Diagnostic instrument | Prevalence (%) |
|------|---------------------------|---------------------|-----------|-----------|----------------------|----------------|
| 1982 | 14 schools in 2 regions | 344 | 7–9 | 158/186 | ATRS | 12.0 |
| 1991 | 9 schools in 2 cities of 2 regions | 232 | 8–10 | 105/107* | ad hoc TQ (DSM III-R based) likely cases 3.9 possible cases 6.9 | 10.8 |
| 1995 | 6 schools in 1 province | 160 | 6–12 | 21/139 | TRS-C | 2.0 |
| 1995–6 | 2 schools in 2 towns of 1 region | 973 | 7–10 | 463/510 | TRS-C; SDAI; DBL | 1.5 |
| 1999 | 3 family paediatric clinics in Rome | 794 | 6–15 | 380/414 | TRS-C; PSQ-C; WISC-R | 1.5 |
| 2002 | 21 schools in 5 cities of 5 regions | 1,085 | 7–11 | 596/489 | DBD; PICS-IV | 1.5 |
| 2003 | 40 schools in 7 cities of 6 regions | 3,437 | 10–14 | – | CBCL; HoNOSCA; C-GAS; DAWBA | >2.0 |
| 2003 | 1 local health unit | 131** | 7–14 | – | RPTS; HoNOSCA | 1.1 |

ATRS: Abbreviated Teacher Rating Scale; TQ: Teacher Questionnaire; TRS-C: Teacher Rating Scale-Conners; SDAI: Teacher Rating Scale for Disorders of Attention and Hyperactivity; DBL: Daily Behaviour Checklist; PSQ-C: Parent Scale Questionnaire-Conners; WISC-R: Wechsler Intelligence Scale for Children-Revised; DBD: teacher and parent ratings for Disruptive Behaviour Disorders; PICS-IV: Parent Interview for Child Symptom; CBCL: Child Behaviour Check List; HoNOSCA: Health of Nation Outcome Scales for Children and Adolescents-Reduced; C-GAS: Children-Global Assessment Scale; DAWBA: Development and Well Being Assessment; RPTS: Rutter Parents' and Teachers' Scales.

* For 20 children sex was not reported. ** Reference population: 11,980 children.

*Table 8.2* Characteristics of the Italian population-based surveys on ADHD involving family paediatricians

| Year | Setting | Population size (n) | Age (yrs) | Retrieval instrument | Prevalence |
|------|---------|---------------------|-----------|----------------------|------------|
| 1998 | 56 paediatricians in Turin | 47,781 | 0–14 | Interview to paediatricians | 2.5 |
| 2002 | 74 paediatricians of 1 region | 64,800 | 0–14 | Questionnaire to paediatricians | 0.4 |
| 2002–3 | 3 paediatricians in Rome | 1,586 | 6–15 | Clinical form review | 1.1 |

European children and adolescents (www.who.int/topics/global_burden_of_disease), mental disorders affect around 20 per cent of the Italian population aged 4–14 years. However, the accuracy of such estimates is weak because of the numerous limitations in controlling for the variables involved (i.e. patients' age, setting, diagnostic criteria and instruments, etc.). Once again, the conventional 1994 watershed, based on DSM-IV publication, can be useful. During the 'past era' ADHD was covered more thoroughly in the literature by anecdotal cases (case reports) than by systematic, population-based evaluations. Two epidemiological studies were conduced in Italian schools using teacher questionnaires, but the methodological limitations compromised the findings (Table 8.1). Six studies using standardized screening or diagnostic instruments established ADHD prevalence in the Italian paediatric population. Despite the diversity in instruments used and the settings involved, the prevalence values were close. The disorder is estimated to affect 1–2 per cent of Italian school-aged children and adolescents (6–15 years), and is more frequent in males than females. Similar estimates (Table 8.2) were observed in three population-based surveys by submitting questionnaires or interviews to family paediatricians, or reviewing their clinical forms.

## National level management of ADHD: new directions

Methylphenidate (Ritalin®) was withdrawn from the market in Italy in October 1989 by the manufacturer (Ciba) because of low sales and, probably, also because of its increasing illicit use. Since then, the majority of children treated for ADHD have been given tricyclic antidepressants, benzodiazepines, and many questionable, not evidence-based drugs. During this following decade, the lack of availability of methylphenidate and other psychostimulants for therapeutic use was not perceived as a need. It was only in October 2000 that this situation led a group of parents of ADHD children and their paediatricians to lobby the Ministry of Health for the immediate reintroduction of methylphenidate. As a consequence, a neurodevelopmental disorder that had almost been ignored until then by the Italian health community (obviously not by the families), became apparent. The pros and cons discussion on the use of stimulants in children grew widely. In March 2003, a national Consensus Conference that focused on therapeutic strategies for children and adolescents with ADHD was held. Suggestions for the planning of future interventions, as part of a comprehensive, diagnostic, therapeutic and follow-up approach aimed at providing appropriate, standard care to ADHD children and their families were made and shared widely (Table 8.3). In the same year, national guidelines for ADHD diagnosis and therapy were also produced by the Italian Society of Child and Adolescent Neuropsychiatry (SINPIA).

The national Drug Regulatory Agency began dealing with the complex situation that also needed legislative measures and, in 2003, transferred methylphenidate from the Table I list of the Italian Pharmacopoeia to the Table IV list. The latter is less restrictive and acknowledged the drug indication for ADHD treatment in children (≥6 years), based on individual therapeutic schemes and the compulsory

*Table 8.3* Proposals from the National Consensus Conference on ADHD

**Suggested undertakings**

- A census of the existing, reference care centres and the patients currently under care. This task should be carried out by the SINPIA (Italian Society of Child and Adolescent Neuropsychiatry) and by the parents' associations.
- A formal, epidemiological study to estimate the national ADHD and associated disorders rates and the diagnostic and therapeutic approaches in use.
- A national registry of ADHD cases related to methylphenidate prescriptions when the drug is reintroduced onto the market.

**Directions**

- The diagnosis of ADHD and other disorders with similar symptoms must be made by child and adolescent mental health physicians and should involve the child, the parents, the teachers, and the family paediatrician from the beginning.
- The treatment scheme must involve proper guidance and support for parents and teachers, as well as specific psychological interventions. Pharmacological treatment should be pursued only when suggested by a child and adolescent mental health physician, and should be based on the evidence acknowledged by the international community. The physician should also coordinate and monitor the child's welfare together with social workers and the family.
- It is necessary to lay out a national scheme (with district and regional connections) especially designed for diagnosing ADHD that will allow an accurate evaluation in order to provide the best care to children and their families.

registration in the national registry. Stimulants should, in fact, be prescribed judiciously and monitored carefully, also to prevent overuse. This possibility is worrisome in Italy, given the lack of knowledge about the syndrome's incidence, the lack of awareness of diagnostic criteria and therapeutic guidelines in general practice, and the documented adverse reactions that require systematic monitoring. In 2004, a strategic, national-level intervention was therefore planned, involving the setting up of a prospective registry of ADHD cases treated with methylphenidate, through which data on ADHD diagnosis and management could be collected and monitored. This intervention was based on the suggestions and indications of the Consensus, and was coordinated by a commission and the Italian Health Institute (ISS). At the beginning of 2005, the marketing authorization was granted for methylphenidate. The drug was to be placed on the market (by Aventis) and the national registry was to be activated with the cooperation of the local child and adolescent mental health services.

## The political context

The cultural context plays an important role in structuring the environment in which the mental health condition is understood and treated. The cultural environment may therefore affect the attitudes of parents, clinicians and society towards ADHD. Given the complexity of a behavioural disorder such as ADHD, which affects children in particular and for which no specific cognitive, metabolic or neurological markers nor medical tests exist, it is not surprising that the debate within the social society (including in Italy) is heated and often scantly scientific. At present, three main groups are the protagonists of the Italian discussion concerning ADHD: AIDAI (www.aidai.org), AIFA (www.aifa.it), and 'Giù le mani dai bambini' (www.giulemanidaibambini.org). AIDAI (Associazione Italiana Disturbi di Attenzione/Iperattività) is a non-profit association founded in 1996 by a group of child psychologists and psychiatrists and parents of ADHD children. Its mission is: to provide accurate and effective information for parents, teachers and health professionals; to set up a network among families, schools, social-health services and universities; to organize courses, meetings and scientific congresses concerning ADHD; and to promote research on ADHD. Its general approach is characterized by a psychological (behavioural, cognitive and dynamic) more than a psychiatric and psychopharmacological attitude.

AIFA (Associazione Italiana Famiglie ADHD) is a non-profit association founded in 2002 by a group of parents of ADHD children. The core of the association's mission is based on the 'Parents for parents' project, whose main objective is to help parents through lobbying and different educational initiatives. Its activities are based especially on the availability and use of psychotropic drugs in children with ADHD as part of the disorder's therapy.

'Giù le mani dai bambini' is a movement organized in 2004 by a few thousand lay people and a few health professionals concerned about the potential abuse of psychotropics in children and adolescents. It is a lobby group that organizes initiatives, especially through the media, against the pharmacological treatment of ADHD in children. Its activities are supported by a few politicians of differing political stances who have asked questions or raised the issue in the Parliamentary Chamber or regional and local authorities.

## Conclusions

Although methylphenidate is the first-line pharmacological treatment for ADHD, its use should be limited to cases in which it is strictly necessary and should be part of a multimodal therapeutic approach based on the different forms of the disorder. ADHD prevalence in Italian children (6–15 years old) is seen to be 1–2 per cent. Methylphenidate was withdrawn from the Italian market in 1989 and no other stimulant is available. Methylphenidate will be reintroduced in 2005, and a prospective national registry will be set up to collect data as part of a plan to monitor its use and safety as well as the diagnosis and management of ADHD in general. An educational campaign for physicians, psychologists, school-teachers and parents is, however, necessary to overcome the gap between the need for care and the neglected rights of Italian children with ADHD and their families.

## Notes

1   It is under the leadership of Giovanni Bollea that, since the end of the Second World War, the child neuropsychiatry discipline has grown in Italy. For the first time, Bollea introduced the psychoanalytical approach and group psychotherapy with children in practice and in the academia. His approach, way of teaching and mission remain a reference point for professionals and lay people.

## Bibliography

American Psychiatric Association (1994) *Diagnostic and Statistical Manual of Mental Disorders*, 4th edition. Washington, DC: APA.

Basaglia F. (1968) *L'istituzione negata*. Torino: Einaudi.

Bert, G. (1978) 'Preface' to Schrag, P. and Divoky, D., *Il mito del bambino iperattivo*. Milano: Feltrinelli. [Italian translation of: *The Myth of the Hyperactive Child and Other Means of Child Control* (1995). New York: Pantheon Books.]

Besana, D., Bonati, M., Calzone, C., Carpiniello, B., Cianchetti, C., Cornoldi, C., Curatolo, P., Dessi, F., D'Errico, R., Drago, F., Fratta, W., Garattini, S., Gessa, G.L., Marzocchi, G.M., Masi, G., Morosini, P., Omerini, M., Pancheri, P., Pintor, C. and Zuddas, A. (2003) 'Indicazioni e strategie terapeutiche per i bambini e gli adolescenti con ADHD'. *Medico e Bambino*, 22: 383–386.

Besoli, G. and Venier, D. (2003) 'Il disturbo di attenzione con iperattività: indagine conoscitiva tra i pediatri di famiglia in Friuli-Venezia Giulia'. *Quaderni acp*, X: 8–9.

Bonati, M. and Clavenna, A. (2005) 'The epidemiology of psychotropic drug in children and adolescents'. *International Review of Psychiatry* (in press).

Buitelaar, J.K. and Rothenberger, A. (2004) 'Foreword – ADHD in the scientific and political context'. *Eur. Child Adolesc. Psychiatry* 13[Suppl 1]: I/1–I/6.

Camerini, G.B., Coccia, M. and Caffo, E. (1996) 'Il disturbo da deficit dell'attenzione-iperattività: analisi della frequenza in una popolazione scolastica attraverso questionari agli insegnanti'. *Psichiatria dell'infanzia e dell'adolescenza*, 63: 587–594.

Ciotti, F. (1989) 'Il bambino iperattivo: una esperienza italiana'. *Acta Paediatr. Lat.*, 42: 340–348.

Ciotti, F. (2003) 'La sindrome ipercinetica 'pura' fra gli alunni nel territorio cesenate'. *Quaderni acp*, X: 18–20.

Corbo, S., Marolla, F., Sarno, V., Torrioli, M.G. and Vernacotola, S. (2003) 'Prevalenza dell'ADHD in bambini seguiti dal Pediatra di Famiglia'. *Medico e Bambino*, 1: 22–25.

Dwivedi, K.N. and Banhatti, R.G. (2005) 'Attention deficit/hyperactivity disorder and ethnicity'. *Arch. Dis. Child*, 90: i10–i12.

Ferrara, M. (1995) 'The rise and fall of democratic universalism: health care reform in Italy, 1978–1994'. *Journal of Health Polity Policy Law*, 20: 275–302.

Gallucci, F., Bird, H., Berardi, C., Gallai, V., Pfanner, P. and Weinberg, A. (1993) 'Symptoms of attention-deficit hyperactivity disorder in an Italian school sample: findings of a pilot study'. *J. Am. Child Adolescent Psychiatry*, 32: 1051–1058.

Levi, G. (1973) 'Comportamento ipercinetico e percezione'. *Neuropsichiatria Infantile*, 141(2): 131–143.

Levi, G. and Penge, R. (1999) 'Un'esperienza italiana pilota nel campo della salute mentale'. In Levi, G. (ed.) *Una finestra sull'infanzia*. Roma: Borla: 9–17.

Maio, V. and Manzoli, L. (2003) 'The Italian health care system: WHO ranking versus public perception'. *PandT*, 27: 301–308.

Marchini, L., Puzzo, F., Pirella, A., Pandolfini, C., Campi, R., Impicciatore, P. and Bonati, M. 'Se non sta fermo solo in USA scatta la ricetta'. *Occhio Clinico Pediatria*, 4: 12–14.

Marzocchi, G.M. and Cornoldi, C. (2000) 'Una scala di facile uso per la rilevazione dei comportamenti problematici dei bambini con Deficit di Attenzione e Iperattività'. *Psicologia Clinica dello Sviluppo*, IV: 43–63.

Molteni, M. *et al.* (n.d.) Progetto PrISMA (Progetto Italiano Salute Mentale Adolescenti) Irccs Eugenio Medea – La Nostra Famiglia: Bosisio Parini (LC).

O'Leary, K.D., Vivian, D. and Cornoldi, C. (1984) 'Assessment and treatment of "hyper-activity" in Italy and the United States'. *Journal Clinical Child Psychology*, 13: 56–60.

O'Leary, K.D., Vivian, D. and Nisi, A. (1985) 'Hyperactivity in Italy'. *Journal of Abnormal Child Psychology*, 13:485–509.

Panei, P., Arcieri, R., Vella, S., Bonati, M., Martini, N. and Zuddas, A. (2004) 'Italian Attention-Deficit/Hyperactivity Disorder Registry'. *Paediatrics*, 114: 514.

Rappley, M.D. (2005) 'Clinical practice. Attention deficit-hyperactivity disorder'. *N. Engl. J. Med.*, 352: 165–173.

Sarno, V. (2003) 'Il pediatra alle prese con i problemi psicorelazionali: uno studio pilota'. *Medico e Bambino*, 1: 9–12.

Società Italiana di Neuropsichiatria dell'Infanzia e dell'Adolescenza (2004) 'Linee-guida per il Disturbo da Deficit Attentivo con Iperattività (ADHD) in età evolutiva. Diagnosi e terapia farmacologia' (a cura di Masi, G. e Zuddas, A.) *Giornale di Neuropsichiatria dell'Età Evolutiva*, 24(1): 41–87.

World Health Organization (1992) *International Classification of Disease*, 10th edition. Geneva: WHO.

World Health Organization (2001) *The World Health Report 2001 – Mental Health: New Understanding, New Hope*. Geneva: WHO.

Zuddas, A., Marzocchi, G.M., Oosterlaan, J., Cavolina, P., Ancilletta, B. and Sergeant, J.A. (2005) 'Factor structure and cultural factors of Disruptive Behaviour Disorders Symptoms in Italian children'. *European Psychiatry* (in press).

# Chapter 9

# How does the decision to medicate children arise in cases of 'ADHD'?

## Views of parents and professionals in Canada

*David Cohen*

In 1998, the author and his colleagues conducted the first survey of the use of stimulants in public elementary schools in Canada. We had been asked by the regional planning board of the city of Laval, Quebec, to help devise effective ways to deliver health and social services to families living in the Laval area. The controversy over the diagnosis of ADHD and the use of stimulants had been underway for years, yet, besides occasional press releases from commercial medical information firms, no data revealed the proportion of Canadian children receiving stimulants. Surveying all public elementary school teachers in Laval, where approximately 28,000 children between the ages of 6 and 12 were attending public schools, we calculated that 2 percent of girls and 7 percent of boys were taking prescribed stimulants (Cohen *et al.* 1999). These figures, the first solid prevalence estimates of stimulant use in Quebec, were widely cited in media reports. Because the figures suggested a situation comparable to what had often been painted in the media as 'excessive' prescription rates existing in the United States, they sparked even more controversy.

For this author, these figures pointed to the singular absence of data or perspectives on a simple question: just *how* did the option to medicate children with stimulant drugs arise in typical settings such as schools, where children were identified as being affected with the condition ADHD? Were teachers directing children manifesting obvious symptoms of ADHD in schools to the proper authorities who would confirm the diagnosis and prescribe the proper treatment? By the late 1990s, although issues surrounding ADHD and its drug treatment had been receiving a phenomenal amount of public attention in North America, few empirical observations published in scientific or professional journals enabled us to provide an adequate answer to this question.

The issue then required, and still requires today, much more study. Indeed, in the United States and Canada, widely disparate rates of the use of stimulants were reported within neighboring counties, provinces or states (Rappley *et al.* 1995; Rees 1999) and between different racial or ethnic groups within the same states (Zito *et al.* 1998; Lefever *et al.* 1999; Cohen 2000). Of course, the same large disparities were reported between North America and the rest of the world (International Narcotics Control Board [INCB] 1999).

Evidence from some large-scale surveys showed that family practitioners in the United States were more likely than either pediatricians or psychiatrists to prescribe stimulants, and less likely than their colleagues to provide counseling or recommend follow-up interventions (Hoagwood *et al.* 2000). Of course, physicians wrote prescriptions, but other professionals, including teachers, educational psychologists, special educators, social workers, child care workers, and nurses were and are involved in identifying, assessing, diagnosing, and treating children who manifest behavioral or other problems (Damico and Augustine 1995). It seemed to this author that, by virtue of training, experience, and socialization, these professionals might possess different outlooks on ADHD and its treatment. The school setting is obviously an area where these professionals interact. Reviewing the published literature at that time, I found only a handful of studies exploring how various problems of children at school became identified as 'ADD' or 'ADHD' and were dealt with by professionals and parents in their interactions with each other. This dearth of research is unfortunate, given, for example, recent legislation in some American states prohibiting school employees from recommending to parents that a behavior-altering drug be prescribed to a student (Walker 2001; 'Michigan lawmakers debate Ritalin' 2001).

By the time our survey was conducted, we counted only four studies giving us some indication of how different professionals approached the issue of ADHD. Power *et al.* (1995) had surveyed 147 teachers on the acceptability of behavioral and pharmacological interventions. Drug treatment was acceptable only if combined with other interventions, an attitude unrelated to knowledge of ADHD or teaching experience. Damico and Augustine (1995) conducted individual interviews with 33 parents, teachers, physicians, and other professionals, then did some participant observation of the labeling process of three children. They concluded that the actual labeling of children as ADHD occurred primarily outside of the school system and that parents and school professionals held an adversarial attitude when ADHD was discussed. The label was seen to act as a catalyst to provide services not previously offered to the child and parents. Reid *et al.* (1996) interviewed 20 parents of ADHD-diagnosed children about their experiences obtaining services in schools. Parents reported working insistently but unsuccessfully to 'educate' professionals, from year to year and school to school, about their children's special needs. Finally, Doré and Cohen (1997) interviewed 12 parents, teachers, and physicians to explore the dynamics of the medicalization of hyperactivity. Parents and physicians reported experiencing pressure from schools to seek medication for children considered by teachers to be 'hyperactive.' Teachers felt pressured to maintain classroom discipline and deal with 'new' problems of children, and saw stimulants as very useful in this respect. Juxtaposing these observations with data on increased stimulant prescriptions, the authors suggested the need for more research about the actual workings and the actual functions of the treatment system.

That the functions of a system that produces substantial numbers of children on behavior-altering medication may be mostly unrelated to the treatment of medical disorders is a valid possibility, given various arguments questioning the use of medication. As reviewed by McCubbin and Cohen (1999b), arguments found in the literature included: the questionable validity of the ADHD diagnosis, the paucity of long-term research on the safety and efficacy of stimulants, the paucity of evidence for positive effects on learning, the adverse effects caused by stimulants, and the social and ethical problems involved in medicating children in order to control their behavior or improve their educational performance.

To better understand how medications might come to be used with children who manifest certain behaviors in school settings, I adopted an analytical framework derived from ongoing analysis of medications as social and cultural phenomena (Cohen *et al.* 2001). In this framework, individuals are seen to use psychotropic medications partly because of the meanings (emerging from dynamic social interactions at micro, meso, and macro levels) that they attribute to health and illness, pain and suffering, body and identity (Vuckovic and Nichter 1997). In turn, the use of medications influences social interactions and modifies these meanings. The framework is influenced by systems thinking, relying on concepts such as complexity (multiple causality), dynamism (internal and external changes of systems over time), and uncertainty (participants within systems make 'strategic' choices because of incomplete knowledge of the future and of the intentions of other participants). The framework is also constructivist, positing that much of 'reality' and human experience are constructed through sociocultural practices and by means of language (Velody and Williams 1998). Individuals create and interpret knowledge, thus individuals' accounts of their situations are emphasized. Finally, the framework is critical, inviting researchers to overcome definitional and conceptual biases by stepping outside of the usual ways of conceiving the topic under study. It also means considering power distributions between various interested parties involved in the treatment situation (see Cohen and McCubbin 1990; Keen 1998).

## Objectives and study setting

This chapter reports on a study conducted in 1998 in Laval, Quebec. The main objective was to explore systematically *why* and *how* the decision to medicate children with stimulants arises in situations characterized by the involvement of various helping professionals. The review of existing evidence and the analytical framework pointed us toward obtaining the accounts of different participants' perceptions of their constraints and incentives in typical situations involving the identification, assessment, and treatment of children judged to manifest ADHD-like behaviors.

The collaborators made up an interdisciplinary team including a university-based social work researcher interested in the social aspects of medication use (the author), as well as three medical colleagues situated in Laval: a primary care physician specializing in public health administration, a pediatrician working in a private clinic, and a neurodevelopmental pediatrician working in a multidisciplinary clinic of the area's main teaching hospital.

Laval (pop. 285,000 in 1998) is a predominantly francophone city (French being the native tongue of 75 percent of residents), with a homogeneous, middle-class population. Incorporated a few decades ago from many separate municipalities in a large island bordering the city of Montreal, Laval contains urban and semi-rural areas.

## Study methods and procedure

To reach our objective, we chose to obtain data by means of focus group discussions with parents, teachers, school-based psychosocial professionals, and physicians specializing in the assessment and care of children. We chose the focus group format because it is well suited to help understand different perceptions of people concerned by a given problem or issue, and to identify local or specific dynamics around it (Stevens 1995). Previous studies we had reviewed gathered data by means of questionnaires or individual interviews. We felt that the focus group format might add the extra dimension of interaction to the accounts we sought to obtain. We aimed primarily to describe the contents of adult participants' discussions of: (a) how children's problems were first identified, (b) how the children were assessed and diagnosed, (c) what actual interventions were considered, carried out, and followed-up, and (d) how the entire process might be modified or improved. As we could find no strong theoretical guidance for the optimal size of a focus group (Tang and Davis 1995), we decided to try and follow Krueger's (1994) suggestion (between six and twelve participants). In all, we selected and contacted 38 individuals, all of whom agreed to participate; 29 (76 percent) actually participated.

*Parents.* We sought parents of children with a diagnosis of ADHD, currently attending an elementary school in Laval. We contacted the local chapter of a nonprofit association advocating for children with learning difficulties, and a local pediatric clinic. Each source provided four names of mothers willing to be contacted. Five mothers actually attended their focus group (three from the association, two from the clinic). These mothers had one to four children each, the age range for their ADHD-identified child (four boys and one girl) was 7 to 12 years.

*Teachers.* Each of Laval's four school boards suggested two names (seven women, one man, each from a different school); all participated. They had at least five years' teaching experience and were currently teaching at least one child with an ADHD diagnosis. One teacher taught a special class. Two taught in second grade, and each other grade from 1 to 6 was represented by one teacher.

*Psychosocial practitioners* (hereafter called 'practitioners'). In this group we aimed to include practitioners active in schools (though perhaps based in other agencies), as well as school principals. Nine practitioners were suggested by two community health care centers and by the school boards; eight attended (six women and two men, all working mainly in separate schools). They included: two child psychologists, a specialist in learning difficulties, a speech-language pathologist, a school nurse, a community health worker, and two school principals. A social worker was unable to attend the focus group.

*Primary care physicians.* We sought front-line family practitioners and pediatricians with varied experience. Eight local practising physicians known to some of the researchers were contacted. Five (three men, two women) attended: three pediatricians and two general practitioners. Three had over ten years' professional experience.

*Specialist physicians.* This group was not initially planned. However, based on comments about the work of neurologists in the other focus groups, we decided that the input of specialist physicians would be valuable. We contacted three neurologists, a child psychiatrist, and a developmental pediatrician, known to physicians and other professionals to evaluate ADHD cases referred from the Laval area. Two of the neurologists did not attend, leaving three (male) participants, all with over ten years' professional experience.

After an initial brief telephone conversation, all potential participants were informed of the study's objectives and procedure by letter. In order to limit the scope of expected discussions to ADHD-like behaviors rather than any childhood problem behaviors, two brief descriptions of children presenting moderate and severe ADHD-like problems in a classroom were attached to the letter. We also attached a list of a dozen open-ended questions focusing on these main themes:

1   *Identification* (e.g. specific behaviors observed, where and when observed, impact on child and others, views of their nature and origin);
2   *Assessment* (e.g. referral procedures, type and scope of evaluation, tests or instruments used, differential diagnosis, participants in the evaluation);
3   *Intervention* (e.g. treatment plan proposed or initiated, criteria for prescribing medication, place of medication in the treatment plan, positive and negative experiences with various interventions);
4   *Follow-up* (e.g. type, extent and frequency of follow-up of children once treatment is initiated, evaluation and communication of outcomes);
5   *Proposed solutions or improvements.*

Some examples of questions were: 'Do you ever identify children presenting problems of inattention or hyperactivity?'; 'What is your general evaluation or assessment approach in these cases?'; 'Do you use any specific tests or instruments?'; 'What type of intervention do you recommend or use in these cases?'; 'What resources are available to you to carry out this intervention?'; 'What importance do you attach to psychostimulant medication in the overall intervention plan?'; 'What support do you receive from other professionals?'; 'How would you describe the ideal services that should be offered to this population?'

Potential participants were then telephoned to confirm their participation. Two social workers without in-depth knowledge of the research topic but previous experience moderating focus groups received a 90-minute training session on the research objectives, and served consecutively as moderators. The five groups convened on five evenings over a four-week period, in the meeting room in a child development clinic in Laval's main hospital, and were audio-taped. Participants received no remuneration (except reimbursement of parking fees). They were reminded of the objectives and the procedure; each provided informed consent to participate and to be audio-recorded. The group discussions lasted approximately two hours each (70 minutes for the parent group) and covered at least all five themes described above. Audio recordings were of excellent quality and transcribed by a professional transcriber.

## Limitations of the study

Due to obvious difficulties in establishing valid sampling frames for several target groups (e.g. parents of ADHD children, medical providers), a convenience sample was used. This leaves the study vulnerable to various sampling biases and generalization of the findings can only be made to the participants in this study. In addition, a single focus group was convened from each category of respondents, and both the parent and physician groups did not attain the planned composition. This would be expected to limit the variety of comments expressed. Regrettably, no father participated. The five mothers, being at an advanced stage in the intervention process (their child was diagnosed at least one year previously), appeared well informed regarding existing resources in their community. For this reason, they may have been atypical parents.

Despite these limitations, the focus groups exhibited the desired characteristics of being relatively homogeneous and composed of participants who did not know each other (Krueger 1994). Participant teachers came from eight different schools and taught in all grades. In the psychosocial professional group, six different types of professionals from seven different institutions participated. These characteristics suggest that a reasonable diversity of participants, appropriate to the objectives of the study, was obtained.

## Data analysis

The primary aim of the analysis was to describe, in reasonably condensed form, the contents of the transcripts of the focus group discussions, which constituted the accounts of the participants. The analysis consisted of grouping the verbatim contents into categories, then summarizing the contents within each category, then comparing the summaries within and across focus groups (Miles and Huberman 1984). Finally, an attempt at theorizing is offered in this chapter.

For each focus group, verbatim transcripts were first grouped by means of cut-and-paste on a word processor, into the five pre-established discussion themes as well as into several other themes and sub-themes which emerged during this first reading. The thematic groupings were then reviewed, discussed, and debated in sessions involving all collaborators, until complete agreement was reached about which comments belonged under which theme headings. The nature of the comments within each focus group was then examined. We noted *all* comments, whether consensual or not. We aimed to faithfully describe the diversity of views occurring among 'similar' participants within the same group. Succinct summaries of each different statement contained within each theme or sub-theme were then generated. These summaries were also discussed and refined in discussions involving all researchers until full agreement was reached on the exact wording of each summary. Finally, we organized by theme and sub-theme all the summaries across the five groups, to identify the degree of consensus or difference among study participants.

Because no method or data triangulation was used in this study, the accuracy of this analysis is vulnerable to bias. However, the collaborators in this study represented truly diverse approaches, perspectives, and experiences related to the ADHD phenomenon and the use of medication. This led to lengthy, detailed discussions of the data from varied, often opposite perspectives, and thus to a reduction of the likelihood of any persistent bias in the descriptive analysis. However, the interpretation of the findings, presented in the discussion section of this chapter, remains this author's sole responsibility.

## Summary of the findings

### Identification

*First indications of problems.* Three mothers noticed 'learning difficulties,' 'delays' in language or general development, or 'hyperactive behaviors' in their child before kindergarten. These were not too bothersome but became so once the child started school. Two mothers had themselves had experienced similar problems at school, and saw their child's problems as 'hereditary.'

Practitioners and physicians stated observing 'lack of concentration,' 'inattention,' 'disruptive behaviors,' and 'learning difficulties.' Most children seen by physicians for these problems were in first grade – somewhat older for one specialist – though preschoolers and older adolescents were sometimes referred.

*Scope of the problems.* Each physician estimated seeing 'about one child a day' presenting such problems; numbers were highest 'following the first school report card' and peaked again at the end of the school year. Physicians expressed concern about the prevalence of ADHD-type problems and their persistence into adulthood. They felt that problems were more frequent in boys but they questioned lower figures reported for girls, attributing this to their being less disruptive in class. Specialist physicians cited prevalence rates of learning or behavior problems in regular classes of 10 percent of children; one noted that up to 40 percent of children in some classes might be taking stimulants. The practitioners expressed that in special classes a majority of children might be taking stimulants.

*Who refers the children?* All participants agreed on the following sequence: teachers are the first to detect or be concerned by particular behaviors of a child, teachers refer the child to professionals in the school setting, these professionals conduct their assessment and then suggest that the child undergo a medical evaluation, often by a neurologist.

All physicians spoke of 'pressure' applied by 'the school' upon parents to consult a physician. Some physicians said that some schools provide parents with names of physicians known to be favorably disposed to prescribing medication. Parents themselves did not mention the word 'pressure' but said they understood that they must consult a physician or else their child might be placed in a special class or suspended from school.

## Assessment

*The general assessment approach.* Assessment begins once a teacher refers a child to a practitioner. These practitioners and physicians said that a consistent assessment approach was lacking. One practitioner described a community health center's efforts to establish an assessment protocol. Two other practitioners sometimes collaborated with the area's single (hospital-based) multidisciplinary team. Another described one school's attempt to establish priorities for the large number of requests for assessments.

Practitioners named four different standardized assessment instruments they used (but gave no details on the specific functions of each). One practitioner devised his own instrument. Two of the five front-line physicians said they gave weight to the evaluation made by school professionals and then applied their own judgment. Some might refer the child for hearing and eyesight tests. Some named a standardized behavior rating scale. Specialist physicians followed similar procedures: reports from school practitititioners provided an initial evaluation, which specialists completed by means of 'tests,' but neither the nature of the tests nor their duration were specified.

*Participants in the assessment.* Practitioners said that teachers participate in the evaluation process by completing one of the assessment instruments. However, except for the special class teacher, teachers saw their own participation as 'limited' and 'inadequate.' After they request an evaluation, they are 'left to themselves,' their choices restricted to observing how the situation evolves, trying to meet with parents on the issue, and discussing it with colleagues.

*Satisfaction with the assessment.* Every participant in every focus group expressed dissatisfaction with the assessment of children, in school or medical settings. Mothers emphasized their disappointment that tests and evaluations did not consider 'social and family' dimensions, and only occurred after 'long delays.' They questioned whether neurological evaluations lasting 15 to 20 minutes were sufficient to diagnose ADHD and prescribe medication. One mother was satisfied with the work of a psychologist in private practice. School principals and several teachers also saw medical evaluations as 'not rigorous' enough.

For their part, given their impressions that ADHD-type problems sometimes arise out of 'situational crises' or 'parental difficulties,' primary-care physicians felt that school-based evaluations of children were not sufficiently 'psychosocial.' These physicians blamed delays on the 'inability of the schools to properly screen children.' As for specialist physicians, they emphasized the shortcomings of popular ADHD rating scales and criticized the approach of psychosocial practitioners, who were said to 'confuse diverse problems of children with attention deficits.'

*Communication of the assessment results.* Practitioners stated that they communicated the results of their evaluations to other professionals but all teachers emphasized these results' 'irrelevance.' According to teachers, practitioners merely repeated back to teachers what information teachers had provided in the first place. Mothers said they felt 'barely informed' by the assessments, especially concerning the children's 'overall situation.'

Front-line and specialist physicians indicated difficulty in obtaining the results of other professionals' assessments. Specialists said they informed parents of the results of their evaluations by meeting them or sending them written reports. One specialist expected parents to inform the school, another left the choice to the parents. All physicians said they required parents' authorization before communicating with the school. One specialist took care not to reveal unnecessary details about the family in his reports; another made such decisions case by case.

*The ADHD diagnosis.* Front-line physicians unanimously described the diagnosis of ADHD as 'ambiguous' and 'complicated.' They identified five reasons for this: absence of biological diagnostic criteria; difficulty in determining causes of the children's behavior; contradictions between different previous assessments; limited access to these assessments; isolation of physicians from the school environment.

Practitioners and specialist physicians did not specifically discuss diagnosis. Only one teacher did, expressing that the diagnostic label is a problem insofar as it 'allows prescription without exploring the child's problems.'

### Intervention and follow-up

*Information about intervention.* Mothers spoke of receiving incomplete or contradictory information from schools concerning what was contemplated for their child. Specialist physicians also emphasized this point, as they understood it from parents' comments during medical consultations.

*Nature of the interventions.* All participants expressed that aside from evaluating a child and prescribing medications, interventions were 'virtually nonexistent' or 'simply unavailable.' Practitioners said that they tried, given time and resource constraints, to 'provide support' to the children and to their families. They mentioned using student internees to observe and interact with children, 'reward systems,' 'workshops,' and occasional individual meetings with the children. One school principal described in detail the involvement with children and families, three days a week, of a school social worker: this resulted in a sharp drop in the number of children on medication, and the principal was satisfied with the behavior of children removed from medication. A single classroom intervention was mentioned by teachers: using the positive influence of peers to modify some children's behavior. Teachers expressed their concern that intervening with some children makes teachers less available to other students.

*Nature and extent of follow-up.* Mothers said that any follow-up to medication was 'minimal' or ill-suited to their children's actual needs or situations; also academic supports were quite limited, and some hired private tutors. Primary-care physicians stated that once a child received medication, 'the school withdraws support' to the child and family as resources are scarce. Physicians 'try' to follow-up medicated children; they did not as a rule follow unmedicated children, though they sometimes tried to persuade their parents that medication might be beneficial. Physicians said that once children are medicated, schools and sometimes parents are less concerned about medical follow-up, the primary expectation being that the physician provide a prescription. Specialist physicians said that follow-up was important, but they could not be responsible for it, and that their remuneration for such tasks was insufficient. For their part, teachers expressed that to their knowledge, the only professionals who actually followed up medicated children were teachers.

## Use of stimulant medication

*Initial discussions.* According to the five mothers, teachers or psychosocial practitioners first raised the possibility of prescribing stimulant medication to their child. Mothers were told that, given their child's problem, they had 'nothing to lose' by trying medication and should consult a physician. Physicians told a similar story about the nature of schools' discussions with parents about medication.

*The role of medication.* An identical and unanimous consensus emerged in each focus group: if medication is to be used, it must be combined with other types of interventions.

*Perceived pressures to prescribe medication.* Both physician groups described 'pressures' exerted on parents by psychosocial practitioners or schools: schools were said to require the taking of a stimulant while parents were unconvinced that this was the best solution. Physicians sensed parents' distress and even panic; some parents expected their physician to intervene directly with schools and 'reassure' schools about their child's capabilities. However, except for one teacher who described how years ago she resisted pressure from her own son's school that he take a stimulant, no participants in the other focus groups – including mothers – spoke directly of such pressure.

Physicians also spoke of pressure put directly on them by schools, such as not getting referrals from school professionals if physicians did not prescribe medication readily. Every physician expressed frustration that other professionals viewed him or her uniquely as a medication prescriber.

*Prescription criteria.* Physicians cited two criteria for prescribing medication: when there is agreement among previous assessments that the child meets DSM ADHD criteria, and to avoid transfering a child to a special class. They said they avoided prescribing to children with normal academic performance. They reported occasionally suggesting that medication be used on a 'trial' basis, especially with resistant parents.

*Effects of medication.* Across the five groups, the main positively valued effect of stimulants was 'calming' children, which 'increases their concentration and attention.' Some also saw medication as 'helping children complete their homework.' Others saw it as 'helping [to raise] self-esteem.' However, some observed that medication improved neither children's agitation or concentration level nor their academic performance.

Negatively valued effects mentioned were more diverse: medicated children might appear 'amorphic,' 'sad' or dysphoric, or agitated if they missed a dose. 'Psychological dependence' was mentioned in several groups as an issue of concern. Physicians added: temporary stunting of growth, headaches, insomnia, and reduced appetite. Specialist physicians said they sometimes prescribed additional drugs to counteract stimulant effects, and one mother reported sometimes giving 'sleeping pills' to put her child to bed. Mothers expressed fewer worries about medication adverse effects than other participants. Some mothers had noticed reduced appetite, insomnia, and 'slowness' prior to drug treatment, though they also observed that medication sometimes worsened these symptoms in their child.

*Concerns about using medication.* Teachers and practitioners expressed several concerns about using medication: no information about long-term effects on children; an 'overblown' perception of medication as a 'miracle solution'; how quickly physicians issue prescriptions; the 'risk of abuse' of stimulants; and 'psychological dependence.' Physicians expressed a concern about the 'stigmatizing of medicated children.'

### Lack of cooperation among professionals

A constantly repeated observation in each group was the isolation and lack of collaboration between most of the different professionals involved with children.

*Absence of teamwork.* All participants acknowledged the importance of conducting contextual and multidimensional assessments of children. Nonetheless, all agreed that contacts between different professionals were 'infrequent and limited,' with 'no real cooperation' and 'very little multidisciplinary teamwork' – thus that the 'flow of information' was too 'constrained' to allow for effective helping practices. All but psychosocial practitioners stressed that they felt 'isolated' from other players.

*Lack of professional resources.* All agreed about a 'glaring' absence of professional and academic personnel and resources in schools, causing delays at every step. Physicians in particular complained of excessive workload. They complained of finding themselves dealing too often with 'poorly informed' parents to whom they must repeat the same explanations and await a decrease of 'resistance to medication.' They believed that their remuneration, based on discrete medical acts, was not geared to intervention in cases requiring extensive work with families.

## Proposed solutions

Five suggestions to improve the system were raised in the discussions. First, all the groups believed that schools must provide better academic services to children, including help with homework. Second, the need for health practitioners and schools to provide supports to families was emphasized, by means of 'support groups' and 'specialized programs' focusing on parents' needs. Third, in each focus group it was strongly suggested that other professionals' assessments of children should be 'more rigorous.' Mothers stressed the need to 'sensitize teachers and other school professionals' to children's 'psychosocial problems.' Primary-care physicians added that their own evaluations needed to be improved, notably by finding tests to increase the validity of their diagnoses. Fourth, these physicians opined that referrals to neurologists should be less frequent, since causes of ADHD are 'not neurological.' Pediatricians felt that their specialty should participate more in the care of ADHD-type children, justifying their role on the basis of 'the trust people have in their physicians' and because only physicians may prescribe drugs. Finally, calls to 'increase solidarity' between teachers and other professionals, to 'increase the number of teachers and professional resources' in schools, and to improve 'cooperation between organizations' were voiced in all groups.

## Discussion

This section first summarizes and characterizes the views emerging most commonly and forcefully from the discussions, sometimes counterpoising them with what was *not* said. Finally, I attempt to link the study's findings to operations of complex systems of care.

### Key findings

The discourses of the participants in this study suggest that in some public elementary schools in a medium-sized suburban, mostly French-speaking Canadian community, candidates for a diagnosis of ADHD and stimulant medication are mainly boys disturbing classrooms and failing in school. However, although various academic and personal difficulties of children were noticed by the participants, these difficulties were not described in detail nor were distinctions made between different types of difficulties. This suggests that our participants may have been inappropriately grouping heterogeneous problem behaviors under the ADHD label.

Virtually all participants judged assessments of children as inadequate. Indeed, even three successive evaluations of a child (by a school psychologist, a front-line physician, then a neurologist) did not ensure that any participant would be satisfied with the understanding achieved of the child's difficulties or the course of action recommended. Besides calling for more exactness in the evaluation and more emphasis on psychosocial factors in children's lives, participants specified no specific *purposes* of the assessment. It remained unclear whether these professionals assessed alternative hypotheses besides ADHD to explain the children's presenting problems.

Despite physicians' detailed accounts of 'pressures' that schools put on parents to medicate the children, mothers did not speak of such pressure. This discrepancy could be a clue as to how parents perceive themselves in the system, e.g. assuming a reduced or perhaps powerless role (see below) vis-à-vis the schools. On the other hand, as previously noted, these mothers did display fairly extensive involvement in and knowledge of community resources, and may have been more confident in their dealings with schools.

Relative to other participants, primary-care physicians expressed more honesty about the limits of their own work, plainly describing factors that weaken the soundness of their assessment. Their discourse on ADHD may be seen to reflect the ambiguity of the diagnostic category itself as well as intra-medical rivalries. Indeed, these front-line physicians doubted neurology's pertinence in the matter of ADHD and expressed frustration that ADHD was perceived as a *neurological* problem and neurologists as its true experts. For their part, specialist physicians criticized the work of psychosocial practitioners but refrained from specifying the nature of their own assessment and diagnostic methods.

It may be helpful here to raise the issue of the *function* of the medical consultation. One may argue, based on the present findings, that criteria and tools to diagnose ADHD varied among physicians yet the main outcome – prescription of medication – was largely invariant. Did the medical consultation serve therefore mainly to justify the outcome? In other words, was the decision to prescribe medication made 'independently' of physicians by other concerned professionals, who then directed the child to a physician for the official ratification of the decision? In this study's findings, three elements in the physicians' discourse suggest a positive answer to this question (as well as directions for future research). First, although they were critical of most aspects of the diagnostic and assessment process, the physicians did not question their *own* prescription of medication. Second, they stated that non-medical professionals viewed them as serving solely to dispense prescriptions. Third, to justify their decision to prescribe, they identified largely *educational* criteria (e.g. whether or not child was failing in school).

Paradoxically, although participants stated emphatically that interventions with children must not rely only upon medication, they recognized just as emphatically that interventions consisted almost exclusively of medication. Although participants identified five different forms of direct intervention as appropriate for ADHD, no participant spoke of their involvement in any form besides medication. Psychosocial practitioners described their work as centering on assessment and referral; physicians on diagnosis and prescription. The one positive note sounded for psychosocial intervention came from a school principal who felt that a social worker's involvement with children and families was directly responsible for lowering the rate of medicated children in that school. In contrast to the observation of Damico and Augustine (1995) that parents used the ADHD label to pressure schools into providing services to their children, some participants in our study decisively affirmed that the prescribing of medication constituted the pretext for schools to *avoid* securing services that parents and professionals considered essential.

Participants' comments about stimulant medication reflected the range of observations found in the professional literature. Most participants appreciated the calming effects of stimulants. Most mentioned adverse effects, but were not unduly worried by them. They also described rebound effects – agitation following a missed dose, for example – but did not identify them as such, raising the possibility that these effects were attributed rather to ADHD. Judging from the absence of comments on specific medication objectives, frequency of follow-up, withdrawal issues, or occasional placebo substitution, it appeared that the effects of medication did not seem to be carefully evaluated by these participants.

Solutions proposed by participants underscored the complex web of institutional relationships bordering assessment and intervention: few and poorly organized services and resources, overwork, inappropriate remuneration structure for physicians to undertake multidisciplinary work. The lack of cooperation among participants may have explained the accessory observation that, generally, whatever beliefs participants thought other participants held about them were unconfirmed by the others. The solutions also suggested that the professionals in this study felt that they functioned in a context they themselves described as unfit to respond adequately to the needs of children. Moreover, participants expressed powerlessness, discouragement, and pessimism about the possibility of effecting change. If the proposed solutions could improve particular aspects of the assessment and intervention process, no participants (except perhaps primary-care physicians) expressed what they *themselves* could do to reach that goal. Almost invariably, the solutions were expected to originate from and involve other actors than those who proposed them.

## Acting within complex systems of care

Controversy over the use of stimulants by children is not new (e.g. Schrag and Divoky 1975) and despite nearly three decades of sustained use in North America, several issues still remain unresolved – including the exact nature of the behavior cluster known as ADHD, the validity of this cluster as a genuine disorder, its developmental consequences, as well as the effects of prolonged stimulant use in children ('Diagnosis and treatment' 1998). These uncertainties raise doubts, regularly expressed in professional and popular publications, about the *systemic* value of using behavior-altering medication with children. Given such doubts, it is reasonable to demand that in *individual cases*, professionals charged with caring for children weigh the issues carefully, in consonance with conceptual/clinical frameworks and protocols that can be clearly explained and justified to others and that can serve to evaluate the effects of interventions on each child. Phrased differently, given the controversies surrounding the diagnosis of ADHD and the use of stimulants, most of the legitimacy of prescribing stimulants to children rests on the judgment and professionalism of the experts involved in the screening and assessment that lead directly to the prescription. The results of this study, however, suggest that – at least in the public school system of a medium-sized suburban city in Canada in the late 1990s – such professional practices largely escaped the power or intentions of the professionals themselves.

The findings described a poorly controlled process of assessment, intervention, and follow-up, lacking *explicit* guiding or consensual principles. A complex dynamic was put into play, in which individuals acted in isolation of each other yet were severely constrained to take into account the actions, or inactions, of others (see Crozier and Friedberg 1980). As a result of this particular dynamic, individuals' expectations of each other were rarely satisfied.

What did appear to unite these different participants' discourses from the start was their reference to the concept of ADHD. A strength of that concept may lie in its ability to connote different things for different individuals evolving in different environments. The same label seemed to be applied to different problematic behaviors, and seemed to allow divergent assessment practices to co-exist amicably. It was surprising to this author that, in this study the validity of the concept of ADHD was questioned most by physicians, least by psychosocial professionals.

The findings of this study pointed to the idea that because a school tolerates or encourages medication without requiring or encouraging other interventions, medication becomes the only available intervention (unless parents are able to hire private professionals or tutors). This would result in each step of the assessment process of a child suspected of exhibiting ADHD symptoms becoming subservient to the known likely outcome – prescription of medication – and each step proceeding even if performed perfunctorily. Thus, in the minds of the professionals involved, the issue of medication could have been present *as soon as a child was first identified as presenting a problem in class.*

The exploratory findings of this study indeed raise the possibility that the use of medication constituted the *implicit* purpose, function, and outcome of the work of identification and assessment for all the professionals involved, even if such use was *not explicitly* 'intended' as its goal by any of these professionals. This is evidently a paradox, but understanding how it could arise is facilitated if one looks primarily at the level of the system itself, and only secondarily at the level of individual responsibilities of actors within that system. McCubbin and Cohen (1999b) noted that, 'As social systems become increasingly complex there is always the danger that they adapt to the complexity by increasing mechanization – reducing the role of human agency – or by losing control of important elements of their systems – reducing the role of collective human agency' (p. 70).

'Increasing mechanization' may be manifest today in North America in the widespread reliance on medication as the main solution to the problem termed 'ADHD,' or inversely, in the non-availability of multimodal interventions (which rest on making fine determinations of children's problems and proposing individualized intervention plans requiring frequent evaluations and modifications, e.g. Maag and Reid 1996). Prescribing medication does respond to the initial request by teachers that something be done to ensure orderly functioning of the classroom or to intervene with a given child. In the short term, medication use by the child will tend to reduce pressure on the teachers and the school, who are likely then to reduce pressure on the parents. However, medication use by the child might also be expected to decrease the burden of responsibility as well as the incentives upon each professional to implement rigorous assessment and intervention alternatives. Instead, assessment may need only address whether children could 'benefit from medication.'

In this study, given all participants' statements describing schools as definitely supporting the use of stimulants, these drugs were likely to be prescribed by overworked physicians having any uncertainty about what to do in complex psychosocial situations involving children and who knew that this was the *standard* practice of their medical colleagues. Indeed, by the time the parents consulted physicians after a possibly lengthy delay – resulting partly from a lack of resources and partly because some parents resisted investigation of their child's behavior or academic problems – little support had been offered to the child/family and the situation had in all likelihood worsened. At that point, neither parents nor physicians would have expected to possess a realistically large margin of action. In these circumstances, the medication could be said to have appeared as the 'last recourse' to avoid transferring the child to a special class or to avoid failing the child. Furthermore, given professionals' isolation from each other, even a very dissatisfied professional might not discuss his or her concerns with an appropriate colleague. 'Reducing the role of human agency' may be discerned in participants' comments expressing their powerlessness and inability, as individuals, to effect change in directions which these individuals explicitly and repeatedly stated and agreed were desirable and necessary.

'Reducing the role of collective agency', another characteristic of certain complex systems of care, emerged in two distinct realms in the findings of this study: general (though implicit and not unanimous) acceptance of the ADHD construct as valid and useful to organize the work of professionals, and general (though implicit) acceptance of schools as unchangeable. Indeed, while 'the school' occupied a pivotal place in all participants' comments and its influence was criticized by many, participants did not discuss any school-, education-, or teacher-related factors possibly contributing to the onset or maintenance of disturbing behavior or inadequate learning by children, that professionals might need to address (e.g. Gatto 1992). This omission might serve both to indicate and reinforce a view of ADHD-like behavior as difficulties intrinsic to the children and unrelated to culture and environment, a view which – combined with the dearth of published children's perspectives on ADHD and on the use of medication – suggests that practitioners and researchers redouble their efforts to explore whether children's interests are being served by the overall process of assessment and intervention for ADHD.

Of course, the findings from this study cannot generalize to service providers in school settings. They provide only a partial, static picture of the individual participants' views and perceptions with respect to the management of ADHD-type problems. They also exclude from consideration many wider systemic factors – cultural, economic, and bureaucratic – contributing to the medication outcome (e.g. Kiger 1985; DeGrandpre 1998; Lloyd and Norris 1999). However, they converge with other recent research and personal accounts (e.g. Baldwin 2000), and highlight the need to persist in inquiring about the rationality of the overall treatment system, at least as it is described to operate in some public schools in North America.

Notwithstanding their limitations, these findings suggest that even the best intentions of individual actors can become warped or coopted by the requirements of a system whose purposes are rarely analyzed explicitly. Clearly, the outcomes of the system might be more rational if all professional actors involved in it assumed more responsibility for the results of their own professional actions – but it may be unreasonable to expect them to do so as long as their actions and their results remain, basically, unexamined.

## References

Baldwin, S. (2000). 'Impact evaluation of a mass media public education campaign on clinic service provision for minors diagnosed with ADHD/ADD: Audit survey of 100 index cases'. *International Journal of Risk and Safety in Medicine*, 13: 203–219.

Cohen, D. (2000). *Sociocultural Determinants of Stimulant Prescriptions: Prevalence among primary school youths in Quebec and France.* Presented at the 128th Annual Meeting, American Public Health Association, Boston, MA, November 15, 2000.

Cohen, D. and McCubbin, M. (1990). 'The political economy of tardive dyskinesia: Asymmetries in power and responsibility'. *Journal of Mind and Behavior*, 11: 465–488.

Cohen, D., Clapperton, I., Gref, P., Tremblay, Y. and Cameron, S. (1999). *DAH: Perceptions des acteurs et utilisation de psychostimulants* [ADHD: Actors' perceptions and use of psychostimulants]. Laval, QC: Regional Health and Social Services Board of Laval.

Cohen, D., McCubbin, M., Collin, J., Pérodeau, G. (2001). 'Medications as social phenomena'. *Health*, 4: 451–474.

Crozier, M. and Friedberg, E. (1980). *Actors and Systems: The politics of collective action* (translated by A. Goldhammer). Chicago, IL: University of Chicago Press.

Damico, J.S. and Augustine, L.E. (1995). 'Social considerations in the labeling of students as attention deficit hyperactivity disorders'. *Seminars in Speech and Language*, 16: 259–274.

DeGrandpre, R. (1998). *Ritalin Nation: Rapid-fire culture and the transformation of higher consciousness.* New York: W.W. Norton.

DeGrandpre, R. (2000). 'ADHD: Serious psychiatric problem or all-American cop-out?' *Cerebrum*, 2(3): 12–39.

'Diagnosis and treatment of attention deficit hyperactivity disorder' (1998, November). *NIH Consensus Statement 16–18*, 16(2): 1–37.

Diller, L.H. (1998). *Running on Ritalin: A physician reflects on children, society and performance in a pill.* New York: Bantam.

Doré, C. and Cohen, D. (1997). 'La prescription de stimulants aux enfants 'hyperactifs': Une étude pilote des incitatifs et des contraintes pour les parents, les médecins et les enseignants' [Prescription of stimulants to 'hyperactive' children: A pilot study of incentives and constraints on parents, physicians, and teachers]. *Santé mentale au Québec*, 22: 216–238.

Gatto, J.T. (1992). *Dumbing Us Down: The hidden curriculum of compulsory schooling*. Gabriola Island, BC: New Society Publishers.

Hoagwood, K., Kelleher, K.J., Feil, M. and Comer, D.M. (2000). 'Treatment services for children with ADHD: A national perspective'. *Journal of the Academy of Child and Adolescent Psychiatry*, 39: 198–206.

INCB (1999, February 23). 'Europeans take tranquillisers, Americans stimulants'. Press Release No. 4, INCB Annual Report for 1998. Vienna: United Nations Information Service. Available online: http://www.incb.org/f/press/1998/f_rel_04.htm.

Keen, E. (1998). *Drugs, Therapy, and Professional Power*. Westport, CT: Praeger.

Kiger, G. (1985). 'Economic transformation and processing of hyperactive school children'. *Mid-American Review of Sociology*, 10: 65–85.

Krueger, R.A. (1994). *Focus Groups: A practical guide for applied research*. Thousand Oaks, CA: Sage.

LeFever, G.B., Dawson, K.V. and Morrow, A.L. (1999). 'The extent of drug therapy for attention-deficit/hyperactivity disorder among children in public schools'. *American Journal of Public Health*, 89: 1359–1364.

Lloyd, G. and Norris, C. (1999). 'Including ADHD?' *Disability and Society*, 14: 505–517.

McCubbin, M. and Cohen, D. (1999a). 'Empirical, ethical, and political perspectives on the use of methylphenidate'. *Ethical Human Sciences and Services*, 1: 81–101.

McCubbin, M. and Cohen, D. (1999b). 'A systemic and value-based approach to strategic reform of the mental health system'. *Health Care Analysis*, 7: 57–77.

'Michigan lawmakers debate Ritalin' (2001). Retrieved on December 24, 2001 from http://www.newsmax.com/archives/articles/2001/12/24/132353.shtml.

Maag, J.W. and Reid, R. (1996) 'Treatment of attention deficit-hyperactivity disorder: A multi-model model for schools'. *Seminars in Speech and Language*, 17(1): 37–58.

Miles, M.B. and Huberman, A.M. (1984). *Qualitative Data Analysis: A sourcebook of new methods*. Beverly Hills, CA: Sage.

Power, T.J., Hess, L.E. and Bennett, D.S. (1995). 'The acceptability of interventions for attention-deficit/hyperactivity disorder among elementary and middle school teachers'. *Journal of Developmental and Behavioral Pediatrics*, 16: 238–243.

Rappley, M.D., Gardiner, J.R. and Jetton, R.C.H. (1995). 'The use of methylphenidate in Michigan'. *Archives of Pediatric and Adolescent Medicine*, 149: 675–679.

Rees, A. (1999, August 9). 'Boys will be boys: That's why we've got them popping pills'. *The Province* (Vancouver): A14–A16.

Reid, R., Hertzog, M. and Snyder, M. (1996). 'Educating every teacher, every year: The public schools and parents of children with ADHD'. *Seminars in Speech and Language*, 17: 73–90.

Schrag, P. and Divoky, D. (1975). *The Myth of the Hyperactive Child, and Other Means of Child Control*. New York: Pantheon Books.

Searight, R. (1996). 'Perceptions of attention deficit hyperactivity disorder and its treatment among children and adolescents'. *Journal of Medical Humanities*, 17: 51–61.

Sherman, C. (1998). 'Stimulant prescribing rises for Medicaid children'. *Clinical Psychiatry News*, 26: 14.

Stevens, P.E. (1996). 'Focus groups: Collecting aggregate-level data to understand community health phenomena'. *Public Health Nursing*, 13: 170–176.

Tang, K.C. and Davis, A. (1995). 'Critical factors in the determination of focus group size'. *Family Practice*, 12: 474–475.

Velody, I. and Williams, R. (eds) (1998). *The Politics of Constructionism*. London: Academy of Hebrew Language.

Vuckovic, N. and Nichter, M. (1997). 'Changing patterns of pharmaceutical practice in the United States'. *Social Science and Medicine*, 44: 1285–1302.

Walker, S. (2001, October 28). 'Yes: Legislature must reassess policies on controversial use of potent drugs'. *Detroit News*. Retrieved February 17, 2002 from http://detnews.com/2001/editorial/0110/29/a19-328930.htm.

Zito, J.M., Safer, D.J., dosReis, S. and Riddle, M.A. (1998). 'Racial disparity in psychotropic medications prescribed for youths with Medicaid insurance in Maryland'. *Journal of the Academy of Child and Adolescent Psychiatry*, 37: 179–184.

Zito, J.M., Safer, D.J., dosReis, S., Gardner, J.F., Boles, M. and Lynch, F. (2000). 'Trends in the prescribing of psychotropic medications to preschoolers'. *JAMA*, 283: 1025–1030.

# Chapter 10

# ADHD from a cross-cultural perspective

## Insights into adult–child power relationships

*Ken Jacobson*

In January 1999 I went to Oxfordshire, England to begin conducting what I thought would be a field study in England and the United States evaluating mostly non-diagnosed 10- and 11-year-old children for the diagnostic characteristics of Attention-Deficit/Hyperactivity Disorder (ADHD). The project turned out to be much more extensive than I imagined. In this chapter I will first explain the scope of the research and the methodology used. I will then cite some results with respect to ADHD. These results suggest that while it is likely that ADHD-like behaviours on the part of children do not necessarily signal that the children have a disorder, they do signal something significant about power relationships between children and adults generally. At the project's end, it came to encompass power relationships expressed in school and home settings. This chapter will focus on the in-school relationships. Here, the results suggest that even though teachers and administrators spend much time and effort trying to maintain order, and consequently disciplining children, those efforts are effective – if at all – only for brief periods of time. Moreover, those efforts impact materially on the schools' educational mission. The chapter concludes with a suggestion as to how schools might be more effective in their educational role.

## Research scope and methodology

As reflected by extensive clinical and popular literatures (Diller 1998), ADHD has the highest profile of the 'mental disorders' for which children in the United States are diagnosed and treated. The *Diagnostic and Statistical Manual of Mental Disorders, Fourth Edition* (DSM-IV), used by mental health practitioners in the United States as the definitive source for information on mental disorders, defines three sub-types for ADHD: inattention; hyperactivity-impulsivity; and a combined type in which both inattention and hyperactivity-impulsivity are expressed (American Psychiatric Association 1994: 81) The exact rate of ADHD diagnosis is subject to some speculation. A recent Centers for Disease Control and Prevention (CDC) publication reports, 'Among children 6–11 years of age, nearly 7 percent were reported to have a diagnosis of ADD' (Pastor and Reuben 2002: 3) If the CDC figure is accepted, then clearly a substantial number of children in the United States have been diagnosed. The most popular remediation for the 'disorder' is the use of amphetamines or stimulants like Ritalin.

Interestingly, in many other countries, the rate of diagnosis is far lower than in the United States. Since no definite neurobiology or physical markers of ADHD have emerged, much controversy exists about the nature of this 'disorder'. In 1999, England was one of the Western countries in which ADHD was diagnosed much less frequently than the United States. My initial research aim was to try and understand the reasons for this difference. Over time, the research aim evolved to trying to evaluate children's behaviour in these two countries to see if I could identify differences that might explain the different rates of diagnosis. To my knowledge, this is the first anthropological cross-cultural study of ADHD-like behaviour using a checklist for lengthy individual observations as well as group observations and interviews in general school samples.

The research was primarily conducted at three locations: a publicly funded primary school in Oxfordshire, England (which I call 'Riverton School'); a public middle school in a New England (US) town ('Farmdale School'); and at a specialist school for dyslexic children in England (all names of schools, children and teachers have been changed). Over 100 children aged 10 and 11 were observed. Formal observations were made for approximately 16 months, although I was in touch with both Riverton and Farmdale for much longer. At the Riverton School, there were 32 year 5 and year 6 children in one classroom. Two teachers shared responsibility for that classroom. Mrs Bridge, the school's Deputy Head Teacher and special education needs coordinator (SENCO) taught on Monday, Tuesday and Wednesday. Mrs Pegg taught on Thursday and Friday. At the Farmdale School three subject teachers, Mrs Young, Mrs Church and Mrs Winter each equally saw on a daily basis the 65 fifth graders from which the participating population was drawn. Since the children could be observed interacting with several different teachers, a natural experimental situation presented itself.

The project utilized four different methodologies. The first two were qualitative: participant observation, during which I immersed myself in the schools and class-rooms and recorded my observations as field notes, and interviewing. I also utilized two quantitative methodologies, focal individual sampling (FIS) and diagnostic questionnaires.

## Focal individual sampling

This approach was chosen because 'it can provide relatively unbiased data relevant to a wide variety of questions about spontaneous social behaviour in groups' (Altman 1974: 247). FIS methodology is also used extensively by primatologists and others to study behaviours of interest in various species of animals. I chose this methodology because I thought it would allow me to observe children in their classrooms for the diagnostic criteria of ADHD in a systematic manner, something that had not been done before.

If children were observed for those behaviours considered characteristic of

ADHD, what would one see in classroom settings? The answer to that question proved somewhat elusive. Several published checklists for practitioners are designed to facilitate the diagnosis of ADHD (Barkley and Murphy 1998). These are all couched in generalized language of DSM-IV. Based on the literature, a 34-item grid checklist was designed. That checklist was broken down into five potential behavioural categories. Ultimately, only three of those categories were used in the analysis.

1   Focusing: Where are the child's eyes looking?
2   Talking: Is the child vocalizing in any fashion?
3   Movement: Is the child moving in any way?

I decided to observe each child with respect to the 34 potential behaviours on a 15-second by 15-second basis over a total sample time of 15 minutes. Each child was observed a minimum of five times. Each notation on the checklist had to be classified as either appropriate or inappropriate. FIS observations were balanced as much as possible between teachers, time of day, and task, and at Riverton, because the children regularly either sat 'on the carpet' in front of their teacher or at multi-person tables, balance was maintained with respect to location.

I quickly learned that no absolute objective standards exist by which to judge the appropriateness or inappropriateness of any specific behaviour. One determining factor became whether a behaviour was social, involving more than one child, or personal. Some social behaviours, whispering, for example, were clearly inappropriate. However, during group work, some talking was appropriate. Some determinations were easier to make than others: if, for example, several girls working on an authorized project started talking about boys then returned to the project, that extraneous talk was inappropriate (if the observer sat close enough to overhear their conversation). However, often children would talk while they were supposed to be working independently. Should they be held to a strict standard? What if a child was asking a peer for help, which children often did? Advice from teachers at Riverton suggested I should base my determination on the reaction of the teacher in the room. If the teacher let a behaviour continue, it was appropriate. If the teacher told the children to stop, singly or as a group, then a continuation was inappropriate. Since different teachers applied different standards, social appropriateness was situationally relative.

Regarding personal behaviours: When should I judge it appropriate, for example, for a child to open a pencil case and when should it be seen as fidgeting, or a sign of inattention and/or impulsivity? That is, when might that or any other behaviour – such as moving or squirming in their seat, moving around the classroom, staring into space – be interpreted as off task and inattentive and/or hyperactive-impulsive, and when not? Context became crucial in making my determinations.

At the beginning of the study I assumed that my observations would allow me to establish a baseline separating 'normal' children from 'disordered' children.

Currently, no such baseline exists, even though according to DSM-IV diagnostic criteria for ADHD, children must exhibit 'a persistent pattern of inattention and/or hyperactivity-impulsivity that is more frequent and more severe than is typically observed in individuals at a comparable level of development' (APA 1994: 78) Thus, when clinicians diagnose ADHD, they are making clinical/subjective rather than objective determinations as to how a particular child compares with his/her peers.

Before I present the results of the FIS observations I must explain two decisions with respect to the data analysis. First, one of the 34 behaviours recorded was 'daydreaming.' I innocently inserted it as a catchall to cover any time a child was not looking at anything specific. A problem arose in trying to specify whether 'daydreaming' was ever appropriate. It appeared to me that when taking a quiz or test or creative writing, for example, a child would essentially look into space and then immediately return to their work. On the FIS form I recorded all those instances as appropriate. However, since there is no scientific way to show that a child is 'thinking,' I analysed these data both ways: assuming daydreaming was appropriate as recorded, but also considering all of it to be inappropriate. Second, because of the complexity of the statistics involved, I decided that I would analyse inappropriate behaviours in terms of their frequency – as a percentage of behaviours observed – rather than in terms of their duration within the total observational period.

## Researcher persona

When I began this project I was 55 years old. I had been a single parent for years, taught in college classrooms, run several businesses, and been elected to public office. My natural tendency toward children was to adopt an authoritarian but benevolent attitude. On my first day in Mrs Bridge's class at Riverton, that attitude, at least toward the children I worked with, changed irrevocably. Trevor looked over at me while he was supposed to be paying attention to Mrs Bridge. I smiled, looked at Mrs Bridge, looked back at him, and gave a little shrug. My message, which Trevor understood, was: 'not now, we'll get in trouble.' From that point on I adopted, and grew deeper and deeper although not perfectly into, the role of non-judgmental uncle. I witnessed amazingly bold acts of inappropriate behaviour, and never once intimated to another adult at the school what I had witnessed. The kids and I developed a teasing, almost peer-like relationship. They mostly trusted me. Sometimes, despite my resolve to be the children's friend, I was put into positions of authority – watching a class while the teacher was out of the room, coaching an after-school basketball programme, field trips. On those occasions, I was in the awkward position of having to tell the children to calm down. I'm not sure they obeyed me any more or less than any other adult. However, even in those situations, I never reported their transgressions to anyone. Likewise, if a child was doing something that might cause them physical harm, I would try to get them to stop, but again, with the attitude of a benign uncle.

## Field notes

Taking field notes is an integral aspect of participant observation. Rather than carry a small pocket notebook into which I could surreptitiously write key thoughts to be expanded on returning to home base, I decided to take notes openly and continuously (Emerson *et al.* 1995). I did this simply because I did not believe I would remember enough detail or even be in a position to make the initial notes frequently enough to develop a rich set of field notes. In this manner, I recorded over 2,500 8.5 by 11 inch pages of notes. Because of the relationships I developed with the children, and because mostly I arrived at and left school when children did, I believe these notes serve as a rich catalogue of what occurred in the classrooms during my presence and in general. As in all participant observation, my presence and continuous note-taking had the potential to influence the behaviour of the children and teachers. However, I made myself as unobtrusive as possible, and carried out my observations over an extended period of time. I believe this turned me into a benign human fixture in the classrooms, thus lessening any serious accommodation that the children and teachers had to make to my own behaviour. The notes serve as primary data for the conclusions I have drawn regarding power relationships between adults and children in school settings.

## Results

As noted, data were gathered at three research sites. In Tables 10.1–10.3 (see appendix), the Riverton site is named 'England'; the Farmdale site 'US'; and the specialist dyslexic school in England, 'Dyslexic.' As Table 10.1 indicates, several interesting findings emerged. First, the Dyslexic group, which the school's head teacher had represented to be especially prone to ADHD-like behaviours, actually had the lowest FIS scores of the three groups. Second, although scores for the two English groups differed significantly from each other only with respect to hyperactivity-impulsivity, both these schools' scores differed significantly from the US schools' scores across the board. Third, since the Dyslexic group was shown considerably more video than the other two groups, I wondered whether the significant differences in inattention and hyperactivity-impulsivity between the various classes would remain if time spent watching video was not counted. Excluding time spent watching video ('No Video' counted, Tables 10.1 and 10.2) eliminated any significant difference in scores for inattention between all the schools. Fourth, even after video was isolated, the Dyslexic scores for hyperactivity-impulsivity were still much lower than those of the other two schools.

Before any compensation for video, from the data seen in Table 10.1 one might conclude that the attentive behaviours of school children in the United States and England differ. After the pedagogical differences of video use are eliminated, that conclusion becomes more doubtful. The conclusion can be rejected completely, however, when the children's mean FIS scores are classified by teacher (teacher data not collected for the Dyslexic school) and put in rank order (inappropriate behaviours in Table 10.2, appropriate behaviours in Table 10.3). If the behaviour differed by country, FIS scores for the two English teachers' school should differ significantly from scores for the three American teachers, which is not the case. For example, the behaviour of the English children in Mrs Pegg's classes was similar to the behaviour of the American children. In reality, Mrs Bridge from the English school maintained a much more draconian classroom atmosphere than her colleague Mrs Pegg, such that averaging their scores creates a misleading appearance of a potential cultural difference. This suggests that the major factor influencing the level of a child's ADHD-like behaviours is that child's reaction to the teacher in the room. A second point to be noted from Table 10.3, which I discuss below, is that on the average only 50 per cent of the children's behaviour was appropriate (low of 44 per cent for Mrs Church and high of 58 per cent for Mrs Bridge).

Since no teacher data were recorded for the Dyslexic school, explanations for these student's lower scores for hyperactivity-impulsivity can only be speculative. Class sizes were much smaller at the Dyslexic school, and individual attention was a major part of the teaching methodology. Further, the students sat next to each other, not at square tables, an arrangement less conducive to leaving one's seat than the arrangements prevailing at the Riverton and Farmdale schools.

## Creating a baseline

As noted, one of my goals was to create a baseline of ADHD-like behaviours, using the FIS data, by which children could be distinguished as either 'normal' or 'disordered.' Making this distinction was far from simple. Logically, a baseline could be constructed in one of several ways. I could choose a representative sample of the highest individual scores, but balance by teacher and time of day would be lost. Alternatively, I could pick a sampling of children with the highest average scores but this might skew the baseline to an unreasonably high level by ignoring a great many lower scores. Finally, I could use the whole data set. The second and third approaches would also require me to add a reasonable two standard deviations to the raw averages to ensure that only children with extreme scores would be considered for ADHD diagnosis.

When baselines were calculated using each of those approaches, two major problems emerged. The larger the data set used, the lower – even after adding two standard deviations – the baseline became. At those lower levels the FIS scores of many of the children in the sample would make them eligible for ADHD diagnosis. If only the highest individual scores are used, none of the children would be eligible for diagnosis. However, for inattention and/or hyperactivity-impulsivity, the minimum scores necessary for diagnosis would be approximately 72 per cent of observed behaviours, and for the combined type of ADHD, approximately 80 per cent of observed behaviours. I find the likelihood of any child exhibiting ADHD-like behaviours at those levels unrealistic. Therefore, based on these data I do not think it scientifically possible to separate 'normal' from 'disordered' levels of behaviour. Clearly, I find it unreasonable to believe 7 per cent (or more) of the school-age children in the United States exhibit ADHD-like behaviours at anywhere near those levels. Accordingly, I find it reasonable to conclude that, at best, ADHD is grossly over-diagnosed in the United States. In fact, it may well be that based on the data presented in this chapter no child should be labelled for that disorder.

## The children's world and the 'default'

Table 10.3 shows that on average, only 50 per cent of the children's behaviour was 'appropriate.' If these children did not all have ADHD, then what was the explanation? Examination showed that the children's behaviours were not random, but fell into patterns. Further, those patterns reflected clear strategies. In the present section, I summarize extensive observations and interpretations that appear in the original report of my study and refer interested readers to that report (Jacobson 2003).

On the surface, adults have an inordinate amount of leverage over children. In general, although clearly each family is somewhat different from other families, adults control the purse strings and dictate all major structural elements in children's lives: where they live; how many siblings they have; whether or not they have medical or dental care; how long they must remain in school (until age 16 in England, 18 in America); when they can legally hold a job; and even at what age their consenting sexual behaviour is legal. Yet, this adult structural power does not translate into controlling implementation. Adults dictate where children live but they cannot control children's friendship relationships. Adults try to dictate what foods children eat but children will refuse to eat what's put in front of them. Adults may need to pay for children's clothes but children decide their own styles. Adults can try to regulate children's access to movies, music, computer games, and TV but they cannot do so effectively, and popular culture makes up much of children's dialect. Adults control children's access to money but kids find many ways to get money – chores for parents, presents from many sources. Kids do not seem particularly deterred by legal niceties from engaging in sexual experimentation. Nor, just because they have to attend school, is there a way to mandate their good achievement. Further, controlling children's behaviour requires a way to control their minute-by-minute activity. Adults establish 'rules' as the means by which they attempt to turn their structural leverage into that minute-by-minute control, but children do not necessarily follow those rules or submit to adult authority.

As the research progressed, I was reminded of something that adults might tend to disregard: children organize themselves socially in the same ways adults do. Children establish similar rules reflecting and enforcing shared values (norms); positions within the social group (statuses); and behaviours, obligations, and privileges attached to those statuses (roles) as found in adult worlds. Children's groups positively and negatively reward their members for conforming to the rules/norms (sanctions). For example, peers are extremely important in children's lives, but not necessarily in ways that adhere to conventional understandings. That is, even though children influence each other to behave in ways disapproved of by adults, children's behaviours do not necessarily hurt them. Peers encourage and facilitate the development of a child's personality. It has been argued, indeed, that peers are the primary influence on a child's personality (Harris 1998).

My point is not to argue the primacy of adult versus peer influences on children. Rather, it is to suggest simply that children are not passive recipients of socializing influences from either peers or adults. Rather, children (and adults) behave as they do because of the totality of their individually unique experiences, the perceptions and interpretations of which are influenced in an infinite number of ways by the groups to which they belong. I do not think it is possible to attribute a one-to-one causality to any pattern of behaviours any individual child exhibits. Accordingly, the most accurate way to characterize the relationship between children's groups and adult authority may be 'symbiotic.'

I found the children's resistance most evident in the strategies they use when adults try to implement specific 'rules.' Thus, the groups into which children organize themselves act as vehicles for effective counter strategies to adult authority because they empower children's resistance to adult efforts to enforce those rules. As we will see below, in schools, that empowerment means that adults do not have any means of effectively disciplining children. I have labelled this unique set of norms, roles, statuses, and positively and negatively sanctioned behaviours 'the children's world.'

*When adults are close, the children's world tends to become secretive.* I believe that, as non-judgmental uncle, I gained privileged access to a world that may be usually denied adults. I did not have full access, but it seemed to me that nothing much changed when I wandered over to join a group of children; nor did their lunchroom conversation appear to change because I was sitting there with them. They did keep secrets from me. In fact, when I asked a 10-year-old Farmdale boy if he had secrets that he shared only with his friends he replied: 'I do. But if I told you I'd have to kill you.'

It turned out that what I have interpreted as children's resistance fell into patterns, which I label as 'default behaviour' or more simply as 'the default.' Below I cite specific examples from my field notes of the default in action in the classroom, but first I will speak about it in general terms. Even though the analogy to computer software nomenclature and function breaks down in the fine detail, I called it the default to signify the basic 'order' or 'state' of children's relationships to their environments. The five characteristics of the default explained below should help clarify its nature. Two defining characteristics of the default are that it is a continuum and that it is social. Ten- and 11-year-old boys and girls regularly roughhouse with each other: sometimes it's a sneaky push in the back, sometimes it looks like a wrestling match, and sometimes it looks like real fighting. Unauthorized communications with peers can be quick whispers or extended conversations. A kid might throw one spitball or an extensive series of projectiles.

The default is social because the children's world is mostly peer-oriented. When showing off or challenging adult authority, kids are playing to peer audiences.

Children of course socially interact with adults, but successfully manipulating adults is the *raison d'être* for the default behaviour. For example, acting responsibly so as to be trusted to be sent on errands out of the classroom is all well and good, unless the child happens to detour by her friend's homeroom, the friend signs out for the bathroom, and they converse. Any excuse to be out of one's chair, sharpen a pencil, ask the teacher or a peer a question, leave the room for the bathroom or a drink, collect assignments or books, usually is used to visit with friends.

Three other qualities are equally important to what I saw to be the default's effectiveness: flexibility, resilience, and daring. By flexibility, I mean that the default is a constant condition subject to large swings with respect to degree of expression. For example, as a child or a group of children challenges an adult's authority, his/her peers gauge the adult's response, always poised to go toward the more extreme end of the default. *Flexibility means that the default is like a constant drip of water, which can easily turn into a stream or a flood.* Most substitute teachers elicit high degrees of expression of default behaviours. Music and art classes at Farmdale also registered very high on the default meter.

Of the three default behaviour qualities, resilience is perhaps the easiest to misinterpret as confrontation. No matter what efforts adults make to stifle it, the default will re-emerge. If a teacher changes the seats of particular children to separate them from allies with whom they are 'acting improperly,' they will soon initiate new alliances (while continuing to maintain contact with their former partners). Even wholesale seat changes lead to new friendships, not a more disciplined class.

Children are daring in two broad ways: in defying adult authority, or outrageously imitating older peers and/or siblings. As we will see in one of the transcripts below, children can be brutal when they feel motivated to be so. Prattfalls are mostly appreciated by peers. Arguing or just refusing to stop some behaviour when threatened, and thus forcing the teacher to send you from the room, is common. Even pushing a teacher into losing her cool and yelling serves the default well as it disrupts the educational flow in the room. If not positively sanctioned by peers, however, daring cannot be sustained. I observed time and again in my field work that peer credit, positive sanctioning, is the currency through which daring is rewarded.

Peer credit is also given for daring by imitation; and that credit increases if a child is one of the first of their peer group to do something they probably should not be doing. Behaviours with sexual implications (such as using swear words or telling dirty jokes, daring to wear clothes that expose belly buttons or underwear, age-inappropriate sexual experimentation, grinding against your boyfriend/girlfriend while dancing) make up a large part of daring. I think we adults would tend to label those most daring children 'bad.'

Gaining popularity seemed a major motivator for daring behaviours. Popularity, for the children in this study, meant that the child knew and was known by many peers who were or considered the popular child to be their friend and wanted to hang around with him/her. The most popular boys tended to be boyfriends with the most popular girls. A Riverton year 5 girl defined the popular person as 'funny, attractive, doesn't stromp [sulk] off when he doesn't get his way, nobody can fall out with him because if they do he soon makes up.' 'Funny,' as defined by the children's world, often entailed public displays that may not be appreciated by adults.

While the children did not characterize it as such, popularity also meant peer leadership. Somewhat paradoxically, to grow, to assume more ability to be responsible for themselves, children need to practise being older. The problem becomes whether or not the new behaviour is age-appropriate. Usually, to get the ball rolling, someone needs to dare to exhibit age-inappropriate behaviours (and once enough children follow that person's lead, the behaviour becomes age-appropriate and the next group of 11-year-olds needs to think of something different as a dare). *Thus, acts of badness are also acts of maturity, and those daring to be daring are also leading.*

When dealing with adults, the default uses three main strategic tactics that blend into each other: behavioural/symbolic negotiation, active negotiation, and direct confrontation. Symbolic negotiation means that a child or group of children are doing what they want to do and ignoring implicit adult desires not to do it (because they are supposed to be doing something else or are breaking some rule). Active negotiation results when adults make explicit requests but the children do not immediately comply. Confrontation begins when a child (or group) specifically told not to do something argues with the person forbidding them. *My observational data suggest that in school situations children always seem to win out against adult authority.* (My interview data seem to indicate that children mostly always win outside of school also.) No adult disciplinary tool, no punishment or threat of punishment stops all default behaviours completely, and those behaviours return over time to pre-discipline levels. *Ultimately, I concluded, children will do what they want.*

Adults in school situations aid and abet the default in two general ways. Looking at a whole class period, we see clearly that teachers tolerate much before they try to enforce order. The default is not suicidal, but no teacher is ever in a default-free situation, no classroom is ever totally under any adult's authority. For example, even Mrs Bridge, the most draconian disciplinarian, appeared to tolerate noise in her classroom only up to a particular level. One way to describe the phenomenon is to note that it was as if she had a mental sound meter set to that particular level of noise. When the noise level reached that point she would say 'right,' a signal that the children needed to quiet down. Interestingly, I became able to anticipate within a minute or so the point at which she would say right. Thus, even in her classes, the default gradually escalated.

Yet, if the children find the material intrinsically interesting and/or in their self-interest to learn, they will negatively sanction their peers in an effort to maintain the flow. Most children sense when their disruption will not receive positive peer sanctioning. Conversely, absent that negative sanctioning, adult authority becomes fair game, and the reward is often peer credit. A teacher's simplest way to maintain reasonable order in a classroom is to make the class interesting. Effective teachers seem to sense that an increase in default behaviours means that they are losing students' interest. One way to define effective teachers, then, is to note that they seem to understand that learning is a cooperative effort between teacher and student; that the teacher's task is to maintain student involvement and interest. When a teacher feels forced to threaten to use a particular disciplinary tool, or stop the class to make good on the threat (move a child, send him/her out of the room, impose a penalty to be served later), he/she will probably lose more of the class's attention or stop the teaching momentum dead in its tracks.

The second way that adults aid the default is subtler: teachers and administrators structure the school day so as to afford many opportunities that almost defy order. Any activity that does not have students sitting in a fixed place working quietly by themselves is an invitation for wholesale default behaviour. Since sitting in fixed places actually forms a minority of the school day, the default is fully licensed to express itself far more than it is structurally stifled. For example, group activities are part of the formal curriculum. During group projects – prime invitations for default behaviour – teachers allow students a great deal of latitude, mainly because they cannot enforce strict discipline without curtailing the activity. Even if a teacher wants to monitor formal group activities, he or she, unlike an avuncular researcher, will seldom get close enough to a student conversation to know whether or not it is about the task at hand. Further, non- or semi-academic activities like art, music, computer instruction and physical education are by definition 'fun' activities, and 'fun' is the default's middle name. Even further, once the default has had free reign for a long period of time, it is difficult to get the children to take seriously an adult's desire to return to a more authoritarian mode, unless the teacher can convince them that paying close attention is essential to learning interesting material.

Based on the fact that her mean FIS scores were the highest of the five teachers, Mrs Church (who had been teaching for over 30 years when I worked with her) appeared to have the least control over her classes. Interestingly, she believed that school should be fun for fifth-graders; she felt the atmosphere should be such that the children enjoy learning. Accordingly, she had made the loosening of the reigns of authority into a science: she established an exchange economy allowing the children to acquire points, in the form of stamps or stickers for good academic performance (which was defined very liberally, such as re-doing one's homework correctly after having had it explained, or giving an interesting answer during a current events discussion). That currency could be traded for snacks and sweets that she kept in her classroom. Of note, Mrs Church's students had as high or higher academic achievements than the other grade 5 students. One isolated FIS score may hint at an explanation. Compared with their colleagues, Mrs Church (highest mean FIS score) and Mrs Bridge (lowest mean FIS score), both scored highest for 'appropriate paying attention to teacher,' and 'appropriately talking to teacher.' My data suggested that, from totally different disciplinary positions, both teachers were able to get their student's attention when they needed to.

## Some field note transcripts

The following three partial/edited transcripts from my field notes were picked almost randomly from my data. I wrote down what caught my eye at a particular moment, but since I spent so much time at the schools, and, consequently, took so many notes, I am reasonably certain that my notes reflect what typically was occurring at those schools when I was present. They serve to illustrate some of the general points I made in the preceding sections. I follow each transcript with some interpretations of their significance to understanding the 'default'. The first transcript focuses on one child, the other two give broader snapshots of the behaviour of a number of children in those classrooms.

> *Riverton, March 3: Mrs Pegg Mid-Morning after recess*
> FIS observation of Trevor
> Sitting on carpet while Mrs Pegg explained assignment.
> Exchanged punches with Adam.
> Started pulling shoe apart.
> Used pieces of rubber as objects to be hit back and forth with Adam and
>     several other year six boys.
> Eventually, collected pieces and threw in trash.
> Took quite a bit of time going and returning from trash.
> Mrs Pegg still explaining lesson.
> Trevor constantly looking at, talking to, and giggling with his buddies.
> I noted that he may have glanced at Mrs Pegg twice.
> Children move to assigned seats.
> Trevor asks year five Emily what the assignment was.
> Takes a long time settling down.
> Finally focuses on work.
> But only puts border on sheet of paper and writes a title.

Recording the observation had been demanding because Trevor exhibited just about every inattentive and hyperactive-impulsive behaviour on the FIS checklist. These were not isolated observations of Trevor; they reflected some 'consistent' behaviour that I observed with Trevor, and many other children. I then asked: Is Trevor a typical pre-teen, or is he 'ADHD'? The children at Riverton were required to take their regular shoes off upon entering the school, and to wear special almost slipper-like shoes with very cheap rubber soles in school. Trevor was not the only child to destroy his, but according to the DSM-IV, at least solely on the basis of the number and frequency of the presenting behaviours themselves, one would certainly consider his behaviour as inattentive and/or impulsive; one might also characterize it as symptomatic of Oppositional Defiant Disorder, a condition said to be commonly associated with ADHD. The above description is more than typical of Trevor's in-class behaviour. However, he was an average student, a superior athlete, considered the most popular boy in year 6 because he was so well adjusted socially. Yet I have no doubt that, at least in America, Trevor would have been diagnosed with ADHD and put on a drug regimen.

The field notes on Trevor illustrate Mrs Pegg's ineffectiveness at controlling the children's behaviour, as all of Trevor's fooling around was taking place within ten feet of Mrs Pegg. It also illustrates well just how bold the default can be. Mrs Pegg had essentially lost control of the class by then, and the default had responded accordingly.

*Farmdale, November 3, Mrs Winter's English class*
12:00 silent reading:
FIS observation of Bambi
Bambi sitting next to Paige, plays with binder for a while, then focuses.
[*Paige*] distracts her repeatedly by talking to her.
Some of the children much less focused than Bambi
1:15 Going over homework assignment with Mrs Winter:
Half the children did not have what they were supposed to have done.
Turns out only four people followed assignment correctly.
Mrs Winter sharply rebukes the class. She is 'very disappointed.'
Mrs Winter is angry, almost yelling.
Mrs Winter tells the rest to get their parents to sign their assignment books.
Ryan is next to Jay who is totally unfocused.
Jay infectious, even though Ryan tried to focus.
Ryan eavesdrops on Grace, Kaitlyn, and Evan conversation at next table.
Kaitlyn flirting with Evan in whispers (some children so adept at whispering can't even see lips move).
Mason definitely not on task.
Luke told to either focus or go to principal's office. (I didn't see what he was doing.)
Mrs Winter again demands silence.
Whispering continues.
Kaitlyn can't find assignment page, Evan finds for her in her book.
Nick putting assignment away even as Mrs Winter continues to try to teach.
1:35 Mrs Winter reading story out loud:
Bambi all over room.
Bambi talks with Grace about her hand cream.
Bambi signs out for bathroom . . . uses as excuse to talk to Amanda.
Bambi right back, about four minutes, I note scepticism she went to bathroom.
Joe to bathroom . . . also comes back after about four minutes. (Maybe kids are just quick.)
Mrs Winter continues reading out loud even after period ends.

Mrs Winter tried to be a strict disciplinarian. She paid for those efforts by earning the children's enmity. The failure of the class to do the proper assignment shows how they ignored her. Despite her effort and its price, Mrs Winter's disciplinary tools were mostly ineffective. She employed a harsh tone of voice accompanied by anger; in the same sequence she mentioned being 'disappointed,' using guilt. When the children clearly weren't paying attention, as evidenced by the noise level in the room, she had to call for silence – but repeatedly. Finally, she tried to set an example by threatening Luke with the principal's office. In the end, she doggedly continued reading out loud even after the period had ended. This last act was her way to exert the one authority younger children do not dare to defy, the right to dismiss the class. It was, I suspect, a Pyrrhic victory.

The students exhibited the default tactics of passive and active negotiation. Passively, they whispered, left their seats for non-authorized reasons, and socialized rather than pay attention to Mrs Winter. Actively, they continued to whisper even after being explicitly told not to. Though I did not see what Luke was doing to warrant Mrs Winter's threat, pushing an adult to the point of being threatened by teachers' most powerful disciplinary tool would be an act of rebellion. This transcript also illustrates that the lines between the different tactics are not clear.

I should note that Mrs Church considered Bambi as the best student in the fifth grade. That Bambi chose to break the rules so blatantly is itself close to rebellion. That Joe (also an above-average student but also one of the 'bad' boys) picked up on the 'go to the bathroom' game shows something about how keenly aware children are of current default activities by their peers. I should also note that Luke was new to Farmdale and his major goal was to be popular. He had adopted a bad-boy attitude, and greeted Mrs Winter's threat with an 'oh please don't throw me in the brier patch, Brer Fox' attitude. In short, this transcript is an accurate example of the level at which Mrs Winter could control her class. Tables 10.2 and 10.3 show that the mean FIS scores of her students placed her third among the five teachers, and varied significantly from scores of the first two on the list, Mrs Church and Mrs Young. Accordingly, it seems fair to conclude that the mean FIS scores represent an accurate barometer of what was actually occurring in the classrooms I observed.

*Riverton, May 5: Mrs Bridge 9:00 to 10:10*
Students at tables, Mrs Bridge teaching using the flip chart that serves as the room's chalk board.

Adrian FIS observation
Repeatedly turning towards Trevor sitting next to him, talking and smiling.
Smile looks 'distant.'
Looking out window.
Knew answers to two questions.

General observations
Trinity being very dramatic about what brittle means.
Trinity and Gavin sword fighting using pencils.
Trinity and Gavin now playing hockey with pencils and eraser.

Gavin's pencil goes flying; Trinity giggles.

Zoe just stuck tongue out at Rachael, now making faces.

Cadence making faces at Owen.

Gavin balancing back and forth on chair, kicking both legs, then bouncing back on floor.

Owen and Austin in intimate conversation.

Zoe playing with Cadence' hair.

Mary animated.

Neither Wren nor Glen can see board from where sitting.

Trinity focused on ruler which is in her mouth. She is squiggling, making discernable noise singing to herself, totally unfocused.

Lilly has her feet up on her chair and is sitting on her haunches. She is playing with Victorian artifacts.

Wren lounging in his chair.

Mrs Bridge says: 'Owen, who isn't looking or listening?' Then she asked Trinity: 'What's another thing you can do?'

Trinity knew answer!

Robin appears to be in own world.

Lauren smiling and talking to Zoe across room.

Bobbi becomes involved in Lauren/Zoe conversation.

Lauren poking cheeks with air in them.

Lauren pretending to be disco dancing with Bobbi.

Mrs Bridge says: 'Put a log on the fire Anna.'

Then she asks: 'Cole what is an irreversible process?'

'Glen an example of a reversible process, or Wren because you're both messing around.'

Time for Assembly: year five boys, with Connor as ringleader, get lined up together. That means they will get to sit together.

As previously illustrated by Mrs Bridge's apparently characteristic level of tolerance for noise in her classroom, even an experienced teacher and good disciplinarian never has complete control of a class. Mrs Bridge only relied on singling out some of the students for a question or an admonition rather than, as she did on other occasions, yelling at the whole class (which was often accompanied by a threat). In fact, since my notes do not single out Owen, Wren, Glen or Anna, then, as the notes do indicate, these children were far from the only people Mrs Bridge could have singled out; although she did catch Trinity. Yet, as I believe the data on Trinity showed quite dramatically, *no matter how poorly a child seems to be attending, there may be no way, without asking him/her a question, to know whether or not that is the case.* It also suggests that hyperactive movements, sitting improperly, bouncing, squiggling, do not necessarily translate into lack of attention.

The transcript also illustrates an earlier point, that many adult-supplied structural opportunities encourage the default. First, the schoolroom had been poorly planned, or perhaps had not been planned for 32 students, such that at least two students could not see what their teacher was writing on her makeshift chalkboard. Second, the subject matter Mrs Bridge was teaching was part of the national curriculum, more specifically 'literacy hour,' a new nationwide mandate introduced at the beginning of that school year. The material was not particularly challenging, as the students did not need to give it their full attention to answer questions. Mrs Bridge, like a number of her colleagues, resented the national curriculum. Perhaps her lack of enthusiasm was why she did not really try to enforce order. In any event, the default saw its openings and took full advantage. Third, the children manipulated who sat with whom in assembly by lining up in a particular order.

## Conclusions

Several conclusions may follow from the research described in this paper. First, it seems clear that ADHD-like behaviours are expressed by all children, irrespective of gender or academic success. As part of the complete analysis of the FIS data (Jacobson 2003), minimum and maximum scores for each child were calculated. These scores showed wide fluctuations within each child: even the most daring children, or those showing the most inappropriate behaviour, would settle down and attend to their work. In fact, only a single of the 600 FIS observations showed a child to be 'inattentive' for the full 15-minute observation, and that child was of one of the most academically advanced student at Farmdale. This suggests that each child's degree of expression of ADHD-like behaviours is so extensive, that any attempt to separate 'normal' expression from 'disordered' expression requires setting a standard for normalcy either so low that large numbers of children would need to be diagnosed, or so high that that current CDC supplied figure of 7 per cent seems absurdly high.

Although the efforts to find biological 'causes' for this 'disorder' may be contributing to fundamental understanding of the functioning of the human brain, I seriously doubt these efforts will ever lead to discovering heritable differences in brain anatomy that will meaningfully differentiate between order and disorder, normal and abnormal. Therefore, it seems fair to ask: Are there any scientific grounds upon which the long-term prescription of powerful drugs to children for these seemingly universal behaviours can be justified? Is the diagnosis of children as ADHD yet one more tool adults are using to try to enhance their power over children? Is drug treatment just as abusive as the physical abuse that is now so heavily monitored and legally penalized? Is labelling a child with ADHD – with potential for stigmatization and negative effects on a child's self-esteem – a form of psychological abuse?

Second, it is not scientifically possible to quantify how much learning is not taking place because school-age children devote as much energy to default behaviours as they do to academics. Likewise, it is not scientifically possible to quantify what educational opportunities are being lost, or what would change in the quality of teaching if teachers were not forced to devote so much of their time to dealing with the default. One suspects, however, that both the breadth and quality of the learning experience would be greatly enhanced if the default were no longer a major impediment. That is not to say that the current system is a complete failure; clearly, it is not. It just seems tragic that so much educational potential is being wasted in the struggle between the default and adult power.

Third, it seems to follow that a redefinition of the roles of both groups might be beneficial, not just for family units or classrooms but for society writ large. Such a redefinition would, hopefully, decrease the need for default behaviours. Summerhill, the school founded by A. S. Neill 70 years ago in Leiston, England, may be where to find such an alternative model. Neill hoped to create a community based on a principle of 'liberty without license,' whereby any member of the school community can do whatever they please so long as they do not impose on the rights of others. During weekly meetings at which the school's business is conducted, students and faculty members all have one vote. Since students outnumber faculty, the student vote decides, and it is binding for all issues (except, perhaps, the very existence of the school). At Summerhill, adult authority had been institutionally abrogated.

In 2000, the English government's school inspection unit, OFSTED, recommended that Summerhill be closed, mainly because class attendance was not mandatory. In 2002 the case was settled after Summerhill appealed to a special court of review in London. Before the settlement became final, the current group of Summerhill students convened a Summerhill meeting in a vacant courtroom, thoroughly discussed the issues, and voted to approve the settlement. If these children and teenagers (the oldest is perhaps sixteen) had not voted to approve the settlement, it would have needed to be renegotiated. Part of the settlement specifically states that any future inspections of Summerhill must strongly take into account the children's opinions as to whether they are benefiting from being at Summerhill. Thus, the ruling upheld Summerhill's contention that learning to be a member of a community, learning to exercise one's democratic rights in a responsible manner, learning to become self-motivated, are as important as any particular academic achievements the school might impart. It also gave legal sanction to the equality of children and adults at that particular school.

Indeed, the negotiated settlement put the British government officially on record as agreeing that: (1) children are capable of making important decisions with respect to their own lives; (2) granting that capability makes implicit their right as citizens of a democratic society to be allowed to make those decisions, free from adult coercion; (3) accordingly, the role of adults (and of older peers) is to mentor, not to control. At its essence, then, this settlement holds that adults can reason with children but cannot *order* them about.

Summerhill has given rise to many schools around the world following democratic principles. Most are small, private institutions but some are publicly funded. Interestingly, some such schools, for example, the Albany Free School, a small inner city school in Albany, New York, do not recognize ADHD as a disorder or allow students to be on drug therapies (Mercogliano 2003). The issue of how to compare student achievement between democratic and conventional schools is beginning to be addressed and more research is needed. Of course, even if democratic education were widely introduced, a broader question is whether it can have a lasting effect on children not raised in democratic families. Yet, the value of learning to be a good community member may well be more important than any specific pedagogical goal. Possibly, conditioning children to a belief that 'might makes right' lies at the root of many tensions between adults and children, as well as between groups – ethnic, local, regional, or national. Anything that can be done to improve conditions leading to this belief may lessen these tensions and conflicts.

# References

Altman, J. (1974) 'Observational study of behaviour: sampling methods'. *Behaviour*, 49: 227–267.

American Psychiatric Association (1994) *Diagnostic and Statistical Manual of Mental Disorders, Fourth Edition (DSM- IV)* Washington, DC: American Psychiatric Association.

Barkley, R. A. and Murphy, K. R. (1998) *Attention-Deficit Hyperactivity Disorder*. New York: The Guilford Press.

Diller, L. H. (1998) *Running on Ritalin*. New York: Bantam Books.

Emerson, R. M., Fretz, R. I. and Shaw, L. L. (1995) *Writing Ethnographic Fieldnotes*. Chicago, IL: University of Chicago Press.

Harris, J. R. (1998) *The Nurture Assumption*. New York: Free Press.

Jacobson, K. (2003) 'When order becomes disorder: A cross-cultural study of attention deficit hyperactivity disorder and its implications for the social construction of "normal"'. Doctoral dissertation, Department of Anthroplogy, University of Massachusetts-Amherst.

Mercogliano, C. (2003) *Teaching the Restless: One School's Remarkable No Ritalin Approach to Helping Children Learn and Succeed*. Boston, MA: Beacon Press.

Pastor, P. N. and Reuben, C. A. (2002) 'Attention deficit disorder and learning disability: United States, 1997–98'. *National Center for Health Statistics. Vital and Health Statistics*, 10(208).

# Appendix

Table 10.1 Children's ADHD-like behaviour in different schools (as percentage of all 'inappropriate' behaviour)

| School | N | Mean FIS score ± Standard deviation | | | | |
|---|---|---|---|---|---|---|
| | | Inattention (all daydreaming) | Inattention (some daydreaming) | Inattention (no video) | Hyperact/impulsivity | Appropriate score 'video' |
| Dyslexic | 16 | 24.9 ± 5.9 | 22.5 ± 6.3 | 28.1 ± 7.3 | 27.7 ± 7.9 | 9.6 ± 7.3 |
| England | 33 | 28.8 ± 8.7 | 24.7 ± 9.5 | 28.8 ± 8.7 | 34.8 ± 5.6 | 0.20 ± 1.17 |
| US | 48 | 32.8 ± 6.8 | 31.3 ± 7.0 | 32.8 ± 6.8 | 39.5 ± 7.0 | 1.21 ± 2.72 |
| $P$ * | | DY-EN: 0.20 | DY-EN: 0.635 | DY-EN: 0.937 | DY-EN: 0.002 | |
| | | DY-US: 0.001 | DY-US: 0.001 | DY-US: 0.08 | DY-US: 0.000 | |
| | | EN-US: 0.048 | EN-US: 0.001 | EN-US: 0.05 | EN-US: 0.007 | |

* Probability, using Tukey's HSD test, that observed differences are due to chance; $p$ values $\leq$ 0.05 suggest that observed differences are statistically significant.

Table 10.2 Children's ADHD-like behaviours (as percentage of all 'inappropriate' behaviours) with different teachers

| Teacher | N | Mean FIS score ± Standard deviation | | | | | | | |
|---|---|---|---|---|---|---|---|---|---|
| | | Inattention (all DD[1]) | Teacher rank* | Inattention (some DD[2]) | Teacher rank* | Inattention (no video) | Teacher rank* | Hyperact/ Impulsive | Teacher rank* |
| Mrs Bridge-EN | 32 | 25.7 ± 9.9 | 1 | 21.4 ± 10.9 | 1 | 25.7 ± 9.9 | 1 | 31.6 ± 5.9 | 1 |
| Mrs Pegg-EN | 32 | 34.7 ± 11.0 | 4 | 31.1 ± 11.9 | 3 | 34.7 ± 11.0 | 4 | 40.1 ± 9.2 | 4 |
| Mrs Young-US | 47 | 29.5 ± 8.6 | 2 | 27.9 ± 8.5 | 2 | 29.5 ± 8.6 | 2 | 36.7 ± 8.8 | 2 |
| Mrs Church-US | 47 | 37.2 ± 10.0 | 5 | 35.9 ± 10.7 | 5 | 37.2 ± 10.0 | 5 | 43.7 ± 11.3 | 5 |
| Mrs Winter-US | 48 | 33.2 ± 12.7 | 3 | 31.3 ± 12.7 | 4 | 33.2 ± 12.7 | 3 | 39.4 ± 11.6 | 3 |

* 1 = lowest; 5 = highest; 1: daydreaming; 2: only 'inappropriate' daydreaming

*Table 10.3*  Children's 'appropriate' behaviour (as percentage of all behaviour) with different teachers

| Teacher | N | Mean FIS score ± Standard deviation | | | |
|---|---|---|---|---|---|
| | | 'Appropriate' behaviour | Teacher rank* | 'Appropriate' behaviour (excl. 'appropriate' daydreaming) | Teacher rank* |
| Mrs Bridge-EN | 32 | 58.7 ± 8.9 | 1 | 54.3 ± 8.3 | 1 |
| Mrs Pegg-EN | 32 | 52.7 ± 10.1 | 3 | 49.2 ± 9.7 | 3 |
| Mrs Young-US | 47 | 54.4 ± 8.8 | 2 | 52.8 ± 8.9 | 2 |
| Mrs Church-US | 47 | 46.0 ± 10.9 | 5 | 44.8 ± 10.4 | 5 |
| Mrs Winter-US | 48 | 49.6 ± 11.9 | 4 | 47.7 ± 11.5 | 4 |
| **Total** | 206 | 51.8 ± 11.0 | | 49.5 ± 10.4 | |

\* 1 = highest, 5 = lowest

# Chapter 11

# Pedagogy in the 'ADHD classroom'

## An exploratory study of 'The Little Group'

*Eva Hjörne*

The aim of this chapter is to explore the pedagogical practices developed in a Swedish school in response to the diagnosis ADHD/DAMP.[1] Thus, I focus on what educational strategies practitioners consider relevant when organising teaching and learning activities for children diagnosed with ADHD/DAMP.

At present, this diagnosis is one of the most commonly used categories when accounting for failure in school. The prevalence of children classified as having ADHD/DAMP is estimated at about 10 per cent by the National Board of Health and Welfare in Sweden (Socialstyrelsen 2002). The estimates vary widely, though, from about 1 per cent (Elinder 1997; Kärfve 2000) to above 20 per cent when including concentration difficulties in general (Kadesjö and Gillberg 1998: 799).

Children diagnosed with ADHD/DAMP are usually described as having considerable difficulties managing their schooling (Gillberg 1996; DuPaul and Stoner 2003). They are claimed neither to fit into a normal school, nor into already existing classes specially organised to meet the needs of other children with special needs. This dilemma is something schools currently face, and it has to be handled in some way. As a consequence, different pedagogical practices specifically directed towards the needs of this group of children are organised. For instance, so-called DAMP classes, and even DAMP schools, have now appeared in many communities in Sweden.

However, although such practices emerge as solutions, there is little known about how this kind of education is organised. There are very few, if any, studies conducted in the classroom 'regarding instructional, curricular, or classroom environment manipulations aimed at enhancing the learning and academic performance of these children' (DuPaul and Stoner 2003: 174). The main focus of the study on which this chapter is based is to make visible the classroom practices assumed to suit children assigned the diagnosis ADHD/DAMP. It is a case study, and the following, largely descriptive, questions are focused on: What educational strategies correspond to the diagnosis ADHD/DAMP? What practices unfold, and what do these imply for the pupil's educational career and for his/her identity?

## Strategies for compensating for the slow learner – normalising practices in the classroom

The usual educational strategy for pupils who are categorised as slow learners or learning disabled, or who are claimed to have other problems adapting to life in school, is to compensate by arranging special teaching groups or classes with suitable educational activities (Haug 1998). Offering special teaching groups for pupils who do not fit into the normal school is by no means a new phenomenon. For example, in Sweden there is a long history of organising such classes. In the national curriculum for the comprehensive school of 1962, there were eight different types of special classes, each of which was intended to match the needs of children with some kind of special need. There were for example, school readiness classes, remedial classes and classes for children with cerebral palsy (CP-klass) (LGR 1962: 64–68). And the pedagogical strategies recommended in such special classes were, for example, to practise motor and linguistic skills, and to train children in various kinds of social behaviours.

At present, the strategy of organising special classes of this kind is no longer recommended in the curriculum. Instead, one frequently used model for dealing with teaching and learning problems is to organise small groups. These groups, which may be more or less temporary, are referred to in a number of different ways, for example: 'the little teaching group', classes for 'reading, writing and learning problems', 'speech and language classes', 'preparation classes', classes for pupils with 'social-behavioural problems', and classes for children with 'neuropsychiatric impairments' such as 'DAMP/ADHD classes' and 'Asperger's groups' (Blom 1999: 26).

The ambition behind many of these arrangements with special teaching groups is that they should serve as normalising practices. The idea has generally been to compensate for the disabilities and problems of the children, so that they will later be able to return to a normal class. However, one interesting observation is that often, perhaps in a majority of these cases, there has been no clear link between the diagnosis of the pupil and the teaching supplied. As Haug (1998) expresses it, what characterises the situation is a 'great variety of diagnoses and a low number of pedagogical strategies' (p. 16) that correspond to the diagnoses. This is a very critical issue from both an educational and a democratic point of view, since diagnoses are used in segregating pupils from the mainstream of schooling in a school which, by law, has to serve the needs of all children. The arguments used in this process of segregation, as well as the pedagogical strategies employed for helping children to return to their regular class, have to be carefully scrutinised. The purpose of this study is to look into the pedagogical strategies of such special teaching groups for children assigned the diagnosis ADHD/DAMP.

## The category ADHD/DAMP and its behavioural manifestations

To give a brief background, it should be pointed out that ADHD is claimed to be a neuropsychiatric disorder characterised by *inattention, hyperactivity*, and *impulsivity*. The criteria are described in the diagnostic manual DSM-IV[2] (Diagnostic and Statistical Manual of Mental Disorders), 'which defines psychiatric disorders as fixed measurable categories' (Lloyd and Norris 1999: 512). Children who exhibit the behaviours characteristic of ADHD are said to be 'more likely than their peers to have academic problems' (Reid 1999:1). Many of the described symptoms of ADHD/DAMP 'take the form of overt behaviours that typically are viewed as disruptive in classroom and school environments' (DuPaul and Eckert 1997: 369).

It is also worth noting that boys are more often claimed to have these kinds of difficulties than girls. The ratio of boys to girls supposed to have ADHD/HKD[3] is 'between 3:1 and 9:1 but this may decrease with age. Part of the differences between the sexes may be referral bias related to symptoms of disruptive behaviour since boys have more hyperactive/impulsive symptoms and more conduct and oppositional symptoms than girls' (Swanson *et al.* 1998: 429). This gender imbalance is visible in the present case study as well, since 'The Little Group' I have followed consists of boys only.

In this chapter I will not raise the issues around diagnosis, since these are discussed elsewhere in this book. However, it should be pointed out that in Sweden a heated debate concerning the status of the diagnosis ADHD/DAMP has been going on for many years. The debate has been polarised, with some arguing that this syndrome cannot be considered an identifiable and verifiable condition at all, while others argue that this is one of the most significant health problems of our time. The topic, thus, is very sensitive for those involved, including teachers and parents. It is important to emphasise that I am not taking a stand on the controversial issues of the nature and aetiology of this condition. Rather, my focus is on the concrete uses of the diagnosis as an account of school failure (cf. Hjörne and Säljö 2004), and what pedagogical interventions are considered to match this diagnosis.

## ADHD/DAMP and its pedagogy: solutions suggested

Medical researchers have prescribed pedagogical strategies suitable for children claimed to have ADHD/DAMP. For example, Gillberg (1996), a very influential medical researcher in Sweden within this field, recommends the following strategies when teaching children claimed to have ADHD/DAMP:

- Teaching in a small group;
- Individual instructions in basic subjects such as mathematics, reading and writing;

- Short concentration period, only a few minutes at a time during the first school years;
- Breaks with regular intervals;
- Practice of motor skills (Gillberg 1996: 165–167, my translation).

The term 'structure' appears frequently in descriptions provided by medical scholars as advice to teachers. 'Giving structure to the child's everyday life implies that adults with external frames, rules, and changes in the setting around the child reduce the number of situations where the child has to choose' (Kadesjö 1991: 20, my translation). The preferred structure is described in terms such as 'firm' or 'clear'. In concrete terms, this implies having the same schedule every day in school, having short working periods, and frequent and short pauses (Kadesjö 1991). Furthermore, a prominent argument in this biomedically based philosophy of teaching is to practise various kinds of skills and behaviours; motor skills and skills that have to do with the ability to concentrate, to pay attention, to manage social interaction, and to handle impulses (Kadesjö 1991, 2001).

## Research design

The study reported here is a case study carried out in a classroom with children diagnosed with ADHD/DAMP. The class is locally known as 'The Little Group'. The class includes six boys between 7 and 12 years of age. The pupils are: Per (12 years of age), Peter (10), Paul (9), Pierre (8), and Peo (7) and Pontus (7). The pupils mostly stay three years in the class. There are five adults in the classroom (see below).

I visited the class two days a week during one and a half semesters, and one day every fortnight over a period of two months, sometimes half days and sometimes full days. In all, I visited the classroom on forty occasions from September to May, during the school year of 2000–2001. Thus, I have followed the daily life in this classroom over an extended period of time observing teaching and learning activities. Data were produced using a microethnographic approach (Mehan *et al.* 1986), which implies that the generation of data has been performed through participant observation, field-notes, informal conversations, audio-recorded interviews and by analysing the so-called Working Plan for this class. Other documents, such as training programmes for the children and evaluation documents, have been treated as support data. The interviews with the teachers have been transcribed. There are two and a half handwritten notebooks of field-notes, later transcribed with a word processor. The choice of a participant observation approach represents an attempt to catch such practices as they evolve rather than, for instance, hear how they are described by various actors and stake-holders.

The study has followed the ethical rules for research in the humanities and social sciences adopted by the Swedish Research Council. For the purpose of this study I have focused on the institutional practices and the discourse and meaning making that unfold in these settings.

## Empirical setting

The South Valley Comprehensive School has about 170 pupils from preschool to grade three. None of the children in the class studied live in the reception area for this particular comprehensive school. Rather, they come from other parts of the school district (which is the whole town). The class observed is taught in a room on the fringes of a regular comprehensive school for children between the ages of 6 and 9 years in a medium-sized town (see Figure 11.1).

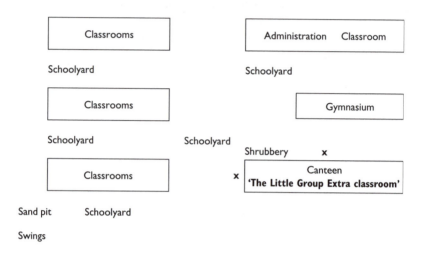

*Figure 11.1* The South Valley Comprehensive School, Grades 1–3.

The mode of organising the setting is characterised by:

- A high teacher/pupil ratio (five teachers and six boys);
- Six desks along the walls, separated from each other;
- The use of shields to separate the children from each other;
- The availability of an extra classroom to be used when there is a need to separate a pupil or a group of pupils from the others;
- A smaller room with a computer next to the classroom. This room is used by the oldest pupil.

Thus, the physical setting is designed on the basis of the idea of separating the children from each other by using shields (see Figure 11.2). The pupils are therefore separated from their regular school and their regular class. They are also separated from the other pupils in this specific school, and they are separated from each other in the classroom as well. This strategy of separating the children from others is claimed by teachers to be an important element in the provision of education for children categorised as having ADHD/DAMP. Along the same lines, the environment is designed to be without external stimulus, that is, devoid of any pictures and other items that might attract attention.

In addition, as can be seen in Figure 11.1, there is an extra room in the same building, but on the opposite side of the classroom. This is used when the group is divided for specific activities. The pedagogical practices that unfold in the classroom are strictly framed by the principles of separation and, as I will show, the idea of 'structure'.

In the classroom (see Figure 11.2), there are, as already mentioned, five adults: two assistants, ARON and AILEEN, two pre-school teachers, PIA and PERNILLA, and one teacher, THEA, trained for junior-level children.[4] The teachers usually take responsibility for one pupil each.

During the lessons, the teachers stand next to the pupils' desks, and during sharing-time the teacher responsible sits next to the pupil. One of the boys normally does not have a teacher next to him. The pupils sit close to the walls far away from each other during all activities except during sharing-time, when they all sit around a big oval table with eleven chairs. There is also a sofa in the room where the teachers, after the meal, read fantasy stories for the pupils. In the cloakroom there is a trampoline, a hula hoop and a skipping-rope to be used for motor exercises during the lessons. Shields are used when the curriculum says 'Work'. These are set up ahead of such a period and separate the children effectively from each other. During the lessons, the pupils have an individual schedule to follow.

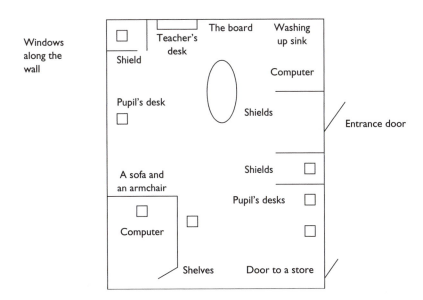

*Figure 11.2* The ADHD/DAMP classroom.

## Research findings

The research findings will be presented in three sections. The first concerns the learning and teaching practices in the ADHD/DAMP classroom. In the second part, I will focus on the teachers' accounts of what they do, including their interpretation of the pedagogical ideas they are attempting to implement. Finally, I will summarise and discuss some of the organising principles and strategies used in the practices of educating pupils with this diagnosis.

## Learning and teaching in an ADHD/DAMP classroom

The task of the teachers is to organise educational activities relevant for pupils diagnosed with ADHD/DAMP. Preferably, this should be done in such a manner that the children can return to a normal class at a later stage. The question is how this is done in the daily work, and what knowledge the activities are based on. In order to make the pedagogical practices visible, I have followed one boy (Pontus, 7 years old) during one day and I will present a relatively detailed description of this day in the classroom. Nothing exceptional happened during this particular day. It followed the schedule closely.

### The 22nd of January: a day in 'The Little Group'

The day begins at 8.10. The class is divided into two groups. One group, Per, Peter, Paul and Peo, stay in the regular classroom. The other group, Pierre and Pontus, go to the smaller classroom together with PIA and PERNILLA. I follow them. They are to stay there between 8.10 and 9.30.

*A. Greeting ceremony, at 8.10*

*B. Today's date and schedule, at 8.14*

They all sit around a table, and Pontus reads the date and some other information from the calendar. PIA writes this information on the board: 01–01–22. PIA also writes the schedule of the day on the board:

|       |               |
|-------|---------------|
|       | Work          |
| 9.30  | Break         |
| 10.00 | Sharing-time  |
|       | Newspaper     |
|       | Your own work |
| 10.40 | Lunch         |
|       | Reading       |
|       | Short break   |
|       | Game          |

12.00   – – (Two pupils finish their school-day, among them Pontus (my comment.))

*Figure 11.3* The schedule as presented in the smaller classroom.

## C. Sharing-time 1, at 8.20

Next it is sharing-time. The talk is about what happened during the weekend. The pupils have to talk one at a time, and they are not allowed to interrupt each other. The teacher reads the pupils' individual schedules before handing them over. The pupils are expected to follow the schedule and work on one task at a time beginning from number 1. PIA instructs them to work five minutes on each task.

1.  My letters Jj
2.  Maths, p. 39
3.  Lyckos 4 c
4.  Computer
5.  Jigsaw puzzle
6.  Maths, pp. 46–47
7.  Hula hoop
8.  Computer
    If you have time, cut Pokemón

*Figure 11.4* The individual schedule for Pontus.

The individual schedule illustrates the nature of work in this class. The working periods are very short. In between, the pupils have to do motor exercises. The activities consist of a mixture of games and academic exercises. The work period that followed will be illustrated by Pontus' activities.

## D. Work, at 8.30

At 8.30 the schedule says 'work'. During this period, the pupils are to work with the tasks described in their individual schedule. They work for one hour, and Pontus is assisted by PERNILLA, who stands next to his desk. There are shields around the computer table and around the pupil's desk.

### EXAMPLE 1: LEARNING LETTERS, AT 8.30

The first task for Pontus is to practise the letters J and j (see Figure 11.4). This task is accomplished in five steps through successive exercises. Pontus gets a set of sheets to complete. The first step in this activity is to choose five colours, and to colour the letters J and j printed on a sheet of paper. A large capital J is printed on one side of the sheet, and a large lower-case j on the other side. Pontus starts to argue with the teacher about how and in what way the task is to be carried out. Pontus wants to start from the bottom when colouring the letters, but PERNILLA tells him that *you always start from the top*. He continues to argue with the teacher.

> Pontus: I don't need any help
> PERNILLA: but we have to see that you're doing the right thing
> Pontus: I decide when you are to leave

Pontus then starts colouring from the top. After a while he has finished this task. He gets a new sheet. This time he is supposed to find the letters J and j on a sheet of paper with many different letters. There are fourteen on the sheet.

The next step is to read words and find out where in the words you hear the sound of the letter J; at the beginning, in the middle, or at the end. Today, Pontus will only do three of the five exercises intended for learning letters.

From a pedagogical point of view, this is a traditional exercise when learning letters, and it is used in many classrooms. The main difference from a regular classroom activity is that the pupil is alone with a teacher standing next to his desk and monitoring his activities. However, this particular arrangement is not always appreciated by the pupil. As can be seen, there is a moment when the social order is negotiated by Pontus. An interesting observation is that Pontus works on this task for fifteen minutes instead of the five that were intended according to the schedule.

EXAMPLE 2: LEARNING TO READ, AT 8.55

The next task for Pontus is 'reading-cards'. This activity is like a memory game, where the task is to match a sentence, for example, 'A black cat is under the table', with a card showing a picture. PERNILLA tells Pontus to put the pencil away. *I think with it*, he answers. He continues holding the pencil, then drops it on the floor and picks it up. He lies on the chair and seems frustrated. PERNILLA and Pontus start playing the reading cards together, and PERNILLA counts at the beginning to see who will be first to take a card. Pontus starts to argue about this. He wants to decide.

> PERNILLA: you decided yesterday so today it's my turn
> Pontus: this is not fair, can't we do 'stone, scissors and bag' [a game]
> PERNILLA: that's a game so we'll do it during the break

Pontus is cheating when playing reading cards. He is turning a card halfway, and then choosing a different one. PERNILLA tells him to stop cheating. They quarrel most of the time they are playing.

In this instance, there is once again a moment when the social order is negotiated. The teacher refers to 'stone, scissors and bag' as a game and it therefore cannot be part of a lesson, although it could be argued that they are playing what must be considered a game. However, this particular 'game' qualifies as schoolwork, since it is connected to teaching of Swedish through reading the cards. The boy, however, seems to be rather frustrated. He starts to disrupt the game by cheating when playing, and the teacher and the pupil continue to negotiate the social order.

### EXAMPLE 3: LEARNING NUMBERS, AT 9.03

When Pontus has finished reading cards, he goes to the cupboard to get 'Lyckos', which is the next task. Lyckos is a game where the children practise reading words or numbers and matching these with pictures on a board. In this case, Pontus is going to match numbers with pictures. When PERNILLA instructs him, he says *be quiet* to her all the time.

> Pontus: you're not to tell me
> PERNILLA: you don't talk like that
> Pontus: but stop pointing out

This is another instance when the social order is openly negotiated. Pontus does not want the teacher to help him, and he tells her to be quiet. The teacher answers by instructing the pupil not to talk to a teacher as he does. In this way, she explicitly keeps to the 'structure' and the social order. She also instructs him about the expected roles of being a teacher and a student, respectively (Freebody and Freiberg 2000; Austin *et al.* 2003).

The task again is a sort of game but alludes to schoolwork, since it is about recognising numbers. It is a simple task, well structured and clearly defined.

### EXAMPLE 4: SKIP THE ROPE, AT 9.10

Pontus has finished 'Lyckos'. The next task, according to his schedule, is 'skipping-rope'.

> PERNILLA: you have to put it back before you skip the rope
> Pontus: the hula hoop you mean (?)
> PERNILLA: no it [the schedule] says skipping-rope, later on you can choose the hula hoop

Pontus goes out to the cloakroom to skip rope.

The teachers consistently enforce the 'structure' by limiting the possibilities for the pupils to choose. If the schedule says skip rope, hula hoop is not an option, though both are motor exercises. Through comments of this kind, the roles of teacher and student are effectively maintained.

## EXAMPLE 5: PRACTISE READING, AT 9.10

Pierre is doing the next task on his individual schedule: 'practise reading'. He starts to read in his book. He reads in a loud voice in the presence of PIA. After a minute, Pontus returns from the cloakroom. He gets the jigsaw puzzle and starts to turn over the pieces. Suddenly Pierre calls out:

> Pierre: can't you [addressing Pontus] work a bit more quietly(!)
> PIA: he's got to turn over the jigsaw pieces [addressing Pierre]
> Pierre: shut up you [addressing Pontus] little monkey (!)
> PIA: be quiet (!)[addressing Pierre]

Pierre reads the letters in a louder voice. PIA tells him that *you're just fooling around*. Pontus is calling out *be quiet* all the time, and Pierre is calling back *be quiet*. Finally, the teachers manage to get both of the pupils quiet.

All the participants in the classroom are involved in negotiating the order of the classroom. The pupils make breaches of discipline and they display various kinds of behaviours that break the norms of what is expected behaviour of a student in a classroom. And the teachers remind them of what is proper behaviour.

## EXAMPLE 6: LEARNING MATHS, AT 9.14

Pontus has now finished the jigsaw puzzle and lies down on the chair. He is making a lot of noise, singing and shouting. PERNILLA tells him that if he continues doing that, he will have to go out [to the cloakroom].

Again, social order is on the agenda but this time the teacher threatens the pupil by telling him that he will have to go to the cloakroom if he is not quiet. This threat of reprisal is probably a common way of correcting and punishing pupils in many classrooms. It is not an exceptional method for the treatment of pupils diagnosed as ADHD/DAMP-pupils.

## EXAMPLE 7: MOTOR PRACTISING, AT 9.24

Pontus continues to do his maths (item 6 on his schedule). When he is ready, the schedule says hula hoop.

> PERNILLA: we won't do that now since Pierre is there [in the cloak-room], could you manage to do the computer before we go out so you can do the computer before the break (?)
> Pontus: yes

Pontus goes to the computer. PERNILLA puts Pontus' maths book into his desk. This time, the teacher negotiates the 'structure' with the pupil and he accepts this. In this way, they change the 'structure' and switch the order in the individual schedule.

At 9.28 Pontus goes out to do the hula hoop. At 9.30 the lesson ends and it is break time.

As can be seen, Pontus did not manage to complete his individual schedule; he did not manage his very last point, cutting Pokemón pictures.

An illustration of the importance of complying with the 'structure', in this case the individual schedule, is when Pontus goes to the cloakroom for motor exercises two minutes before the break. In many instances, it would seem somewhat strange to start with motor exercises two minutes before a break.

The pedagogical practices that unfold during the working period mainly focus on the social order and the behaviours of the pupils. It seems more important that the pupils are *occupied* with something rather than *what* they are doing. There is very little interaction about the contents of the various tasks.

## E. Break, at 9.30

During this break, the pupils usually play on their own, although under close surveillance.

## F. Sharing-time 2, at 10.00

The pupils and the teachers gather in the regular classroom. All the pupils and four of the teachers are here. According to the schedule it is sharing-time. Everybody is supposed to say something about what happened during the break. Pontus raises his hand.

> Pontus: first Paul, Pierre, Peo, and myself we were pals and then we start to quarrel with each other –
> Peo: yes we–
> PIA: Pontus has to finish his story first
> Pontus: we can tell it together
> PIA: you tell it one at a time, that's how you do it in school

In this case, the teacher does not comment on the content of what is being said, but again it is the social order which is focused on. She makes the rules explicit about how to tell a story in school by instructing the pupils. Thus, she makes use of the opportunity to point out what is expected and what is 'normal' behaviour in a regular classroom.

## G. Newspaper, at 10.15

The next point on the schedule of the day is 'newspaper'. At this point, the teacher reads aloud from a newspaper. Afterwards the pupils are supposed to draw a picture based on the story just read. Today, PIA reads from a newspaper, first the headline; 'Man died, fell from the balcony'. She continues:

> PIA: he lay on the ground and there was blood there and you can't survive if you fall from such a high height, the police were called and another man was arrested, crime was committed, it was murder [shows a picture from the newspaper]

The pupils talk about the event and raise some questions. PERNILLA, the teacher, takes a sheet of paper and shows the pupils what to do.

> PERNILLA: here you can draw a high-rise building with many storeys and balconies

PIA writes on the board: 'Man died, fell from a balcony'. She tells them to start drawing with the pencil and then to paint it. The pupils are painting. At 10.35 they have finished.

This illustrates that the teachers structure and define the schoolwork fairly strictly, even the simplest tasks. During the newspaper lessons the teachers generally read about accidents, violent deaths and similar dramatic news. The teachers account for this by arguing that this is a means of gaining the pupils' attention; *otherwise we won't get their attention*. Lack of attention is held to be a characteristic feature of children belonging to the category of 'ADHD/DAMP pupil', and the teachers in this sense account for their practices by referring to this attribute. The lesson in some respects is reminiscent of a regular lesson with clear teacher/student roles. The teacher is standing in front of the pupils, reading something, which the pupils afterwards are expected to comment on. The difference in this classroom is that this interaction takes place in a context where there are five teachers and six students.

### H. Break, at 10.40

The schedule says it is time for lunch. The school canteen is situated just outside the classroom cloakroom. The pupils from this class do not have to queue. They enter the dining-hall before the other children at the school have access.

This strategy of giving the pupils from 'The Little Group' priority for lunch is connected to the assumptions about the symptoms associated with the diagnosis of ADHD. It is assumed, according to the teachers, that the pupils will misbehave if they have to wait in a queue. The teachers, are therefore trying to prevent trouble from occurring. The teachers argue that these pupils are not able to wait for their turn but there are no comments on how to prepare the pupils for future situations of this kind.

### I. Sharing-time 3, at 11.00

Immediately after lunch the schedule says sharing-time. The group splits into two groups again; one consists of the older boys, and the other of the younger boys. The teachers read aloud from a book.

## J. Short break, at 11.15

At 11.15 the teachers have scheduled a break. This implies that the teachers decide the content of the break. Sometimes they play football and sometimes basketball. The idea is, according to the teacher, that the pupils will be *practising social rules such as turn-taking and learning to score a goal*. Today, they are throwing the ball towards the basket. The teachers instruct them to stand in a queue and wait for their turn to throw the ball. Pierre, Peo and Pontus start to discuss and bump into each other. The atmosphere becomes a bit tense. When Pontus laughs at Pierre, when he misses the basket cage, the teachers intervene. *Now you're doing wrong*, PERNILLA says to Pontus, who continues to provoke Pierre. Finally, Pontus is not allowed to participate any longer and PIA takes Pontus inside.

This lesson shows that the teachers try to keep the same order when throwing the ball as they have in the classroom. And when the pupils do not do as they are told, they are reprimanded in the same way as in the classroom. The pupils have to learn that sometimes the breaks are similar to lessons, where the roles of teacher and student, respectively, are maintained.

## K. Games, at 11.30

Immediately after the break, the schedule says 'games'. During this lesson they play different kinds of games. For example, they play Uno (a card game), Bamse-game (a character in a children's book), Letter-Bingo, bowling with toilet-rolls and so on. The children again are divided into two groups, the younger and the older. I stay in the classroom where the younger pupils are; Pierre, Peo and Pontus. Today, PERNILLA decides that they will play Letter-Bingo. All the pupils get their counters. Pierre is dissatisfied with his and throws a counter at Pontus.

> Pierre: DAMP kid(!)
> PIA: that was an impulse . . . children with DAMP have impulses

This short sequence illustrates a feature of this specific context. In a regular classroom situation, the teacher would probably have instructed the pupils to be quiet and continue to work or to raise their hand. But in this case, the teacher makes use of what happened when Pierre refers to Pontus as a *DAMP kid*. She reminds the children of their handicap by saying *that was an impulse . . . children with DAMP have impulses*, which is one of the symptoms associated with the ADHD/DAMP diagnosis. By making use of this predicate of a 'DAMP child', the social identity of the handicapped pupil is openly communicated and confirmed (Hester 1998; Freebody and Freiburg 2000).

They start to play Letter-Bingo and after six rounds the children have won twice each. At 12.45, Pierre and Peo want to play Uno instead. Pontus, however, still wants to play Letter-Bingo. They quarrel a while about this but finally they all play Uno. PIA helps Pontus, PERNILLA helps Peo and Pierre is playing by himself.

All of the pupils are noisy and the teachers tell them to *be quiet and concentrate*. There is no time to complete the game since the time is 12.00.

Again, the teachers make the pupil aware of their identity by pointing at another predicate typical for the diagnosis – lack of concentration– which confirms their status as 'ADHD/DAMP pupils'.

It is the end of the school day for Pontus, and he goes by taxi to an after-school centre situated where he lives.

## Learning to be a (deviant) pupil – some observations

How can one make analytical sense of what happens in this classroom? One general conclusion is that the pedagogical activities in some respects are not very different from the activities one finds in regular classroom.

However, there are several pedagogical practices that clearly differ from those employed in a regular classroom:

1   The separation of the children from each other by means of shields. This is motivated by the assumption that the children need to be in an environment where they are not distracted by external stimuli.
2   The ratio of teachers to pupils is in this case 5:6. This can be compared to a regular classroom where the ratio is about 1:25.
3   The activities are organised in a specific manner. There is a schedule that is repeated every day. The working periods are very short. This structuring of the work, the teachers argue, reduces the complexity for the children, fosters routines, and prevents them from getting into situations where they have to choose. This pattern represents the local interpretation of the recommendations on how to organise pedagogy given by the medical expertise in the literature (cf. Kadesjö 1991; Gillberg 1996). However, as I have shown, during these periods of 'structured' work, a considerable proportion of the time is spent on negotiating social order in the classroom.
4   A prominent strategy is to practise what is described as *concentration skills and social skills*. This is done in order to prepare the children for adaptation to a normal class. During the periods when the pupils work for five minutes on each task, the teachers argue that the children practise 'concentration'. And they add: *they are not capable of more* (field-note, 26/10/2000). However, during the period I followed this class, these concentration periods were never extended. This implies that after three years the pupils still work for five minutes on each task. The necessity of practising 'normal' classroom behaviour in order to better adapt to a regular classroom is made explicit in the conversation between teachers and pupils several times during the day. Thus, the pupils are told what behaviours are unacceptable in a regular classroom or they are told that a particular activity, such as raising one's hand before talking, is something one must learn before one can return to a normal class.

5    A further element of these training practices is that the teachers intervene and comment on the pupils' deficiencies by pointing out that a particular behaviour is characteristic of an ADHD/DAMP diagnosis, and thus something that is unacceptable in class. These reminders might be seen as elements in the constitution of an identity of being a deviant pupil of a particular kind. As we saw, the negative nature of this identity is clear to the children. For instance, children use the expression DAMP kid (cf. section K, Games, in the previous description of a day in the classroom) when teasing each other.

6    The pedagogical content of the tasks is rarely discussed. There is a clear focus on drill-type exercises, which one could probably find in many other classrooms. However, in this context drill exercises seem to dominate teaching and learning activities in a manner that one would not find in most classrooms. There is very little evidence of innovation with respect to pedagogy.

One conclusion regarding the nature of the pedagogical practices implemented, and the ideology that teachers build on, is that the concept of 'structure' plays a very important role as a guiding metaphor. 'Structure', which is recommended in the biomedical literature, results in short working periods, frequent breaks, motor exercises and sessions of sharing-time, and in the dominance of routine tasks in which children work with exercises involving copying. Social intercourse and concentration are also seen as skills that have to be practised through specific exercises.

In the next section I will give a brief description of how the teachers account for their ambitions and the pedagogical practices in the classroom.

## Teachers' accounts and perspectives

The teachers continuously account for the educational activities by bringing up the Working Plan and specific medical literature. The Working Plan describes what goals are supposed to be achieved and how to achieve them. According to this document, the overall purpose of the arrangement providing an education for children having ADHD/DAMP is to 'help the individual pupil so that he can work socially and pedagogically in a way that enables him to fit into a regular school' (quoted from Working Plan, my translation). The prescribed goals are specific:

1    To help the pupil acquire a decent attitude to his/her handicap;
2    That each pupil will be able to read, write and do maths in relation to their ability;
3    To develop the communicative ability of the pupil;
4    To ensure that he/she is capable of working in a group (quoted from Working Plan, my translation).

Most of the goals may be considered relevant for a regular school as well. However, the first goal is clearly different. It points to the importance of making the pupil aware of his/her handicap. In the day described above, this could be seen, for example, in K (Games, at 11.30), where the teacher reminds the pupil about his 'DAMP' diagnosis and that he must control his impulses. The ambition to prepare the pupil for a return to his/her regular class is visible in the daily activities in the sense that it is pointed out to the children that various behaviours and activities are to be expected in a regular class, for instance, that one is supposed to tell *one at a time* when telling a story (in F: Sharing-time, at 10.00 above). This goal, in turn, is an indication that the teaching and learning practices should serve as a compensatory and normalising practice.

When producing the educational activities in the classroom, the teachers use the term 'structure' as the most important element in what they refer to as *DAMP pedagogy*.

### Excerpt 1

> THEA: DAMP pedagogy is when everything looks the same all the time . . . in order, one thing following the next; simply structure (field-note, 19/12/2000).

The teacher gives some examples of what is meant by 'structure' in this case.

1  THEA: Structure is vital for how the schedule and everything is planned and every spell of work in the same way, it is recurrent so they will feel secure in the external structure
2  (. . .)
3  THEA: clarity in most things and that there are limited goals and it varies very much, you can't do maths for a whole lesson and then Swedish for a whole lesson but it's short passes, which are they change rather often but they –, it is the *variation* (. . .) that is the – and they have goals which they reach and when they are supposed to do a task that we help them to structure that first you do this and then you do that
4  PERNILLA: and that it is sharply marked off
5  THEA: that here is the beginning and here is the end
6  R[5]: concerning the variation, how do you mean then(?)
7  THEA: well, that they get tired of doing maths then
8  PERNILLA: they have to do something else
9  THEA: yes they're doing maths then they lose their concentration after a while then we usually put in a motor spell (interview, 29/11/2000).

It is *when everything looks the same all the time . . . in order, one thing following the next*. This is illustrated by the use of the schedule and the repetition of activities. It is obvious that 'structure', as used by the teachers, concerns the form of the lessons and not the content. In the following excerpt, the teachers give further explanations of their views about what characterises *structure*.

## Excerpt 2

The teachers point to the individual work periods where the teachers *help them to structure that first you do this and then you do that*, as a central element in this pedagogy. That is, the teachers have to help the pupils at a very concrete level and *sharply mark off that here is the beginning and here is the end*. This implies that, again, it is the form of the lessons or the work periods that is in focus, i.e. how one works seems to be given more emphasis than what one learns.

In the Working Plan 'a distinct structure and firm routines' are recommended as ways of reaching the prescribed goals. This implies that there is a clear correspondence between the teachers' explanations of what they are doing and the practices that follow. And the Working Plan, in turn, reflects the voice of the medical literature. Thus, there is an intertextuality in which the teachers adopt modes of reasoning from the medical perspective and attempt to organise the pedagogical practices on this basis.

However, 'structure' does not fit every pupil, according to the teachers. 'Structure' as a strategy when teaching children having 'ADHD/DAMP' sometimes becomes a problem.

## Excerpt 3

> THEA: about the 'DAMP pedagogy' that you should do this and that and not more of that now, it doesn't work with Per; he's stressed by structure(.) this doesn't work with him you have to negotiate with him all the time (interview, 8/12/2000).

In Excerpt 3, one boy is held to be *stressed by structure* and some children are talked about as being in need of space for negotiation rather than *structure*. However, the belief that children with ADHD/DAMP represent a homogeneous group that should be taught in special classes is accepted by the teachers (Haug 1998).

Thus, a conclusion is that many features of teaching and learning in the ADHD/DAMP classroom can be found in mainstream classrooms as well. However, when the teachers interpret and explain what they are doing, they emphasise the differences from a regular classroom. More specifically, they point to strategies recommended in the medical literature, for example, imposing 'structure', working in short periods, predominantly with drill exercises, and making the pupil aware of his/her identity as a handicapped child. The long-term consequences of these strategies for pupil identity and for the possibilities of reintegrating the pupil into his/her class of origin could be important to study.

# Basic organising principles of classroom life

The purpose of this chapter has been to make the pedagogical practices in an ADHD/DAMP classroom visible with some basic organising principles, sometimes contradictory, occurring in practice:

1   The first organising principle relies on the metaphorical construction of 'structure', which is a polysemous metaphor. However, in this praxis it is an overarching argument, which is accepted as having a rather precise meaning. It communicates a perspective of how to use time in school, how to organise work tasks, and how to behave. However, the ambiguity of the metaphor occurs when the teachers point to the dilemma of having pupils who become *stressed by structure*. This implies that the idea of 'structure' contains contradictions, since 'structure' – as a member's concept (Sacks 1992), i.e. as the concept is used by the teachers in this setting – does not fit everyone as presumed.

2   The second principle concerns the nature of the training and tasks offered. Routine tasks, drill exercises and repetition of activities dominate the pedagogy, strategies with a long history in special needs schools (Ahlström *et al.* 1986). This heavy emphasis on routine tasks seems to be conceived as a necessary element in the building up of the competence of the individual student. It is also clear that innovation in terms of the content of the tasks is not prominent. There are few signs of actively searching for tasks that would be educative and still connect to the interests of the boys.

3   Yet another important principle in this normalising practice is the idea of practising social skills. In the case here, it concerns an idea of making implicit rules explicit. Rules concerning how to behave, when and how to talk, and when to engage in various activities, are to a large extent implicit in social interaction. Here, continuous attempts are made to make rules explicit. The children practise how to follow rules in social situations as if these were transferable to all situations. For example, the children practise turn-taking and how to follow instructions as if these were unambiguous and always the same. An interesting issue is whether the rules taught are transformed into implicit rules, i.e. if the children learn to 'do' school in the manner intended. It remains an open issue as to whether the pupils are better prepared when they return to their 'normal' class again. In these teaching practices, challenging institutional rules on how to behave continues to be a frequent activity.

4   A further metaphor that plays a somewhat contradictory role is the idea of homogeneity in needs and abilities among the children. In this class, homogeneity seems to be accepted as a principle for teaching the boys in the same class. However, at the same time, the idea 'that certain intervention strategies are universally effective for all students diagnosed with ADHD' (DuPaul and Eckert 1997: 370) is refuted in teachers' accounts of what they do. Rather, the teachers argue that the children differ in many respects, and that one thus has

to adapt to the individual. There is no one specific pedagogical strategy, which fits everyone. Some pupils need 'structure', others are stressed by it.

## Conclusions

Segregating pupils from regular school through the use of this medical diagnosis seems to result in dilemmas and contradictions. In the present case, educational practices adapted to the needs of children assigned with the diagnosis ADHD/DAMP have been studied. This mode of educating children has been inspired by a medical perspective on disability, and it is not grounded in a pedagogical analysis of the pupils' difficulties, needs and strengths. The impact of the medical discourse is decisive and visible in most of the accounts given by the teachers of what they are doing. The strategy adopted implies using distinct routines, control of the pupils' activities and behaviour, frequent training of 'concentration' and other individual and social skills and attempts to avoid all kinds of distractions. The form of schooling seems to be the object of concern rather than considering what students learn in terms of skills such as reading, writing and so on.

Furthermore, the practices deployed are motivated by serving as elements of some kind of normalising procedure. The explicit ambition is to help and train the pupil to function in a normal environment. What remains an open question is whether it is reasonable to assume that practising in such a setting as the one described here will give the child the necessary skills to master a regular classroom environment. As argued by Abbey and Valsiner (2003), the risk is always that such practices 'are severely limited and provide merely a "road to nowhere" for the child' (p. 1). There was little progress in the activities in this respect. For instance, the working periods do not become longer or more similar to what one would expect in a regular classroom. Nor do the pupils learn to work more independently on more complex tasks during their time in this class.

However, it is clear that one of the key ambitions of the practices observed is that the pupils should be made aware of their identity as being deviant and of their belonging to the category 'ADHD/DAMP pupil'. Pupils should also learn to monitor their own behaviours and to filter what they do through their knowledge of what it means to be an ADHD/DAMP pupil. The pedagogical activities and the general organisation of the schooling are thus instrumental in conveying to the pupils, and to others, that they are handicapped in a specific manner. And an interesting contradiction is that to be allowed back into the regular classroom, the pupils must be well trained in mastering their handicap. In some sense, they are learning how to be handicapped in a normal setting.

## Notes

1 ADHD (Attention Deficit Hyperactivity Disorder) and DAMP (Dysfunction in Attention, Motor control and Perception) are used in Sweden for similar difficulties. DAMP is used in Sweden and Denmark (and, to a very limited extent, in Norway and

the UK). ADHD is used in many parts of the world. The National Board of Health and Welfare in Sweden recommends the use of ADHD instead of DAMP (2002). However, in this study I will use the acronym ADHD/DAMP, since the class examined is referred to as a 'DAMP class' and the pedagogy is referred to as 'DAMP pedagogy'.
2   The diagnosis DAMP is, however, not described in any manual.
3   HKD is an acronym for Hyperkinetic Disorder, a diagnosis still sometimes used in Europe, which is similar, in some respect, to ADHD.
4   From now on I will call them all 'teachers'.
5   R is a shortening of researcher.

## References

Abbey, E. and Valsiner, J. (2003) 'Going to no-where: the role of diagnosis in educational practice'. Paper presented at EARLI conference, Padova, August 27, 2003.
Ahlström, K.-G., Emanuelsson, I. and Wallin, E. (1986) *Skolans krav – elevernas behov* [The demands of the school – the pupils' needs]. Lund: Studentlitteratur.
Austin, H., Dwyer, B. and Freebody, P. (2003): *Schooling the Child. The making of students in classrooms*. London: Routledge.
Blom, A. (1999) *Särskilda elever: om barn i särskola: bedömningsgrunder, ställningstaganden och erfarenheter* [Special pupils: children in special school: basis for forming judgements, standpoints and experiences]. Stockholm: Forsknings- och utvecklingsenheten, Socialtjänstförvaltningen.
DuPaul, G.J. and Eckert, T.L. (1997) 'Interventions for students with attention-deficit/hyperactivity disorder: one size does not fit all'. *School Psychology Review*, 26(3): 369–382.
DuPaul G.J. and Stoner, G. (2003) *ADHD in the Schools. Assessment and intervention strategies*. New York: The Guilford Press.
Elinder, L. (1997) 'Friska sjukförklaras i diagnostiskt samhälle' [Those who are well are explained as being ill in a society of diagnosis]. *Läkartidningen*, 94(39): 3391–3394.
Freebody, P. and Freiberg, J. (2000) 'Public and pedagogic morality. The local orders of instructional and regulatory talk in classrooms'. In Hester, S. (ed.) *Local Education Order. Ethnomethodological studies of knowledge in action*. Philadelphia, PA: John Benjamins Publishing Company: 141–162.
Gillberg, C. (1996) *Ett barn i varje klass. Om DAMP, MBD, ADHD* [One child in every class. About DAMP, MBD, ADHD]. Södertälje: Cura.
Haug, P. (1998) *Pedagogiskt dilemma: Specialundervisning* [Pedagogical dilemma: Special needs education]. Stockholm: Liber.
Hester, S. (1998) 'Describing "deviance" in school: recognizably educational psychological problems'. In Antaki, C. and Widdicombe, S. (eds) *Identities in Talk*. London: Sage: 133–150.
Hjörne, E. and Säljö, R. (2004) '"There is something about Julia" – Symptoms, categories, and the process of invoking Attention Deficit Hyperactivity Disorder in the Swedish school: a case study'. *Journal of Language, Identity, and Education*, 3(1): 1–24.
Kadesjö, B. (1991) 'Skolsituation och skolans åtgärder för barn med MBD/DAMP' [School situation and the school's measures for children with MBD/DAMP] (pp. 15–30). In Gillberg, I.C. and Kadesjö, B. (eds) *MBD/DAMP i skolåldern* [MBD/DAMP in the school-age]. (Skolvård) Göteborg: Förlagshuset Gothia.
Kadesjö, B. (2001) *Barn med koncentrationssvårigheter (2nd edn)* [Children with concentration difficulties]. Stockholm: Liber.

Kadesjö, B. and Gillberg, C. (1998) 'Attention deficits and clumsiness in Swedish 7-year-old children'. *Developmental Medicine and Child Neurology*, 40: 796–804.

Kärfve, E. (2000) *Hjärnspöken. DAMP och hotet mot folkhälsan* [Figments of brain. DAMP and the threat to popular health]. Stockholm: Brutus Östling.

LGR (1962) *Läroplan för grundskolan* [Curriculum for the compulsory school 1962]. Stockholm: Kungliga Skolöverstyrelsen.

Lloyd, G. and Norris, C. (1999) 'Including ADHD?' *Disability and Society*, 14(4): 505–517.

Mehan, H., Hertweck, A. and Meihls, J.L. (1986) *Handicapping the Handicapped. Decision making in students' educational careers*. Stanford, CA: Stanford University Press.

Reid, R. (1999) 'Attention deficit hyperactivity disorder: effective methods for the classroom'. *Focus on Exceptional Children*, 32(4): 1–23.

Sacks, H. (1992) *Lectures on Conversation (Vol. 1)* Oxford: Blackwell.

Socialstyrelsen (2002) *ADHD hos barn och vuxna* [ADHD in children and adults]. Stockholm: Modin-Tryck.

Swanson, J.M., Sergeant, J.A., Taylor, E., Sonuga Barke, E.J., Jensen, P.S. and Cantwell, D.P. (1998) 'Attention Deficit Hyperactivity and Hyperkinetic Disorder'. *Lancet*, 351: 429–433.

# Chapter 12

# Managing attention difficulties in the classroom

## A learning styles perspective

*Gavin Reid*

Attention difficulties, particularly those diagnosed as attention deficit hyperactivity disorders (ADHD), have attracted considerable interest in recent years and perhaps because of that, the whole area of attention difficulties has been the subject of confusion and controversy. The aim of this chapter is to focus on the presenting behaviour that may account for attention difficulties rather than the actual label. This is because children with all sorts of labels, and many without a label, can have attention difficulties. Additionally while some children do experience attention difficulties in every area of school, home and play, *most do not*, so their attention difficulties are dependent on many other factors relating to the learning experience, including the nature of the task, how the task is presented, the learning environment and the student's learnt behaviours stemming from past learning experiences.

Montague and Castro (2004) suggest that because of the views held by some regarding the neurobiological nature of ADHD, interventions have tended to focus on pharmacological treatments. They argue however that the current trend is moving away from that perspective and professional organisations such as the 'American Academy of Pediatrics, as well as researchers, psychologists, and counsellors advocate a multimethod, multi-informant, and multidisciplinary approach to treatment . . . and rather than focus on the individual's deficits, emphasis is placed on identifying the strengths of an individual and building on those strengths' (p. 411). Montague and Castro also suggest that school accommodation plans are the key to intervention and these should be multifaceted, involving all teachers, parents and children and that it is important to provide optimal curricular and environmental conditions for learning. They suggest that 'collaboration and cooperation among school, home and community agencies . . . should be the cornerstone of an intervention programme [for ADHD]' (p. 413).

Similarly Lloyd and Norris (1999) suggest that sociological and environmental criteria can be influential factors in ADHD and that dealing with the presenting behaviours and the sociological causes can be more effective than, for example, prescribed medication. This view is also supported by the developmental, contextual perspective (Pellegrini and Horvatt 1995) that acknowledges the interaction between biology and environment as crucial in understanding and dealing with difficulties associated with ADHD.

A programme on ADHD developed by the New South Wales Department of Education in Australia (Talk, Time, Teamwork, Collaborative Management of Students with ADHD 1995) illustrates the multifaceted dimensions of what is known as ADHD. The programme indicates that no single intervention method is sufficient to produce either short- or long-term behavioural change, and interventions for children thought to have ADHD should include individualised instruction; social skills training; behaviour management programmes and family programmes. This is consistent with the views expressed by Grainger (1999) who suggests that it is important to build as many connections as possible addressing all aspects of learning. Therefore, a multisensory and multiconnectionist approach should be utilised.

Giorcelli (1999), who has pioneered inclusive approaches to managing ADHD-type difficulties by considering both within-person factors and systems approaches also suggests that a multifaceted approach is necessary to fully comprehend and advise on the difficulties associated with ADHD.

The perspective put forward in this chapter acknowledges the role of the interaction between the learner and the environment and emphasises that learning styles can have an influential effect on the learning outcome. This can be achieved through reversing any negative learning behaviours and helping to identify and acknowledge the 'optimal curricular and environmental conditions' for learning. It is important to appreciate the role of the environment in learning and a learning-styles approach should consider the learning environment, as well as the cognitive and curricular implications of the learning experience.

## Background to attention difficulties: misperceptions and issues

### What is meant by 'normal attention'?

There are many misperceptions relating to attention difficulties and ideas of ADHD. One of the key issues relates to the question 'what do we mean by "normal attention"?' 'Normal attention' can be seen within a continuum from, on the one hand, 'very attentive' to on the other, 'easily distracted'. This implies that 'easily distracted' is within the bounds of 'normal' behaviour. For that reason it is crucial not to exclude children diagnosed with ADHD from the mainstream classroom experiences, as their attention difficulties may be controlled through manipulation of the learning context with a focus on the barriers the child experiences in the learning situation. Learning styles can help identify these barriers through observing teaching and learning practices. There are, however, a number of other issues that need to be considered and these are discussed below.

## Attributions

One of the key outcomes that can determine success in learning relates to learner autonomy. It is crucial that learners can attribute positive learning performances to factors within their control. If students attribute learning success or failure to extrinsic factors, outwith their control, then they will become dependent on these factors and these factors will determine the learning outcome. One of the key benefits of a focus on learning styles is that it can promote student responsibility for learning. The student becomes aware of their learning style and assumes a responsibility for learning.

Kaider *et al.* (2003) investigated the attributions of a sample of children – half of the sample without the diagnosis of ADHD and the other half with the diagnosis. There were many interesting conclusions from this study that can be followed up, but one of the most relevant was that children with and without the label ADHD did not differ in the behaviours they chose as their most problematic. The most frequently endorsed behaviours by children with the diagnosis of ADHD were losing things, being easily distracted, fidgeting and squirming and talking too much. The behaviours identified as the most problematic for children without ADHD were similar. This study does raise issues about the importance of locus of control in learning. The sample with the diagnosis felt their behaviour was outwith their control and if this is the case this has considerable implications for classroom management and student learning. It suggests that children with ADHD-type difficulties will benefit from learning specific strategies that will help them feel more in control over their learning and subsequently help them become more responsible for their learning behaviours. It follows therefore that classroom management and planning in advance to anticipate the kind of difficulties children with attention difficulties may experience in the classroom are essential. It is also crucial that children with attention difficulties are encouraged to take control over their own learning and behaviour.

Burden (2002) refers to Kelly's Personal Construct theory (Denicolo and Pope 2001) as a means of helping students develop an awareness of their own perception of themselves as learners. This relates to how the individual sees him/herself as a learner and importantly the attributions that they make for their successes and failures in learning. If learners constantly fail at learning they will attribute this failure to themselves and their lack of ability – factors outwith their control. In fact they may be failing because the task or the learning environment is not conducive to the learner's current level of knowledge or his/her learning style. The attributions, that is the reasons children give for failure, are important and can provide useful information on the learner's self-perception and self-esteem. If the learner has a negative perception of their learning abilities, and often children with a diagnosis of ADHD have, this can giver rise to feelings of low self-worth (Covington 1992) and repeated failure can result in the situation that can be referred to as 'learned helplessness' (Smiley and Dweck 1994). This means that the student loses motivation to learn as a result of an accumulation of failures. This has implications for students with attention difficulties.

## Provision and needs

Another issue that can cause controversy relates to provision and needs. The nature of the provision that is suitable for children with attention difficulties can vary. For some, specialised intervention may be appropriate, but for most, differentiation, curriculum and classroom adaptations and acknowledging learning styles will be sufficient. Considering the range of difficulties associated with attention difficulties and the potential behavioural difficulties that can also be associated with attention disorders, this of course provides a challenging situation for teachers.

The remainder of this chapter will focus on these points and in particularly the type of learning-styles strategies and interventions that can be applied to help minimise the effects of attention difficulties through acknowledging learning styles.

## Educational factors

Levine (1997) suggests the following educational factors can be noted in children with attention difficulties:

- Factors associated with free flight – this means that the child will have little control over the thinking process – essentially what may be described as a right hemisphere processing style. This would mean that learners with this style would require some structure to help direct their thinking processes.
- Unpredictability, inconsistency and impulsivity – this again indicates that there is little control over learning and that many actions would be impulsive. Indeed many children with attention difficulties can have 'presenting' behaviour difficulties that have occurred through impulsive actions.
- Pacing skills and on-task factors – these again indicate a lack of control over learning, and would indicate that students with attention difficulties have a problem with pacing the progress of work and therefore may tire easily, or finish a task prematurely.

Based on these views of Levine some possible characteristics of attention difficulties can include the following:

- difficulty sustaining attention during play/learning
- fidgety and restless when sitting
- difficulty being seated for any length of time
- inability to complete tasks
- unable to play quietly
- disruptive when playing with others
- difficulty listening
- answers questions before they need to
- difficulty following instructions
- being easily distracted by external stimuli
- difficulty awaiting turn in group activities

- losing materials necessary for tasks
- unable to consider consequences of actions.

Wearmouth *et al.* (2003) suggest, however, that it is not unreasonable to recognise and address such behaviour within the classroom situation based on an analysis of the task, adaptations to the curriculum and consultative curriculum planning, acknowledging the style and the needs of the learner and considering the nature of the learning environment. All these factors can be complemented through the use of a learning styles framework (see later in this chapter).

## Educational intervention

There is a view that intervention for 'special educational needs', whatever that term might mean, can be approached from a situation-centred perspective (Frederickson and Cline 2002). This view indicates that learning difficulties are in fact environmental and a construction of the education system. This would imply that teaching and curriculum approaches hold the key to minimising the effect on the child of what may be termed a 'special educational need'. Along the same continuum of the environmentally focused approach one can also view the interactional approach to special educational needs. Frederickson and Cline suggest this is the 'complex interaction between the child's strengths and weaknesses, the level of support available and the appropriateness of the education being provided' (p. 420). Dockrell and McShane (1993), like Wearmouth *et al.* (2003), view this in the form of three components – the task, the child and the environment. Although there may be a degree of neurological and cognitive factors associated with special educational needs (Morton and Frith 1995; Frith 2002) it can be argued that these factors are not necessarily fixed and can be manipulated and indeed mediated by the environment. Further the curriculum as the vehicle for the educational experience has a central position in defining success and failure in children. The curriculum in some situations may be prescribed, but the means of delivering the curriculum and the targets set can be flexible. It is important that when planning intervention for children with attention difficulties preparation is made to establish the barriers to learning the child may experience with the task, the curriculum and the learning environment.

Thomas (2004) suggests that the origins of many difficulties children experience lie less in children 'but more in the character of the organisation which we ask them to inhabit for a large part of their lives' (p. 72). In order to establish positive learning experiences for children with ADHD it is necessary to identify their cognitive processing style and the most favoured environmental preferences.

## The role of learning styles in intervention

### Learning theory

There are a number of different theoretical perspectives on how children learn and there are many competing views on learning strategies and how these strategies should be applied. Reid (2005) identifies some points of general importance. These include the following views:

* Learning is a process;
* Learning requires a period of consolidation;
* Learning is more effective when the content is familiar;
* Using the material to be learnt in different contexts and over time enhances the chances of retention and understanding;
* Intrinsic (within child) factors as well as extrinsic (environmental factors) can influence learning; and
* Learning is life-long.

Yet despite these general points there are many areas of uncertainty and controversy about learning. These include, for example, the views that:

* Specific styles of learning should be used for certain types of information;
* Each person has their own style – their own learning fingerprint;
* Learning occurs in age-related stages;
* The role of environment is less important than the cognitive ability to learn; and
* Learning should be differentiated for children of differing abilities.

These points above can be seen as controversial and each has been the subject of various comment and investigation by researchers and by practitioners. This chapter argues that these factors above are of significant importance in learning and have considerable implications for children with attention difficulties.

### Learning needs

Before effective learning can take place it is necessary for the learner to:

* *Understand* the task/information being presented;
* *Recognise* what the task or the information is suggesting;
* *Identify* the key points in the task/information;
* *Implement* the task/use the information;
* *Become 'autonomous'* in accessing the information and carrying out the task;
* *Be able to transfer* the new learning to other learning tasks.

Levine (1997) argues that children with ADHD do not learn effectively because they may have a superficial style of learning: they are 'surface' learners as opposed to 'deep' learners. The effect of this is that they will become uninterested in learning and will be more prone to distraction as they are not receiving the positive self-feedback that one would receive from understanding, appreciating and using new learning. One of the means of achieving this is to help students develop learner autonomy and responsibility for their own learning.

## Autonomous learning

The autonomous stage of learning is extremely important and can be seen as a measure of how successfully the individual has understood the information that has been learnt. Fitts and Posner (1967) suggest that the 'autonomous' stage of learning occurs only after extensive practice. This practice involves the learner using the information and through this use he/she develops 'automaticity' in undertaking the task. At this autonomous stage the learner often loses conscious awareness of how the task is done and it is carried out without too much conscious thought. This leads to automaticity and the learner will have the ability to transfer learnt skills to new learning situations. A crucial index of learning achievement is in fact the extent of the individual's ability to transfer learnt skills.

Nicolson and Fawcett (2004) suggests that this highlights the difference between 'controlled processing' which requires attentional control and uses up working memory capacity, and 'automatic processing, which, once learned in long-term memory, operates independently of the individual's control and uses no working memory resources. Because the learner has control over the process then the learner can be coached and trained to use this process more effectively. Almost everyone has the potential to be trained to become an efficient learner. The learning process therefore needs to be examined in relation to each learner, particularly learners with attention difficulties.

## Learning and self-esteem

Positive self-esteem is crucial for learning, as it can provide the learner with confidence and motivation enabling the learner to utilise metacognitive approaches to reinforce learning. A learner with a low self-concept will very likely have a cautious approach to learning and will have an over-reliance on the structure provided by the teacher. It is unlikely that such learners will develop a high metacognitive awareness, as they will not have the confidence to become responsible for their own learning. It is important that students assume responsibility for their own learning and in time develop their own structures and eventually have the skills to assess their own competencies in tasks.

It is important, therefore, that tasks, indeed all learning and learning experiences, are directed to developing the student's self-esteem. In order to develop self-esteem the learner must have some perception of success. It is obvious that if a learner is continually in a failure situation this will in turn have some influence on the learner's self-esteem. It is crucial therefore that tasks are developed to ensure that the learner will succeed. This may require tasks to be broken down into manageable units for the learner. This would ensure that the learner will achieve some early success when undertaking a task and this will provide motivation for subsequent learning.

## Learning styles and attention difficulties

All the factors discussed thus far in this chapter have implications for learning styles and students thought to have ADHD. It is critical that learners are able to accept responsibility for their own learning and develop metacognitive awareness. Self-knowledge acquired through recognition and use of learning styles can provide a means to achieve this. It is also important that teachers are aware of learning theory and how theory can be of practical use in understanding how children learn and particularly how learning can be made more accessible for learners with specific difficulties and special educational needs. While it is difficult and certainly challenging for teachers to acknowledge individual children's styles in a classroom situation where a wide range of learning needs is evident, it is crucial that some attention is paid to this. By addressing the need to acknowledge style the teacher is assisting the learner to become more aware of him/herself and more aware of how he/she can learn more efficiently and, importantly, more independently. This is the key message in this chapter.

Given and Reid (1999) suggest there are at least 100 instruments designed to identify individual learning styles. A recent study by Coffield et al. (2004) identified 70 learning styles instruments. Attempts have been made to categorise these instruments so that the background influences and psychological and cognitive perspectives can be made more clear. Given and Reid (1999) and Reid (2005) suggested these instruments usually focus on factors that are seen to be influential in the learning process. These factors include:

- Modality preference: the preference for visual, auditory, tactual or kinaesthetic input;
- Personality types: such as intuitive, risk-taking, cautious and reflective;
- Social variables: including the need to work alone or with others;
- Cognitive processes: such as memory, comprehension and methods of information-processing; and
- Movement and laterality such as active learning and left and right hemispheric activities.

Coffield et al. attempted to group 70 learning styles instruments into some form of classification to make sense of the range of instruments and views that contribute to these models. They developed a continuum of models based on the extent to which the developers of these models believed that learning styles represented a fixed trait. At one end of the continuum Coffield et al. placed theorists who believed that learning styles were fixed by inherited traits, and at the other end they placed those theorists who focused more on personal factors such as motivation and environmental factors, and also those who incorporated the influences of curriculum design and institutional and course culture.

At various points throughout the continuum Coffield *et al.* placed models that acknowledge external factors, particularly the immediate environment and models that are based on the idea of dynamic interplay between self and experience.

For the purposes of this chapter it can be suggested that learning styles could be grouped in the following way, categorised by their focus:

1   personality styles
2   environmental influences in learning
3   cognitive styles, and
4   metacognitive influences.

Over and above those factors all styles of learning are mediated by:

1   the learner's culture
2   the classroom and school climate
3   teaching style
4   classroom dynamics and environment, and
5   curriculum expectations.

## Learning styles critique

It needs to be stated that the research in learning styles in peer-reviewed journals is in the main highly critical of the concept of learning styles. The criticism rests on a number of key issues. These include:

- The lack of reliability in many of the learning styles instruments;
- The competing perspectives on what constitutes learning styles, even among supporters of the concept;
- The notion that it is impractical to adhere to the individual learning styles of all children in a class;
- The controversy whether matching individual learning styles to teaching style and teaching materials does actually produce more effective learning; and
- The commercial element that often accompanies a particular learning styles perspective. Usually to implement a specific approach teachers need to attend a training workshop and purchase expensive materials.

As a result learning styles do not have a sound image in the educational psychology literature. However, it is argued here that this is mainly due to a misunderstanding of the purposes and in particular the underlying conceptual understanding of learning styles, certainly as it is applied in the classroom situation.

Many see learning styles as a fixed, perhaps genetically determined, trait like size and hair colour. Using this type of criteria it is not surprising that instruments do not stand up to scientific scrutiny. It is well established that environmental and contextual factors are very powerful in determining a young person's characteristics, both in terms of learning and behavioural factors. Learning styles are therefore no exception to those influences. One is treading on dangerous territory, therefore, when attempting to ascribe a learning style to an individual as a fixed trait. Additionally it needs to be recognised that many, indeed most, of the instruments measuring learning styles are based on self-report and therefore are not infallible, as the accuracy of the data relies on the respondent's awareness and accuracy in identifying that awareness of his/her preferences. If descriptions based on questionnaires were seen as a guide rather than an accurate and absolute picture the questions being put forward by any scientific scrutiny would be qualitatively different (Reid 2005). The key questions would not relate to an investigation of an instrument in isolation, but to the value of the data obtained by that instrument in guiding classroom learning, teaching and curriculum development.

### Given's five learning systems

Given (2002) has developed a comprehensive approach to learning styles by incorporating five learning systems – emotional, social, cognitive, physical and reflective. Learning systems, Given argues, may be guided by the genetic code but are subject to environmental input for their detailed patterns and responses to different learning situations. The key therefore is the interplay, and it is important according to Given that teachers recognise the importance of this interplay and are able to use the natural learning systems to help children develop educationally.

Given outlines the educational implications of these learning systems by suggesting learning goals for each of them. Therefore the learning goals are:

* emotional – self-direction
* social – self-assurance
* cognitive – self-regulation
* physical – self-control, and
* reflective self-assessment.

The learning environment is perhaps one of the most underrated factors in the learning process. Environmental factors can greatly increase or decrease the effectiveness of learning (Reid 2005). Many learners are not aware of this and often just accept the environment as it is, without making any attempt to manipulate it in any way. In some instances it can be difficult to make a choice or to change the environment at all. But this is not always the case and if learners are aware of their environmental preferences then they are in a position to make informed choices when they have some flexibility over learning. In most cases, certainly for younger learners, the learning environment refers to the classroom, but it can in fact refer to the other areas that are used for learning, such as the library, family and community settings. The environment is very influential and should be seen as an important resource that can help to access effective learning for students with attention difficulties.

The key aspects in the learning environment, and how different environments can be more suited to certain types of learning styles, will be discussed in this chapter. This will highlight the view that the learning environment can, to a great extent, influence learning for students diagnosed with ADHD.

There are a number of factors that need to be considered in relation to the learning environment. These include the following:

- design
- colour
- wall displays
- light
- sound
- visual and auditory distractions
- space, and
- other learners in the same environment.

## Organising students with attention difficulties

Students diagnosed with ADHD usually have difficulty with organisation. Although one of the key themes in this chapter relates to the need to develop student autonomy through acknowledging learning styles, it may still be necessary for the teacher to take an active role in helping the student organise their work programme. Such help could include ensuring that notebooks have dividers and that separate folders are used for different activities and that these folders are clearly labelled, in addition to helping the student keep a daily record of tasks to be completed and those that have been completed. It should be acknowledged, however, that there are different degrees of organisation and some students can only tolerate a degree of imposed organisation. Nevertheless it should be ensured that the student with attention difficulties is sufficiently aware of materials they will require and how to access the information they need for learning. There is an ongoing debate in the learning styles literature on whether one should attempt to modify a student's learning style if it is seen to be inappropriate for the type of learning tasks in which the student is engaged. This in fact emphasises the point made elsewhere in this chapter that learning styles should provide guidance, and should not be seen as a form of fixed characteristics. It will be beneficial therefore to discuss the child's learning style with him/her and to identify how this can be advantageous/or otherwise when undertaking certain types of tasks.

## Learning styles using observational criteria

Observational assessment can be diagnostic, because it is flexible, adaptable and can be used in natural settings with interactive activities. Given and Reid (1999) have developed such a framework – the Interactive Observational Style Identification (IOSI). See the appendix for a summary of this.

A framework such as the IOSI can be used as a guide and perhaps be supplemented by more formal measures of learning style. Such a framework examines the actual behaviour and it is crucial to obtain this picture for children who have attention difficulties. It is, for example, very likely that the student with attention difficulties will have a natural style for mobility. This should therefore be incorporated into a learning programme in a controlled manner. Similarly with persistence – it is likely that they may have a low level of persistence and therefore the steps to learning need to be small and the child will need frequent breaks.

In the United States Gadwa and Griggs (1985) reported on the learning styles of students involved in a Washington High School alternative programme who had attention difficulties and were at risk of failure. It was noted that the students showed many right hemisphere, global, characteristics and preferred learning with music, low light, an informal design, short assignments with break time between, and high peer motivation (Dunn *et al.* 1990). Additionally the study showed that this group were not morning-alert learners and required a variety of teaching methods rather than traditional and routine methods. This confirms the findings of Dunn and Griggs (1988) who suggested that seven learning style traits characterise high-risk students from others. These are:

- they need to be mobile while learning;
- they require a variety of teaching and learning approaches and peer learning;
- their most productive learning time is late morning, afternoon or evening, but not early morning;
- they benefit from an informal seating design for learning, not traditional desks and chairs;
- they prefer low illumination;
- they thrive on tactual and kinaesthetic learning, certainly when first learning a new topic or skill;
- they benefit from multi-sensory teaching packages.

(Dunn and Griggs 1988, adapted from Milgram *et al.* 1993)

In a cross-cultural study of high-risk students from seven countries – Brazil, Canada, Guatemala, Israel, Korea, the Philippines and the United States – Price and Milgram (1993) found many similarities to the above study. These studies, and indeed the learning styles literature (Given and Reid 1999; Given 2002; Reid 2005), support the view that classroom accommodations based on the learner's cognitive and environmental preferences can provide the student with autonomy in learning and this can lead to educational success.

## Concluding points

One of the key points in this chapter is that the precise presenting behaviours displayed by the child diagnosed with ADHD need to be identified. Further, these behaviours need to be identified within the learning context in order to establish reasons and strategies for overcoming the difficulties. It is further suggested in this chapter that this should be accompanied by identification of learning styles from both cognitive and environmental perspectives. Much of this information can be obtained from observation of the child within the learning context. It is also important to recognise that learning styles identification will provide guidance on the nature of the classroom, curricular and environmental considerations that need to be made and these should not necessarily be seen in a fixed and prescriptive manner. To do this for children diagnosed with ADHD would merely be replacing one label with another. It is crucial that the intervention for children with attention difficulties is seen as an educational responsibility and one that can be controlled through analysing the learning experience for those children and offering a relevant, individually structured educational experience. Teaching based on the idea of learning styles offers one such means of achieving this objective.

## Appendix: Summary of the Interactive Observational Style Identification (IOSI) (Given and Reid 1999)

### Emotional

Motivation:

- What topics, tasks and activities interest the child?
- What kind of prompting and cueing is necessary to increase motivation?
- What kind of incentives motivate the child – leadership opportunities, working with others, free time or physical activity?

Persistence:

- Does the child stick to a task until completion without breaks?
- Are frequent breaks necessary when working on difficult tasks?

Responsibility:

- To what extent does the child take responsibility for his/her own learning?
- Does the child attribute success or failure to self or others?

Structure:

- Are the child's personal effects (desk, clothing, materials) well organised or cluttered?
- How does the child respond to someone imposing organisational structure on him/her?

## Social interaction

- When is the child's best work accomplished – when working alone, with one other or in a small group?
- Does the child ask for approval or need to have work checked frequently?

Communication:

- Does the child give the main events and gloss over the details?
- Does the child interrupt others when they are talking?

## Cognitive

Modality preference:

- What type of instructions does the child most easily understand – written, oral or visual?
- Does the child respond more quickly and easily to questions about stories heard or read?

Sequential or simultaneous learning:

- Does the child begin with one step and proceed in an orderly fashion, or have difficulty following sequential information?
- Is there a logical sequence to the child's explanations or do her/his thoughts bounce around from one idea to another?

Impulsive/reflective:

- Are the child's responses rapid and spontaneous or delayed and reflective?
- Does the child seem to consider past events before taking action?

## Physical

Mobility:

- Does the child move around the class frequently or fidget when seated?
- Does the child like to stand or walk while learning something new?

Food intake:

- Does the child snack or chew on a pencil when studying?

Time of day:

- During which time of day is the child most alert?
- Is there a noticeable difference between morning work completed and afternoon work?

Sound:

- Does the child seek out places that are particularly quiet?

Light:

- Does the child like to work in dimly lit areas or say that the light is too bright?

Temperature:

- Does the child leave his/her coat on when others seem warm?

Furniture design:

- When given a choice does the child sit on the floor, lie down, or sit in a straight chair to read?

## Metacognition

- Is the child aware of his/her learning style strengths?
- Does the child demonstrate self-assessment?

## Prediction

- Does the child make plans and work towards goals or let things happen?

## Feedback

- How does the child respond to different types of feedback?
- How much external prompting is needed before the child can access previous knowledge?

## References

Burden, B. (2002) 'A cognitive approach to dyslexia: learning styles and thinking skills'. In Reid, G. and Wearmouth, J. (eds.) *Dyslexia and Literacy, Theory and Practice.* Chichester: Wiley.

Coffield, F., Moseley, D., Hall, E. and Ecclestone, K. (2004) *Should We be Using Learning Styles? What research has to say to practice.* London: DfES.

Covington, M.E. (1992) *Making the Grade.* Cambridge: CUP.

Denicolo, P. and Pope, M. (2001) *Transformational Professional Practice: Personal construct approaches to education and research.* London: Whurr Publications.

Dockrell, J. and McShane, J. (1993) *Childrens' Learning Difficulties – A cognitive approach.* Oxford: Blackwell.

Dunn, R. and Griggs, S.A. (1988) *Learning Styles: The quiet revolution in American secondary schools.* Reston, VA: NASSP.

Dunn, R., Bruno, J., Sklar, R., Zenhausern R. and Beaudry, J. (1990) 'Effects of matching and mismatching minority developmental college students' hemispheric preferences on mathematical scores'. *Educational Research*, 83(5): 283–288.

Fitts, P.M. and Posner, M.I. (1967) *Human Performance.* Belmont, CA: Brooks Cole.

Frederickson, N. and Cline, T. (2002) *Special Educational Needs, Inclusion and Diversity, a text book.* Buckingham: Open University Press.

Frith, U. (2002) 'Resolving the paradoxes of dyslexia'. In Reid, G. and Wearmouth, J. (eds.) *Dyslexia and Literacy, Theory and Practice.* Chichester: Wiley.

Gadwa, K. and Griggs, S.A. (1985) 'The school dropout: implications for counsellors'. *School Counsellor*, 33: 9–17.

Giorcelli, L. R. (1999) 'Inclusion and other factors affecting teachers' attitudes to literacy programmes for students with special needs'. In Watson, A.J. and Giorcelli, L.R. (eds.) *Accepting the Literacy Challenge.* Gosford, NSW: Scholastic Publications.

Given, B.K. (2002) *Teaching to the Brain's Natural Learning Systems.* Alexandria, VA: ASCD Publications.

Given, B.K. and Reid, G. (1999) *Learning Styles: A guide for teachers and parents.* St Anne's on Sea: Red Rose Publications.

Grainger, J. (1999) 'Attention deficit hyperactivity disorder and reading disorders: how are they related?' In Watson, A.J. and Giorcelli, L.R. (eds.) *Accepting the Literacy Challenge.* Gosford, NSW: Scholastic Publications.

Kaider, G. *et al.* (2003) 'The attributions of children with ADHD for their problem behaviours'. *Journal of Attention Disorders*, 6: 99–109.

Levine, M. (1997) *Frames of Mind.* Cambridge, MA: Educators Publishers.

Lloyd, G. and Norris, C. (1999) 'Including ADHD'. *Disability and Society*, 14(4): 505–517.

Milgram, R.M., Dunn, R. and Price, G.E. (eds.) (1993) *Teaching and Counselling Talented Adolescents: An international perspective.* Westport, CT: Praeger.

Montague, M. and Castro, M. (2004) 'Attention Deficit Hyperactivity Disorder: concerns and issues'. In Clough, P., Garner, P., Pardeck, P.T. and Yuen, F. (2004) (eds.) *Handbook of Emotional and Behavioural Difficulties.* London: Sage Publications.

Morton, J. and Frith, U. (1995) 'Causal modelling: a structural approach to developmental psychopathology'. In Cicchetti, D. and Cohen, D.J. (eds.) *Manual of Developmental Psychopathology*. Psychological Assessment of Dyslexia. New York: Wiley: 357–390.

Nicolson, R.I. and Fawcett, A.J. (2004) 'Learning from the science of learning: implications for the classroom'. In Reid, G. and Fawcett, A. (eds.) *Dyslexia in Context: Research, policy and practice*. London: Whurr Publications.

Pellegrini, A.D. and Horvatt, M.A. (1995) 'Developmental contextualist critique of attention deficit disorder'. *Educational Researcher*, 24: 13–19.

Price, G. and Milgram, R.M. (1993) 'The learning styles of gifted adolescents around the world. Differences and similarities'. In Milgram, R.M., Dunn, R. and Price, G.E. (eds.) *Teaching and Counselling Talented Adolescents: An international perspective*. Westport, CT: Praeger.

Reid, G. (2005) *Learning Styles and Inclusion*. London: Sage Publications.

Smiley, P.A. and Dweck, C.S. (1994) 'Individual differences in achievement goals among young children'. *Child Development*, 65: 1723–1743.

Thomas, G. (2004) 'What do we mean by "EBD"'. In Clough, P., Garner, P., Pardeck, J.T. and Yuen, F. (eds.) *Handbook of Emotional and Behavioural Difficulties*. London: Sage Publications.

Wearmouth, J., Soler, J. and Reid, G. (2003) *Meeting Difficulties in Literacy Development: Research, policy and practice*. London: Routledge Falmer.

# Chapter 13

# Conclusion

## Supporting children in school

*Gwynedd Lloyd*

Across the world there are children and young people with real difficulties in dealing with their daily lives in school; families who struggle to manage their children; teachers who are faced with challenging behaviour in class. However, contributors to this book have argued that there is a wide and complex range of reasons for these difficulties and that it does not make sense to sweep large numbers of children into one rather over-simple category, labelling and medicating them. This chapter[1] addresses the concerns of educators and others who may accept the critiques of ADHD, of labelling and of the widespread (ab)use of medication but who still have to find the best way to support the particular children and young people in their class and school. The chapter suggests that a range of effective strategies for supporting children and teachers exists but that these should be developed within a more humanistic and less technicist approach to children and young people with difficulties in their lives.

The chapter will begin by briefly discussing the contested nature of ADHD diagnoses, offer a critique of the way that this is often ignored in the literature aimed at parents and professionals, and then look at some broader issues of mental health in education and the 'new' medical model. It will then offer some ideas for more appropriate support for children and young people experiencing and/or causing difficulties in school. I will argue that we should not underestimate the capacity of parents and teachers to understand that ADHD is a contested idea, rooted in complexity. The label ADHD describes a range of aspects of behaviour clustered together by human judgement into a diagnosis. ADHD, as contributors to this book have demonstrated, is not a simply measurable 'condition' but, on the contrary, it is subjectively measured by professionals who are reliant on behaviour checklists.

Sometimes official medical guidelines, such as those here in Scotland, do acknowledge the vague nature of the 'disorders' with which children are labelled. 'Considerable controversy therefore surrounds the extent of these disorders, for which there are, as yet, no robust diagnostic tests; thus their definition continues to be debated' (SIGN Guidelines 2001). However, the substantial literature aimed at parents and teachers (with a few notable exceptions, e.g. Armstrong 1997) often fails to reflect any such debate, presenting clear pictures of an uncontroversial 'disorder', its diagnosis, treatment and medication. This literature describes *the*

ADHD child – how to know when your child has ADHD, how 'ADHD' children should be treated by parents and teachers. The perspective is one-dimensional, failing to recognise the complexities in the lives of individual children and in their relationships with their families, their peers and their teachers.

## ADHD: part of a wider picture of children's difficulties at school

There is a broad consensus that we are diagnosing more and more children as suffering from mental health problems since the Second World War, with numbers often estimated at about 20 per cent of all children (Rutter and Smith 1995; Mental Health Foundation 1999). At the same time there are concerns over the numbers of children being identified as having difficulties in school, failing to attend school regularly, being excluded (suspended and expelled in US terminology) from school, experiencing problems in their family or committing crimes in the community (Munn *et al.* 2000). These are often overlapping populations. Recent Scottish research suggests that some young people may move between different professional settings, attracting different professional labels (Lloyd *et al.* 2001).

Research into exclusion (suspension and expulsion) from school has regularly found that individual, family, neighbourhood and school factors are all important in understanding schooling difficulties (Munn *et al.* 2000). However, the research also clearly indicates that some schools exclude more children than others, even when they have very similar student populations. The ethos, curriculum, discipline and support systems of schools are highly significant in understanding why some schools are able to be much more inclusive.

The relationship between difficulties at school and other problems in children's lives was recognised in a submission by the children's mental health organisation Young Minds to the Department for Education in England. Young Minds argued that many children and young people whose behaviour leads to exclusion, who truant or who perform badly in school are likely to have unmet 'mental health' needs. They perceived considerable overlaps between what schools term emotional and behavioural difficulties (EBD) and health services term mental health problems (Young Minds 1999). The concept of a mental health problem, like that of Emotional and Behavioural Difficulty/Disorder or ADHD is relational; it is socially produced, reflecting the assumptions of the definer. The processes through which some young people become labelled in school as having Emotional or Behavioural Difficulties/Disorders (EBD) are complex.

As other contributors to this book have argued, labels like EBD or ADHD offer a special status to young people and their parents, offering 'labels of forgiveness' – this diagnosis saves them from blame, from being branded 'bad' (Lloyd and Norris 1999). In much professional discourse the concept of 'EBD' is set against the idea of simply 'bad' behaviour. The dominant perspectives on 'EBD' in Britain and the USA are informed by psycho-medical assumptions which both fail to recognise the social context of the production of labels and the power processes involved in the social construction of deviance but also tend to deny agency and individual subject consciousness to students seen to be determined and defined by their disorder. So their transgression of the norms of the school is viewed as inadvertent, not deliberate or conscious. In contrast some of the more sociologically influenced writing may interpret their actions as resistance to oppressive structures and deny any biological or psychological influences (Slee 1995). Others argue that we are seeing a medicalising of 'naughtiness' (Thomas and Loxley 2001).

## The reappearance of the medical model

In the 1970s and 1980s the disability rights movement encouraged educators to reconsider their ideas and practices in relation to the education of students with special educational needs. There was a recognition of the social construction of disability and of the importance of recognising students as whole human beings, entitled to education in terms of their abilities, not their disabilities. This was reflected in legal and policy moves towards, first, mainstreaming and, more recently, educational inclusion. In Scotland, for example, recent legislation has reconceptualised support for learning away from deficit-based ideas of special educational needs towards a much broader idea of additional support needs. There is a broad range of reasons why a student may require additional support for learning, as specified in the legislation, including temporary issues such as family difficulties, interrupted learning, peer difficulties in school. So the legislation recognises that there are many reasons why students may require additional support, not only those associated with identified medically diagnosed conditions or diagnoses. This is compatible with definitions of inclusion that argue for schools to become wider communities able to address the educational needs of diverse students.

Paradoxically, however, there is also, in Britain, the USA and other parts of the world, clear evidence of a significant move towards greater use of psycho-medical explanations, apparent in the 'new medical' and the 'biopsychosocial' models (Slee 1995, 1998; Cooper and O'Regan 2001; Thomas and Loxley 2001; Gresham 2002). The new medical model, discussed for example in the American journal *Behavioural Disorders* by Forness and Kavale (2001), is based on the observation, as outlined by Oswald, that when 'the old medical model' was discarded:

> Special educators, struggling with the challenging behaviours of children with emotional and behavioural disorders (E/BD), came to rely on functional behavioural analysis and positive behaviour support as the sole strategy available for diagnosis and treatment. The new medical model adds to the classroom behavioural armamentarium a contemporary, largely biological, conceptual framework that emphasizes the role of psychopharmacology in the treatment of E/BD.
>
> (Oswald 2002: 155)

The new medical model reasserts the disciplinary supremacy of medical professionals, rejecting the conceptualisations and strategies developed by educators. An analysis of press coverage of ADHD in Britain suggested that there was a hierarchy of experts with hospital-based psychiatrists and paediatricians most frequently cited but that community-based general doctors (GPs in Britain) and educational professionals were not frequently quoted (Norris and Lloyd 2000).

In Britain, Kewley calls for a screening for ADHD at an early age in schools as well as for a range of other 'conditions', SEBD, dyslexia, etc. (Kewley 1999). ADHD is itself considered to be co-morbid with a range of other 'disorders'. Sixty to seventy per cent of those diagnosed with ADHD are thought have one or more co-existing conditions, some of these, like ADHD, imported into Britain from the American DSM-IV. Oppositional Defiant Disorder, Conduct Disorder, Depression, Bipolar Disorder, Tourette's, Obsessive Compulsive Disorder, Dyslexia, Asperger's are all thought to be co-morbid (ibid.). Thus the concept of ADHD is widened to relate to a whole raft of psychosocial problems, involving complex 'cocktails' of medication, not simply those like methylphenidate hydrochloride often recommended for ADHD.

The new medical model in the USA and the biopsychosocial model in Britain clearly can be criticised in that the labels are constructed to focus on the individual and therefore avoid scrutiny of the school environment. The difficulties of children and young people are constructed out of 'assumptions about deficit, weakness, disturbance or vulnerability' (Thomas and Loxley 2001: 88). The US writer Gresham, in a critique of the new medical model, argues that the reasoning involved in explaining disorders like EBD or ADHD is tautologous (Gresham 2002) 'Children have it because they show the behaviours which define it' (Paper 6). Gresham quotes Carson's view that:

> psychiatrists continue to view problematic behaviours as manifestations of a generalised, mysterious intrinsic property – much like a virus – that exists within individuals whose behaviour meet certain classification criteria.
>
> (Gresham 2002: 159)

The procedures for exclusion/suspension from school, in the USA as in Britain, require a consideration of whether the behaviour considered by the school to be unacceptable is a manifestation of their 'emotional disability' (Munn et al. 2000). Gresham suggests that this produces a conceptual quandary in 'manifestation determination' hearings when: 'school personnel involved must decide whether a student's problem behaviour was or was not due to his or her emotional disability' (Gresham 2002: 159). This difficulty follows from a conceptualisation of difficulties as disease, when the disease 'causes' the behaviour, so all actions are therefore a manifestation of the disease. Children in this view are not actors in a social world with feelings, motives, relationships, they are determined by the disease and therefore cannot be held to account for their actions.

Professionals use a range of labels to describe the actions of children considered to be deviant in school. These include EBD, maladjusted, disruptive, disturbed, mental health problems, at risk, in moral danger, out of control, delinquent, phobic, hyperactive, bad, etc. These labels are produced through a discourse of disciplinary knowledge that is constituted by a complex mixture of professional, theoretical and personal perspectives. The labels are not objectively constituted but are relational, they depend on an assumed idea of normality. However, research on classroom disruption and disaffection clearly indicates a significant degree of contextual variation in how such behaviour is construed. Behaviour takes place in meaningful contexts. The mechanistic use by professionals of labels like ADHD robs both the *individual* of agency and the *context* of meaning.

## A broader understanding of students' difficulties in context?

So a more complex understanding of how young people act in school requires a broader understanding of how children grow and develop through social interaction in social settings. It requires recognition of the multiplicity of factors in the construction and labelling of educational deviance. Young people are constructed and labelled in shifting professional discourses. I have argued elsewhere that understanding these processes requires a complex, multidimensional model which recognises the movements of power on and between the different but related levels of the social world, acknowledging the impact on relationships in school of wider structural inequalities, of a range of dominant and minority cultures and cultural sources, like the mass media. Such an understanding involves an analysis of competing policy interests, of professional expert discourses, of financial and funding pressures, of commercial promotion. It requires an exploration of the operations of power in the micropolitics of schools (Lloyd 2005).

A more complex understanding of students' difficulties involves a conceptualisation of young people as *subject to* disciplinary processes but also as *resistant to* these processes, as exerting their own power in school. It views the disciplinary processes of schools as gendered, classed and racialised (Wright 2005). It rejects binary notions of normality, worthiness, sanity and their opposites by recognising that young people move in and out of deviant identities, and that professional discourses also shift and moderate their notions of deviance. To understand the 'deviant student' it is necessary to perceive all these factors in an enmeshed and dynamic relationship with each other and with the individual choices and responses of the young person. Young people respond to these processes with individual human feelings, and these have to be included in the model.

The school and multi-professional processes through which children and young people who are disruptive or disaffected are identified and supported are closely related to those processes in our societies and in our schools that may contribute to the disaffection or difficulties. Education can only be viewed in relation to the wider social world:

[E]ducational issues cannot be adequately understood in merely technical and resource terms. They are fundamentally social questions, involving struggles over, for example, social justice, equity and citizenship.

(Barton 1999: 54)

It is important not to deny the reality of some of the difficulties faced by some families, children and their teachers. I am *not* arguing that these difficulties do not exist, but rather that we need to generate a wider understanding of the range of factors that may contribute to them. Writers in this book have discussed many of these factors, for example the impact of the changing cultural context in the USA and Britain and the impact of the new mass media. Major marketing drives by pharmaceutical companies have promoted not only the widespread use of medication in children but the professional mindset that views children in terms of normality and disorder. New managerial approaches to education in the 1990s in Britain and the USA emphasising the measurement of attainment led to pressures on schools for early attainment in basic skills in and an approach to educational achievement that was test-driven. In the USA 'high stakes' testing impacted strongly on school practice and on children's anxieties about learning (Wheelock 1998). In British primary (elementary) schools there was a reduction in physical exercise, drama and creative arts. Schools were publicly compared in 'league tables' of not only attainment but also school exclusion (Munn *et al.* 2000). There was a much greater focus on formal learning in the early years of school. Children were expected to attend, to concentrate and to keep still for longer. Teachers and other professionals are subject to a greater degree of scrutiny in their work and to frequent policy innovation. There is a substantial research literature that points to the links between inappropriate or overly prescriptive curricula and school disaffection, disruption and school exclusion (Kinder *et al.* 1995; Munn *et al.* 2000).

In both Britain and the USA moves towards developing more inclusive schools, associated with a more social and rights-based understanding of the idea of disability have been paradoxically accompanied by the medicalisation of children's behaviour and by ever larger demands on special education budgets. Teachers often find it easier to argue for funding of support for learning in school when students have 'medical' diagnoses. Parents who had experienced difficulties with their children, often criticised by teachers, felt relieved and supported by this kind of diagnosis. Economically disadvantaged families in Britain could be further supported by a Disabled Living Allowance associated with the diagnosis. These factors add up to a (perverse) incentive for teachers and parents to wish for formal diagnoses.

Such diagnoses, paradoxically, then often create anxieties on the part of educators, concerned that they do not have the special skills or knowledge to support such students. The literature aimed at educationalists, as argued earlier, suggests that there are special methods, a distinctive pedagogy. The next section explores this notion of a distinctive and special pedagogy.

## So what should teachers do: is there an ADHD pedagogy?

The label itself may not lead to improvements in school – one recent large-scale study in England found that the formal labelling of children with ADHD and the communication of this label to teachers was associated with a reduction in attainment (Tymms and Merrill 2004). The same study did find, however, that teachers and students benefited from advice about how to manage ADHD-like behaviour in their classrooms.

There is a huge educational literature on students with ADHD (Cooper and O'Regan 2001; O'Regan 2005). The literature begins with the premise that students 'with' ADHD are distinctively different and that teachers will need particular advice as to how to manage them in a classroom. This is the traditional special educational model – diagnosis followed by a distinctive pedagogical approach tailored to the disability or disorder.

There has been a recent debate over the notion of distinctively different pedagogies for differently classified children. Florian, in a recent paper (2005), observed that, when she began teaching in the USA in the 1970s, thinking about 'special education' had been affected by the consciousness-raising of the civil rights movement and was widely understood to be about social justice. She goes on to outline the subsequent debates over 'place' and 'pedagogy' for children identified with special education needs. Moves on both sides of the Atlantic and in other parts of the world towards education in the 'least restrictive environment' challenge notions that children with disabilities can only be educated in special settings but then created a concern for mainstream teachers that perhaps there was a special and mysterious pedagogy that they needed to learn.

Florian relates the educational debate to a parallel 'development versus difference' debate in the psychological literature as to whether 'children with various types of disabilities and/or learning difficulties are thought to be qualitatively different as learners and therefore in need of educational responses or treatments that are uniquely tailored to those differences' (Florian 2005: 3). This issue was explored by Lewis and Norwich (2000) in a review of pedagogical approaches to a range of special educational needs. They concluded that there was a move away from the idea of pedagogies particular to special educational need and found 'some support for the argument that what works for most pupils works for all pupils though there might be differences in application' (Florian 2005). In England a further study of the research on this issue was commissioned by the Government, with similar conclusions (Davis and Florian 2004).

Florian argues that it is not the differences among children that are problematic but that when the magnitude of these differences exceeds what schools can support, children are considered to have special educational needs. Davis and Florian found that 'sound practices in teaching and learning in mainstream and special education literatures were often informed by the same basic research', concluding that questions about special education pedagogy are not helpful and that we should ask broader questions about how to develop pedagogy that is inclusive of all students (Florian 2005: 11).

The very large literature on methods for 'ADHD students' makes very strong claims for specialist intervention. However, when these are examined *they almost always identify issues and practices that are not particular to diagnoses of ADHD!* Cooper, for example, in a chapter on a pedagogy for ADHD, develops an important critique of the 'factory model' in the education system in Britain, arguing that:

> A key problem with the DSM diagnostic criteria is that they harbour taken for granted assumptions about the kinds of pupil behaviours that are to be expected in properly functioning classrooms. Pupils . . . are expected from an early age to internalise and behave in accordance with a set of rules that derive from constraints imposed by a teacher-centred, curriculum focussed method of teaching pupils in age-related groups . . . Pupils, therefore are required to be expert in following complex instructions and internalising behavioural and cognitive routine.
>
> (Cooper 2005: 128)

Surely this is much wider than simply a problem for the DSM diagnostic criteria? Cooper, however, goes on to suggest that teachers will be able to negotiate these issues more effectively for students if the teacher is knowledgeable about ADHD. He then discusses educational strategies for ADHD, concluding, however, that 'When we look at the classroom with the perspective of the individual with AD/HD we find fault lines that, when addressed, benefit all pupils' (Cooper 2005: 132). We could, however, substitute the terms learning difficulty or behavioural problems and make the same point. The methods of intervention in the many books on ADHD and education are *not distinctively different* from those in books on behaviour management or learning difficulties. O'Regan, who was the head of a special school for pupils 'with' ADHD, in a recent book for teachers entitled *ADHD*, argues that:

> In essence the key factors for ADHD children are clearly specified rules and instructions. In addition, they need immediate and consistent feedback on behaviour and redirection to task. Reasonable and meaningful consequences for both compliance and non-compliance will also be necessary. Finally they will need adults who will deal with their problems in a way that is based on knowledge, compassion and respect.
>
> (O'Regan 2005: 34)

O'Regan also offers six key rules:

1   Completing work and tasks.
2   No physical or verbal aggression to others.
3   Following school policy (e.g. on the use of mobile phones etc.).
4   No eating or drinking in class.

5   Timekeeping.
6   Adhering to the uniform or dress code (if there is one).

(Ibid.: 35)

Flick (1998) in *ADD/ADHD Behaviour Change Resource Kit* adopts the ABC model of behaviour change: A–Antecedent Events, looking at what precedes or precipitates the behaviour, B–Behaviour, describing and identifying 'problem' behaviours, and C–Consequences. This book talks about using rewards and punishments; about writing behavioural plans; about when to ignore behaviour; about time-out and other behaviour modification approaches.

Rief (1993) in *How to Reach and Teach ADD/ADHD Children* writes helpful suggestions about how to engage students' attention, using signals, eye contact, and visuals. She offers tips for helping distractible students, keeping the students' interest. These are useful suggestions that would benefit any student teacher, not specific to children with a 'disorder'.

There is no special technology here. Effective intervention with children with very challenging behaviour, with attention/concentration problems, is about constructing appropriate and meaningful learning experiences. There are no 'ADHD' students; there are individual children with very varied family and educational histories, competences, learning styles and preferences. Teachers and parents need help in developing appropriately supportive interventions that take account of what works for children with complex individual lives, not labels that lead to mass medication of children. Effective pedagogies for classroom management offer a range of approaches. If, as argued earlier, there is a wide and complex range of reasons for these 'ADHD' kind of difficulties then we need an equally diverse mix of possible practice – not one answer or simple solutions but a *large* range of pedagogical strategies, relevant for different students at different levels and at different times. There can be no simple prescription of strategy to fit a category of 'need'.

## Educating diverse and individual students

Children with diagnoses of ADHD will be varied in their previous experiences of life. They will have different family and parenting histories, will have had quite different relationships with different teachers, different classes and peer groups. They may or may not be on medication. They may have very different and, like other children, varying levels of self-esteem. They will have different interests, different preferred styles of learning. Some students are easily distracted, helped by peace and quiet; others work best with 'white' noise or music. They will not all respond identically to a narrow model of teaching for ADHD. Research, mentioned earlier, into effective intervention and support for students with behavioural and other difficulties in school and at home found, perhaps not surprisingly, that some approaches worked for some kids, some places, at some times in their lives (Lloyd *et al.* 2001). It worked when it was the 'right help at the right time'.

Helpful strategies are not different from those established as effective with most children. They suggest that teachers should be well organised and prepared for providing a differentiated curriculum using positive group management techniques. They should give clear instructions, preview and warn of changes in activities. Students should be involved in developing classroom rules that should be clear, minimal and expressed positively. Teachers should, as part of whole-school behaviour policies, develop general strategies to promote positive behaviour, for example using praise and reward.

There are a number of organisations/individuals who make a strong case for diet in understanding ADHD-like behaviour. Some, like the work of Richardson on fatty acids and behaviour in Britain, are establishing research-based evidence (Richardson 2004). Others write about their experience with their own children and the impact of dietary change on their child. There is a wide range of 'alternative' dietary based approaches, and they rely on a systematic programme of allergy-eliminating foods. There does not need to be much research, however, to convince many teachers that how some children eat/drink may contribute to their difficulties. Social and economic disadvantage in Britain and in the USA can be associated with unhealthy diets. Some schools in Britain now have breakfast clubs to ensure that children eat something healthy before class and others are reviewing their catering services to reduce sugary foods and promote healthy eating.

Physical activity is also identified as helpful for some students, not simply in the routine curriculum but also as part of a range of strategies that may help individual pupils deal with excess energy or concentration problems. One research project in the USA has found exercise to be significantly effective in reducing ADHD symptoms in children. Wendt (2005) said that changes in behaviour were generally noticeable between two and four weeks into the exercise programme. The greatest gains were made in the oppositional category of behaviours, which are largely responsible for conflict problems with children.

Wendt indicated that this might be an alternative for parents who do not wish to use medication as a means of modifying behaviour. The side effects of a good exercise programme are far less invasive than the side effects of exposing children to long-term doses of medication.

> An added benefit to an exercise program for children is it may produce a chemically enriched environment that promotes brain growth. The latest research in fitness and exercise implies that an active lifestyle can have a positive effect on brain growth and development. If this is true then keeping your child involved in exercise can be beneficial, especially if it takes place over a number of years.
>
> (Wendt 2005)

Involving students in cognitively based activities where they identify their own solutions and construct their own programmes encourages engagement with educational processes. Teaching metacognitive, problem-solving, visualisation and organisational skills are helpful for all students. Reid's chapter in this book emphasises that all students learn differently. They may learn differently in different settings and when they feel differently about themselves.

Self-esteem/positive self-concept are, equally, much cited as important for children's learning. Self-esteem is now less considered to be a fixed measurable quality but as socially variable. Students who feel labelled as 'dumb', 'stupid' or educationally inferior may not feel like learning. They may also be stigmatised or bullied by other pupils. As I have argued earlier this makes such students and their parents grateful for diagnoses like ADHD. The emphasis on academic attainment in many Western education systems creates dilemmas for schools that wish to be inclusive. Many educators now use the idea of multiple intelligence to demonstrate to students that human beings may have very varied but equally valuable strengths and abilities.

Restorative practices in schools use restorative language, circles and conferences to promote and restore good relationships when there has been conflict or harm between students, between students and teachers. Teachers are experienced as helpful when they offer unconditional positive regard to students and to parents. Students value teachers who maintain classroom control but who know who they are as a person, have a laugh with them. Effective teachers focus on whole individuals with strengths as well as difficulties. They encourage students' self-control/empowerment. Within the group activities of the classroom they are also able to provide 'individual' attention. They also value and recognise students' learning outside of school, within the home, peer group and neighbourhood.

The possible strategies clearly do not have to be complex. Approaches to work with students with difficulties in their lives are often viewed as helpful by the student and their families when they are based in equitable, non-judgemental, genuine relationships, rather than in highly professionalised interventions, and effective if they are rooted in understanding, not only of individual biographies, but of the institutional processes in which they are mutually engaged (Hill 1999; Lloyd *et al.* 2001; Lloyd 2005). Teachers in Britain, the USA and other parts of the world are increasingly, as argued earlier, subject to pressures to demonstrate academic achievement of children, measured in terms of group testing. They manage children in groups, with little time to get to know them and to understand their school lives in the context of their wider histories. They work long hours, planning and delivering curricula without raising their head to reflect on their institutional structures and processes. School managers could explore the possibilities for staff to get to know their pupils as human beings with histories whose actions reflect both their out-of-school lives and their in-school experiences.

Teachers need help and support too, in imagining creative responses to challenging situations and in developing formative assessment processes that point them to educational responses to learning difficulties, rather than, or at least as well as, summative assessment that classifies and reinforces difference between students. They may be supported in this by the presence of additional adults in the classrooms. In Scotland, for example as part of the Better Behaviour Better Learning initiative, and in recognition of the stress experienced by some teachers in facing challenging behaviour, the government has funded more classroom support assistants, who have been largely valued by both teachers and parents (Munn *et al.* 2005). It may be that these additional staff may offer the kind of informal support valued by some parents intimidated by teachers and aware of their own negative experiences of schooling (Stead and Lloyd forthcoming).

The literature on 'ADHD' often suggests that the benefit of a formal diagnosis is that that parents no longer feel blamed by schools for their children's actions and clearly many parents whose children are constantly in trouble in school do feel such blame (Cooper 2005). In this case the diagnosis of ADHD acts as a 'label of forgiveness' (Lloyd and Norris 1999). However, if school staff were able to remain supportive to parents whose children are causing problems in school then this label might be less attractive. In many cases it may be that parents are also experiencing difficulties with their child and a joint approach to the issue may be more effective. It may also, however, be important to engage parents in a discussion of their role in child development and in contributing to children's difficulties. While it is clearly unhelpful to 'blame' it may be equally unhelpful to accept the ADHD diagnosis as an absolution that denies any parenting or family factors in the explanation of difficulties. In any case, whether or not they are to be blamed or to be held responsible, parents need to be engaged and taught to help their children learn.

## Conclusion

Armstrong in his chapter in this book argues that we should use ADHD to develop a critique of contemporary culture and our education system. Rather than simply accepting a medicalising of 'problem' behaviour, students, parents and professionals could reflect on the nature and purposes of our education systems and their relationships to their cultural context. The American writer Wheelock (1998) argues that students need schools characterised by 'rigorous caring' between teachers and students and where they can engage in meaningful tasks to create high-quality work. She argues that students need schools where teachers meet standards of practice in a professional community. Everything in the culture of the school must attend to these purposes.

In this chapter I have argued that an educational response to the kind of behaviour characterised as ADHD should involve the recognition of every child as a whole individual human being who can make choices, rather than as driven by a disorder. If schools can include parents in educational discussion, support and intervention, explain alternatives to medication and avoid blame, then parents may be less likely to look for labels. Schools that recognise the interaction between individual behaviour and the context in which it occurs will review their classroom organisation, curriculum and pedagogy to identify barriers to effective learning. They will explore their inter-agency working and support mechanisms that do not depend on highly professionalised and inaccessible language but talk about children's lives in a way that they and their parents can participate – recognising that children are ultimately the experts on their own lives. We need a redefinition of professionalism in education that requires us to respond to students and parents with respect, to value their individual strengths, to support and work with them in relation to their difficulties and to be reflective about our own institutional processes and practices. This is not easy: there are clear challenges for schools in managing the diverse expectations of governments, communities and the varying expectations of different groups of parents and students. The contributors to this book have demonstrated the importance of reflecting on and challenging received wisdom about childhood 'disorders' such as ADHD. We hope that schools will be encouraged to avoid easy labelling and classification of students, will understand the complexity of the issue but be still willing to explore helpful support strategies in collaboration with other colleagues, students and parents.

## Notes

1   Some of the discussion in this chapter first appeared in my article 'Listening not labelling: responding to troubled and troublesome students', in the first issue of *International Journal of School Disaffection* (2003). Stoke: Trentham.

## References

Armstrong, T. (1997) *The Myth of the A.D.D. Child: 50 ways to improve your child's behaviour and attention span*. London: Penguin.

Barton, L. (1999) 'Market ideologies, education and the challenge for inclusion'. In Cooper, P. (2001) *We Can Work It Out. What works in educating pupils with emotional and behavioural difficulties*. Ilford: Barnardos.

Cooper, P. (2005) *AD/HD in Special Teaching for Special Children?* Maidenhead: Open University Press.

Cooper, P. and O'Regan, F. J. (2001) *Educating Children with AD/HD – A teacher's manual*. London: Routledge Falmer.

Davis, P. and Florian, L. (2004) *Teaching Strategies and Approaches for Children with Special Educational Needs: A scoping study* (Research report 516). London: DfES.

Flick, G. (1998) *ADD/ADHD Behaviour Change Resource Kit*. San Francisco, CA: Jossey Bass.

Florian, L. (2005) 'Reforming Teaching: Is there such a thing as a special pedagogy?' Paper presented at a seminar on Disabled Learners and Social Justice. Edinburgh: CREID.

Forness, S. R. and Kavale, K. A. (2001) 'Ignoring the odds: hazards of not adding the new medical model to special education decisions'. *Behavioural Disorders*, 26: 269–281.

Gresham, F. (2002) 'Caveat emptor: considerations before buying into the "new" medical model'. *Behavioural Disorders*, 27(2): 158–167.

Hill, M. (1999) 'What's the problem? Who can help? The perspectives of children and young people on their well-being and on helping professionals'. *Journal of Social Work Practice*, 13(2): 135–145.

Kewley, G. (1999) *Attention Deficit Hyperactivity Disorder*. London: David Fulton.

Kinder, K., Harland, J., Wilkin, A. and Wakefield, A. (1995) *Three to Remember. Strategies for disaffected pupils*. Slough: NFER.

Lewis, A. and Norwich, B. (2000) *Mapping a Special Needs Pedagogy*. Exeter: University of Exeter and University of Warwick.

Lloyd, G. (2005) '"EBD" girls – a critical view'. In Lloyd, G. (ed.) *'Problem' Girls. Understanding and supporting troubled and troublesome girls and young women*. London: Routledge.

Lloyd, G. and Norris, C. (1999) 'Including ADHD?' *Disability and Society*, 14(4): 505–517.

Lloyd, G., Stead, J. and Kendrick, A. (2001) *Hanging On In There: A study of inter-agency work to prevent school exclusion in three local authorities*. London: National Children's Bureau and Joseph Rowntree Foundation.

Mental Health Foundation (1999) *The Big Picture Report*. London: MHF.

Munn, P., Lloyd, G. and Cullen, M. A. (2000) *Alternatives to Exclusion from School*. London: Paul Chapman.

Munn, P., Riddell, S., Lloyd, G., Macleod, G., Stead, J., Fairley, J. and Kane, J. (2005) *Evaluation of the Discipline Task Group Recommendations: The deployment of additional staff to promote positive school discipline*. A report to the Scottish Executive Edinburgh: University of Edinburgh.

Norris, C. and Lloyd, G. (2000) 'Parents, professionals and ADHD – What the papers say'. *European Journal of Special Needs Education*, 15(2): 123–137.

O'Regan, F. (2005) *ADHD*. London: Continuum.

Oswald, D. P. (2002) 'The new medical model and beyond. A response to Furness and Kavale'. *Behavioural Disorders*, 27(2): 155–157.

Richardson, A. J. (2004) 'Long-chain polyunsaturated fatty acids in childhood developmental and psychiatric disorders'. *Lipids*, 39: 1215–1222.

Rief, S. (1993) *How to Reach and Teach ADD/ADHD Children*. San Francisco: Jossey Bass.

Rutter, M. and Smith, D. (1995) *Psychosocial Disorders in Young People: Time trends and their causes*. London: Wiley.

SIGN (2001) *Attention Deficit and Hyperkinetic Disorders in Children and Young People. A national clinical guideline*. Published by Scottish Intercollegiate Guidelines Network, Edinburgh.

Slee, R. (1995) *Changing Theories and Practices of Discipline*. London: Falmer.

Slee, R. (1998) 'The politics of theorising special education'. In Clark, C., Dyson, A. and Millward, A. (eds) *Theorising Special Education*. London: Routledge.

Stead, J. and Lloyd, G. (forthcoming) 'Supporting our most challenging pupils with our least trained staff? Can behaviour support assistants offer a distinctive kind of help?'

Thomas, G. and Loxley, A. (2001) *Deconstructing Special Education and Constructing Inclusion*. Buckingham: Open University Press.

Tymms, P. and Merrill, C. (2004) 'Screening and classroom interventions for inattentive, hyperactive and impulsive young children – a longitudinal study'. Paper presented at American Educational Research Association.

Wendt, M. (2005) Available <http://www.acalogic.com/adhd_research_summary.htm> (accessed July 2005).

Wheelock, A. (1998) *Safe to be Smart*. Westerville, OH: National Middle School Association.

Wright, C. (2005) 'Black femininities go to school'. In Lloyd, G. (ed.) *'Problem' Girls. Understanding and supporting troubled and troublesome girls and young women*. London: Routledge.

Young Minds (1999) *Response to Social Inclusion: Pupils support consultation document from the DfEE*. London: Young Minds.

# Index

Abbey, E. 195
abuse 71
Adams, D. 66
Adderall 13
ADHD adults 16, 17
ADHD (Attention Deficit Hyperactivity
    Disorder): aetiology 3, 36; as annoying
    behaviour 21–2; background 2–3,
    75–6; characteristics 12, 118*t*, 119*t*,
    120, 201–2, 210, 218; concept 1, 76–9;
    definitions 12, 16, 24, 45, 75, 156; *see
    also* critiques of the 'ADHD' enterprise;
    diagnosis of ADHD; treatment of
    ADHD
adopted children 117
adult–child power relationships 156–75;
    baseline 161–2; the children's world
    162–6; conclusions 171–3; daring
    164–5; default behaviour 163–6;
    effective teachers 165–6; fieldnotes 160,
    166–71; flexibility 164; focal individual
    sampling 157–9; research scope and
    methodology 156–7; researcher
    persona 159; resilience 164; results
    160–1, 174–5*t*
advertising 35–6
Agency for Health Care Policy and
    Research (AHCPR) 27, 29
*AIANMHQ (American Indian and Alaska Native
    Mental Health Quarterly)* 76–7
AIDAI (Associazione Italiana Disturbi di
    Attenzione/Iperattività) 133
AIFA (Associazione Italiana Famiglie
    ADHD) 133
aimlessness 118*t*, 119*t*, 121, 123
alcohol 73–4
Altman, J. 157
American Academy of Pediatrics 36, 198

*American Indian and Alaska Native Mental
    Health Quarterly (AIANMHQ)* 76–7
American Indians 66–79, 79 n2; abuse 71;
    ADHD 67, 69–70, 72, 74, 75, 76, 78–9;
    education 69–72; eugenics and
    oppression 68–70, 75–6; Fetal Alcohol
    Syndrome 73–4; Hopi 77;
    indoctrination of concepts 76–9;
    learning styles 72–3, 79; mothers 68,
    73; oppositional identity 72; psychiatric
    diagnosis as oppression 67; trauma,
    grief and oppression 70–2; Yakama
    Nation 66, 70–2, 74, 76, 78
American Psychiatric Association *see
    Diagnostic and Statistical Manual of Mental
    Disorders*
American Psychological Association 35,
    115, 123
Ames, L.B. 41
anti-realism 87–90
Associazione Italiana Disturbi di
    Attenzione/Iperattività (AIDAI) 133
Associazione Italiana Famiglie ADHD
    (AIFA) 133
attachment 117
attention: 'normal attention' 199; short
    attention span culture 34–5
attention difficulties in the classroom
    198–213; attributions 200; autonomous
    learning 200, 204, 209; characteristics
    201–2, 210; collaboration and
    cooperation 198; control 200, 201;
    educational factors 201–2; educational
    intervention 202–5; learning and self-
    esteem 200, 204–5; learning needs 201,
    203–4; learning styles 199, 200, 201,
    203, 205–13; learning theory 203–5;
    'normal attention' 199; provision 201